ARCHAEOLOGICAL SITE SCIENCE

ARCHAEOLOGICAL SITE SCIENCE

by

FRANK H. GOODYEAR

B.Sc., F.R.I.C.

AMERICAN ELSEVIER PUBLISHING COMPANY, INC.

NEW YORK   1971

First Published in the United States by
American Elsevier Publishing Company, Inc.
52 Vanderbilt Avenue, New York, New York 10017

Library of Congress Catalog Card Number 70–155095

ISBN 0 444 19598 X

Printed in Great Britain

CONTENTS

Part Four

Archaeological Prospecting

LIST OF PLATES

LIST OF TABLES

INTRODUCTION

It is now generally appreciated that the practical archaeologist, whether amateur or professional, needs some basic scientific knowledge, not only to help him to recognize and interpret the complex and diverse materials and features which are revealed during excavation, but also to provide him with some appreciation of the possibilities available through the application of scientific methods in the laboratory. By long experience of excavation one may become accustomed to the general nature of soils, the appearance of buried pottery and corroded iron, but without some knowledge of the scientific background—the mechanism of soil formation and the intricacies of corrosion processes, for instance— interpretation is stifled and only an incomplete picture can result.

More serious difficulties may arise when the excavator is faced with some phenomenon not previously experienced, or an object he does not recognize, and must make a quick decision on procedure; whether or how digging should proceed, or perhaps whether an artifact material might be easily identified or made to yield its secrets by suitable laboratory investigations, and, perhaps more important, whether a knowledge of these secrets would repay all the time and effort involved. A scientist could be expected to know how to make these decisions, but he would merely be working towards the unknown from the known, extrapolating his experience, or, perhaps, making an inspired guess, which is possible only when there is a source of inspiration, in this case his scientific training and knowledge.

But it may be argued that the director of an excavation will have scientific assistants available at any time for consultation and to carry out the necessary tests. This will certainly be so on large professional digs, but in many countries there are hundreds of small excavations taking place every year, by professionals and amateurs, on which it is not possible to employ scientific assistants, so that the director himself must do the best he can. If he is professionally trained in a modern school of archaeology he will have studied certain scientific aspects of his subject, but these are likely to consist of a few more or less unrelated topics, such as the identification of animal bones and the nature of pottery. These will probably have been studied to great depth, but he will not generally have obtained a wide overall picture of the scientific background. The amateur, on the other hand, coming from any walk of life, may or may not have some knowledge of science, but this also will most likely be limited to a smattering of physics and chemistry, or 'general science', which is often more general than scientific.

Archaeology, in one way or another, touches almost every scientific discipline; geology and pedology in the nature of the environment, biology and metallurgy in relation to the remains of animals or artifacts, physics and chemistry in the testing of materials and as fundamental to all the other sciences.

One is thus forced to the conclusion that practically all excavators, not only directors and supervisors but also the man or woman with the spade and trowel, need a certain amount of understanding of some of the basic principles and methods of application of the relevant sciences. It is not necessary to delve deeply into any of the sciences, and, indeed, we shall merely scratch the surface, if an archaeologist may be permitted such a phrase! Only the more important aspects will be considered, in the hope that a little learning will not prove dangerous but may increase the pleasure of many in their already fascinating practical archaeology.

The present work, then, is intended for *practical* archaeologists of all kinds and is mainly concerned with applications on the site, but because excavation may be influenced by, and have its own influence on, laboratory investigations, a brief survey of such methods is included.

The archaeologist rarely discovers artifacts or structures in anything like their original state. Over the years various changes have taken place, some of them rapid, some very slow; some irreversible, others which may be at least partly reversed by careful treatment. Frequently the only traces of an artifact remaining are discoloration or textural variation of the soil, as, for example, for a completely decayed iron object or a post-hole. But such traces may provide valuable evidence, and some understanding of the processes which brought about these results is essential to successful interpretation.

Continuous change is universal. Probably nothing remains completely unaffected by the passage of time, and decay sets in very early in the life of most artifacts, even without the help of modern 'built-in obsolescence'. This is not always appreciated by archaeologists, and there is a tendency, particularly among beginners, to believe that such decay, perhaps the rusting of an iron object, took place at some precise instant of time between its manufacture and its unearthing during excavation. An appreciation of the continuity of such processes will, it is hoped, grow from a study of this book. Above all, it must be emphasized that the decay processes do not cease when an object is removed from the ground; they may, in fact, rapidly accelerate.

It is well known that some otherwise perishable materials may be accidentally preserved by lying in appropriate surroundings, but removal into different conditions causes rapid, often catastrophic, decay. This is well illustrated by ancient wooden objects preserved in waterlogged conditions. To prevent loss the objects should immediately receive scientific treatment or be stored under similar conditions until they can be so treated.

Examples of this kind reveal the close relationship between the condition of an ancient object and the nature of its surroundings. Here we have one of the main themes of this book. It is not sufficient for the practical archaeologist to be familiar with the appearance and properties of ancient man's raw materials; he would like to be able to recognize these same materials at all stages of their decay under various conditions. To do this he needs to know something of the physical and chemical nature of the archaeological environment, and of the interaction between materials and their surroundings.

It has sometimes been necessary to digress from the logical development of a topic in order to explain scientific principles, but in such cases an effort has been made to avoid any irrelevant matter. Explanations have been kept as simple as possible without, it is hoped, over-taxing the patience of those readers with some basic scientific knowledge. Also, whilst the book is mainly designed to be read as one continuous narrative with the main theme of change and decay, it should also have a place as a book of reference. For this reason a glossary has been included and a comprehensive index has been compiled.

The topics discussed above are dealt with in Part I under three Sections: the archaeological environment, the materials of antiquity, and the interaction of the materials with their surroundings. Here the main theme is developed, illustrating the causes, mechanisms, and results of decay.

In Part II a review is made of the kinds of tests and research that can be carried out in archaeological laboratories, or, more commonly, by interested and helpful non-archaeologists in their specialist laboratories.

The more direct applications of scientific methods on the archaeological site are presented in Part III. The aim has been to give just sufficient detail to enable the tests to be carried out and understood, so that correct conclusions can be drawn.

Archaeological prospecting methods are reviewed in Part IV, with brief mention of several methods and more details of the well-established methods and the more promising newer techniques.

It would have been a formidable task to try to quote references for the sources of all the information used, particularly in view of the very wide field covered. If further information is required it will generally be found in one of the publications quoted in the Select Bibliography, or a reference there will lead to the appropriate source.

My thanks are due to the following for kindly supplying photographs for the illustrations: Martin-Clark Instruments of Guildford, Surrey, England, for Plate VIII(a) and Figure II; Varian Associates of Walton-on-Thames, England and Palo Alto, California, U.S.A., for Plate VIII(b) and (c); The Littlemore Scientific Engineering Co. Ltd., of Littlemore, Oxford, England for Plate IX; and to Professor J. M. T. Charlton for kind permission to reproduce an aerial photograph as Plate XI.

I should also like to record my thanks to Mr G. T. Emery, B.D.S., for taking the photographs for the remaining plates, and also for reading through the manuscript and making many useful suggestions.

PART ONE

A. The Archaeological Environment

B. The Materials of Antiquity

and

C. The Interaction of Materials with their Surroundings

A. The Archaeological Environment

ONE

INTRODUCTION

The archaeological environment forms the immediate surroundings of any archaeological feature or artifact. It includes an infinite variety of circumstances, from the atmosphere to airless depths, from arid, almost waterless desert to the depths of the sea, but is rarely as simple as any of these alone.

No two artifacts are in exactly the same environment, though they may lie side by side. In fact the environment of one artifact might not be the same over its whole area, as may be seen from the varying extent of its decay from point to point on the surface.

Soil is undoubtedly the most familiar environment to the archaeologist, and he early realizes its great complexity, even without the interference of man. In the soil may be found every natural chemical element, combined in one form or another, from hydrogen (the lightest) to uranium (the heaviest). But many of these elements are present only in minute traces, which are archaeologically important only in the determination of the sources of materials, or, possibly, in dating.

The almost infinite variety of ways in which even a few of the more common elements may be combined together may be seen in the vast number of rock and mineral types; these are *inorganic* substances, never having formed part of living matter. *Organic* substances are, for our present purposes, those which are or have been part of plant or animal, and, although they are mainly built up from only four or five common elements, they can be extremely complex substances, and their decay processes very difficult to unravel.

Less complex than soil, but far from being simple, is water. Pure water does not exist on earth. It dissolves a certain amount, however small in some cases, of practically every substance with which it comes in contact, so that the purest spring or mountain stream is in reality a complex solution. It is mainly the dissolved substances that are active in archaeological contexts.

The atmosphere is the least complicated of the archaeological environments; at least, it would be if it were not contaminated by man. Even so, we must bear in mind that the air in all but the most arid regions of the world frequently contains quite large amounts of water, not only during rainy seasons but in periods of mist and fog or of high relative humidity. Air also permeates the soil, often to quite considerable depths, so that all three of our main environments meet in the ground. Consequently, it is not strictly legitimate to separate them completely, but in order to make any progress at all in our discussion we must first simplify things; we shall therefore start by considering the simplest conditions and proceed to the more complex in turn.

TWO

THE ATMOSPHERE

Let us first examine the average composition of pure air and the properties of its constituents before considering the effects of contaminating substances.

Almost four-fifths of the air consists of nitrogen, one of the least reactive of gases, which therefore plays no direct part in the normal decay processes nor in the life processes of plant or animal, with very few exceptions (e.g. the 'nitrifying bacteria'). Hence for our present purposes nitrogen can be completely ignored. The remaining one-fifth of the atmosphere contains a variety of gases, as Table 1 shows.

TABLE 1

The Composition of the Atmosphere

Gas	Percentage by volume
Nitrogen	77·32
Oxygen	20·80
Helium, Neon, Argon	0·93
Carbon dioxide	0·03
Water vapour	0·92

We shall have very little to do with the 'inert gases' (or 'noble gases'), as they have very little to do with other substances, not forming normal compounds but keeping themselves very much to themselves. There are six of these gases, the best known being helium, neon, and argon, all used to impart their various colours to the glow of lamps and advertising signs. Helium and argon are of interest in certain dating methods for rocks and might consequently concern the archaeologist, but we shall not consider them any further here.

Carbon dioxide is essential for plant life, since plants obtain practically all their carbon in this form from the atmosphere, and carbon is the fundamental element in all plant and animal tissues. In other words, carbon dioxide is an essential food for plants; they use it in the process of photosynthesis, in which complex compounds are built up from simple ones under the influence of light and with the help of the green colouring matter *chlorophyll.*

But, as is well known, plants and animals in general take in oxygen and give out carbon dioxide during respiration. In these two ways, photosynthesis and respiration, there is a constant interchange of carbon dioxide between living things and the atmosphere, with the oceans acting as a large reservoir, so that the proportion of carbon dioxide in the atmosphere remains surprisingly constant. These exchange processes make 'radiocarbon dating' possible, because during their lifetimes plants and animals maintain the same proportion of 'radiocarbon' in their tissues as in the atmosphere. But after death the 'radiocarbon' steadily decreases in quantity through radioactive decay, so that the decrease in the proportion of radiocarbon to ordinary carbon measures the length of time since the death of the plant or animal. Notice particularly that it does not measure the date of *deposition* of the material in the archaeological context.

Of itself carbon dioxide plays no part in the decay processes with which we are mainly concerned, but when it dissolves in water it partly combines with the water to form carbonic acid. So we must expect to find this acid in all natural waters. However, in many places the acidity due to carbonic acid may be reduced or neutralized by other impurities in the water. We shall return to this later, but for the present we need only note that carbon dioxide will become effective in decay processes only when dissolved in water, whilst recognizing that such water may be in the form of rain or even as minute droplets in a very humid atmosphere or in fog or mist. The formation of caves and potholes in limestone country is due to the action of very small amounts of carbonic acid in the rivers and streams dissolving the basic limestone rocks. When some of the water in such caves evaporates carbon dioxide is released and the limestone is re-deposited as stalagmites and stalactites, extremely slowly.

All living things, with the exception of a few bacteria ('anaerobic bacteria') need oxygen for respiration. Aquatic animals make use of the oxygen *dissolved* in water, and have developed many fascinating ways of extracting it. In the stagnant waters in which captive fish are kept it is very important to ensure an adequate supply of dissolved oxygen by the use of 'bubblers'. Otherwise the lack of water movement and the contamination will rapidly deplete the supply and the fish will suffer.

The familiar example of the aquarium will help to remind us that heavily contaminated water, or, almost the same thing, waterlogged soil, may contain very little oxygen, depending partly on the nature of the dissolved substances. In these conditions normal decay processes may be considerably modified. These changes will be considered later.

Terrestrial animals are adapted for the extraction of oxygen from the much larger amounts available in the atmosphere, but the balance of nature is such that the proportion of oxygen in unpolluted air remains remarkably constant. We need not investigate the biological or biochemical mechanisms by which oxygen is used in the body, but if we consider merely the gaseous input and output we shall find a relationship very similar to those occurring during the burning of solid fuels, oil, coal gas, or natural gas.

All the fuels just mentioned are products of the decay of living things, which means that they are essentially 'organic', and when they are burnt all the complex substances are broken down and all the carbon combines with oxygen to form carbon dioxide. Hence there is an 'intake' of oxygen and an 'output' of carbon dioxide. When a substance combines with oxygen, either during combustion or otherwise, we say it is *oxidized*. We shall find that many decay processes involve oxidation.

In or near industrial areas, or large residential areas where there is no smoke-control order in force, the atmosphere may be heavily polluted, and some of the contaminating substances are extremely corrosive. Coal always contains a certain amount of sulphur, which burns to sulphur dioxide, an obnoxious and corrosive gas familiar to those who remember the smell (or taste) of the fumes from steam locomotives, or to users of coal-gas appliances where the gas has not been thoroughly 'washed' to remove the undesirable contaminants. But sulphur dioxide in extremely small amounts, very much less than can be detected by the senses, is corrosive, with particularly bad effects on mortar, cement, and most building materials.

One tends to overlook the solid constituents of the atmosphere until a fog or 'smog' appears or the hay-fever season starts. It is a simple matter to extract a sample of the air-borne solids by drawing the air through a filter. Apart from soot and dust there may be, at appropriate times, large quantities of pollen and bacteria, though the smaller 'germs', i.e. viruses, pass through the filter. On windy days the air may contain an appreciable amount of very small clay particles, but the larger sand grains will be found only quite close to the ground. These will be important in dry sandy areas, such as dune lands, since blown sand can be very abrasive and cause serious damage to buildings; controlled sand-blasting is now used for cleaning stone- and brick-work and for many industrial purposes.

It is found that only the smaller sand grains are air-borne for any considerable distance; the larger grains bounce or hop along, but, even so, may travel great distances.

The archaeological significance of air-borne bacteria may not be obvious or of great importance, but it must be observed that organic materials will decay by bacterial action when not in contact with the soil and its vast bacterial population. One can only assume that the bacteria reach their 'victims' via the atmosphere.

Pollen also may travel considerable distances through the air, particularly in high winds. This should be remembered when interpreting the results of pollen analysis on archaeological sites. Whereas this movement of pollen will not affect dating procedure, care must be taken not to deduce a very localized ecology from the pollen of a site. Certainly the types of pollen found will give a good idea of the ecology of the *region* and hence its general climate at the time the pollen was deposited, but any evidence for more localized conditions must be looked for in the soil itself. For example, one and the same layer on a site might contain pollen from pine trees of the highlands and from weeds of marshy ground, but the site itself might not fit into either of these categories. If the site had ever been marshy or boggy the colour and nature of the soil should reveal this.

THREE

WATER

In recent years there has been a rapid increase in under-sea archaeological exploration and of excavations of the sea-bed, and we can expect to hear shortly of more such work being done in inland waters, though to date most archaeological materials from fresh waters have been chance finds. It is thus important for the archaeologist to have some knowledge of the nature of both sea-water and the common types of fresh-water in order to be able to understand and explain the condition of artifacts from such environments.

Chemically there is only one kind of water occurring naturally. When one speaks of sea-water, river-water, soil-water, and so on, one is merely indicating, by reference to the source of the water, the kinds of impurities that are likely to be found in it, organic and inorganic, dissolved or suspended, living or dead.

The appearance of a natural water may give some idea of its composition, providing that we distinguish colours due to suspended and dissolved matter from the influence of the structure or colour of the bed. A turbidity resulting from large amounts of suspended clay particles imparts a yellowish colour, marl is said to produce a bluish green, some kinds of plankton brown, and phytoplankton deep green, usually in drifts. The darkest colours are usually found in swamps and bogs, or the streams issuing from them, where the dissolved and the suspended humic material gives a brown colour, but blue, green, and yellow are possible. Iron may produce a yellow to red colour, and associated with this there may be staining of the bedrock if the iron concentration is high.

Turbidity is caused by very small suspended particles scattering the light, i.e. reflecting light in all directions. All natural waters contain suspended matter, but larger pieces settle quickly unless there is a strong current. It has been calculated that, in still water, sand will fall through one foot in a few seconds, and silt in several minutes; clay may take a year and smaller colloidal particles perhaps a century. Water is never really still, but these figures show quite vividly the effect of the size of particles on their rate of settlement and hence that the turbidity of natural waters is mainly caused by clay and other colloidal particles. Included in these there might be some of the bacteria which, when dead, would fall one foot in two or three days, but will remain suspended during their lifetimes. Colloidal material cannot be *filtered* out by normal filtering methods, but by adding salts to the water it may be *flocculated*, i.e. large numbers of the particles are made to come together to form larger particles which, being much heavier than water, will settle out.

It is well known that at or near the surface of the sea there are countless numbers of very small organisms collectively known as *plankton*, but it is not generally realized that practically all natural waters carry plankton, more especially lakes and ponds rather than the flowing waters of rivers and streams. Plankton consists mainly of microscopic plants and animals, most of them with no means of propulsion, but just drifting along with the currents and surface winds. Slightly larger, free-swimming organisms are known as *nekton*.

Bacteria are also present in all natural waters, their numbers being estimated as between forty thousand and two million per cubic centimetre of water. Some of these play essential parts in the 'nitrogen cycle', a succession of processes by which nitrogen from the air is converted into food for green plants, which build it into proteins and other substances on which animals and bacteria feed. Then by other intermediate stages the nitrogen eventually returns to the elementary form and may pass back into the atmosphere, to be re-used over and over again.

Fungi, sometimes called water moulds, grow on all kinds of organic matter in, on, or below most natural waters. Finally there are the larger plants and animals, of practically every family, which may be found in waters of one kind or another; but their archaeological significance is small. Their remains may be found in waterlogged conditions on archaeological sites, and the plants may play some part in the destruction of underwater structures by the penetration of their roots into cracks or directly into the mortar of walls. The purely physical effect may be reinforced by the chemical effects of acids released by the roots.

Of greater general significance are the numerous substances dissolved in natural waters. Even unpolluted waters carry large quantities of material in solution, and it is these which give the water its taste, make it *hard* or *soft*, bland or corrosive. Substances in true solution are usually in the form of single molecules, or occasionally two or three molecules together, intimately mixed in with the molecules of the water. Larger clusters of molecules may form *colloidal* solutions (properly called *sols*), then *suspensions*, and any still larger particles will settle out, or precipitate. It is not necessary for us to detail here the complex rules governing the solubility of substances in water. Some idea of the wide range of solubilities may be seen in the very slight solubility of the igneous rocks and in the amount of sugar that some people manage to dissolve in a cup of tea.

We have seen that the gases of the atmosphere dissolve to a certain extent in water. Dissolved oxygen may also be derived from green water-plants during their photosynthesis, and carbon dioxide from the respiration of plants and animals and from the decay of organic matter in the water. There may be much more carbon dioxide in subterranean waters, with a correspondingly greater solubility of limestone, because calcium carbonate (limestone) is not normally soluble, but becomes dissolved by being first converted to calcium bicarbonate by chemical reaction with carbon dioxide and water. (A bicarbonate contains twice as much combined carbon dioxide as the corresponding carbonate.) We have seen that the reverse of this chemical change can also occur under suitable conditions.

Several other gases are often found in natural waters, such as hydrogen sulphide (the smell of rotten eggs), ammonia, and methane ('marsh gas'). The latter is most common in marshes and bogs, being produced by the decomposition of organic matter on the bottom. The gas rises in bubbles, and sometimes in sudden bursts that bring up large quantities of rubbish. Small amounts of methane may spontaneously ignite, producing the phenomenon known as 'Will-o'-the-wisp'. Methane in coal mines is referred to as *fire-damp*.

Solids dissolved in natural waters may account for over one-tenth of the total weight of the 'water', but this sort of figure would be found only in salt lakes. Other waters are more likely to have from ten to a few hundred parts per million (i.e. up to one-twentieth of one per cent). Rain-water brings down thirty to forty parts per million of dissolved solids from non-polluted atmospheres and very much more from modern cities. The solids in natural waters come from many sources, such as air-borne and wind-blown dusts, soil erosion, soil minerals dissolved in surface water or seepage water, and the decay products of organic matter. There is, perhaps surprisingly, more dissolved *organic* material in fresh-water lakes than in the sea, though the sea will usually contain much more inorganic matter.

It is of interest to note here that modern agricultural methods are causing drastic changes in the composition of rivers, streams, and lakes through the leaching of vast quantities of artificial fertilizers. These provide food for aquatic plants, which are therefore increasing rapidly and choking many waterways, with consequent loss of fish and other aquatic animals and increased risk of flooding. The effect of sewage disposal into such rivers and lakes may be left to the imagination.

The acidity of water may be important, especially in relation to the corrosion of metals and the decay of organic matter. A convenient measure for not too strongly acid or basic solutions is known as the *pH* of the solution (*see* Glossary). This scale ranges from zero to fourteen, with a neutral solution (such as pure water) having a pH of seven, the mid-point of the scale. Acidic solutions have pH values *below* seven, and alkaline (basic) solutions have pH values above seven. On this basis most natural waters will have pH from 6·5 to 8·5, but under rather unusual conditions they may range from pH 3 to pH 11. The pH of a particular stretch of water depends on many factors, including the nature of the rock formations, soil, and vegetation cover of the adjoining land. Many salts that dissolve in water make it acidic or basic, and in addition there are the so-called humic acids, various complex mixtures that are washed out of most kinds of soil.

The pH values of most natural waters are continually changing, but not generally very greatly. They also frequently vary from place to place in the same water, both horizontally and vertically. An interesting situation often arises with bog lakes, where the open water is alkaline but the water in the boggy fringes, where Sphagnum moss is growing, is quite acid, the change taking place across only a few inches of water. This acidity of bog water is fairly common; water from areas of sedge or forest, or where peat has been *deposited*, is usually alkaline, though moorland peats are generally slightly acid.

One of the main criteria of acceptability for drinking water is salinity. Water containing up to 400 parts per million of sodium chloride has no taste, but with more than 5,000 parts per million it is quite undrinkable. A brackish taste appears between 400 and 500 parts per million of salt, and higher concentrations become strongly salty and less bearable for drinking purposes. The salinity of underground waters depends on the rock formation, the climate, and the depth from which the water is drawn. The best water will probably come from boreholes in old rocks such as schists and granites (e.g. in Africa), but in Western and Southern Australia water from boreholes in older rocks is very salty and unusable. Again, in the arid regions of the south-western States of the U.S.A. boreholes can reach good-quality water in crystalline rocks.

This brief review has emphasized the importance of dissolved and suspended matter in natural waters in archaeological contexts—but what of the water itself? Pure water would have no chemical effects on archaeological materials, but would have important physical effects, the most drastic arising from freezing and thawing, especially when frequently repeated. This may have extensive disruptive effects on structures, particularly when porous materials are involved, and comes about because water expands when it freezes, i.e. the ice formed needs more room than the liquid water did. Hence, inside porous solids or in cracks and fissures the tremendous pressures produced by freezing water can cause havoc. The effect on rocks is to open up fissures in vertical or horizontal surfaces and to produce large boulders, as on many mountain tops, or scree below more or less vertical faces. The large numbers of broken pebbles which frequently mislead the beginner in archaeological excavation may be produced largely by this natural process. The stones may be split across, or more-or-less thin layers may be broken off curved surfaces. These thin pieces have often been mistaken at first sight for pottery sherds, and the resemblance can be very close indeed (Plate I).

Physical effects of running water are seen both in natural deposits and artifacts. Boulders, small stones, and sand-grains carried by water become worn and polished, but the process is extremely slow, and a high polish may take thousands of years to produce. The main cause of such transport effects is through the abrasive action of rolling on the river bed, which rubs the sand-grains together and against stationary rocks, knocking off the sharp corners and slowly polishing the surfaces. This gives a distinctive appearance to water-borne sands compared to wind-blown sands, which tend to be more quickly rounded but not polished. Sands deposited from ancient seas have a more or less intermediate appearance, more rounded than river sands and more highly polished. They may also be better sorted than river sands, i.e. grains of different sizes tend to be found in different layers.

Stone tools are often found on river gravels, or on the ancient flood-plains of rivers that have long since ceased to flow, and the extent of rounding of corners and edges can show whether the tools have been transported by water. Strongly abraded tools may be found at great distances from the site where they were abandoned. Only when the edges remain quite sharp can it be assumed that the implement is lying near a human occupation site.

FOUR

THE SOIL

From the archaeological point of view the soil comprises all material from the surface of the ground to the underlying bedrock, though unless he is particularly interested in the Paleolithic period an excavator will often finish digging at some level which he calls the 'natural' (or sterile) sub-soil. This stratum may not always be clearly distinguished, but should be defined from the evidence of a trial hole in a completely undisturbed area near the excavations. In order to understand the natural 'stratification' of soils it will be necessary to consider their methods of formation, bearing in mind that soil formation is a continuing process, and that it will start anew immediately following any man-made disturbance.

First we may imagine a freshly formed (or uncovered) rock, either igneous, sedimentary or metamorphic (see Chap. 2, p. 47). The surface becomes subject to all the various weathering processes, both physical and chemical, with effects varying with the nature of the rock and its constituent minerals. Initial breaking-down of the surface by rain and frost will be helped by the chemical action of acid rain- or surface-water when any basic minerals are present.

Micro-organisms play an important part in soil formation right from the start. Among the first of these to colonize bare rock are the *algae*, either single-cell varieties or those consisting of long green filaments, some of which are familiar in stagnant water. Often algae are associated with fungi to form *lichens*, which cling to the rock and hold a film of water around themselves. This not only helps to break down the rock by dissolving out some of the minerals, but also enables the organisms to extract nutrient minerals by the process of *ion-exchange*. Nitrogen is taken from the air, as also is carbon in the form of carbon dioxide, and the presence of lichens, alive or dead, provides support for other plants or animals.

Wind-blown clay, silt, and fine sand-grains will settle around lichens and in the cracks of the rock, and after a time air-borne seeds germinating there will be able to take hold and find sufficient nourishment to flourish and multiply.

Besides fixing the plant in the soil, roots can exert considerable pressure in forcing their way through cracks, so speeding up the process of comminution of the rock. Further help comes from small amounts of acid substances secreted by the roots.

In the autumn and winter annual plants die and deciduous trees lose their leaves, forming a layer of vegetable matter, which decays at a rate depending on the climate, the nature of the soil, and the presence of bacteria and other flora and fauna.

In passing, we might note that it is largely by the same processes that archaeological sites become covered with soil. It has been suggested that the rate of soil deposition might be worked out, and hence the time since the abandonment of a site, but there are far too many unknown factors involved, and although an average rate might be about one inch per hundred years, there will be large variations, and even variations from point to point on the same site.

Now that a layer of humus covers our soil we shall find that chemical effects increase, largely because humus is acidic and contains iron salts. Rain-water may now wash down the humic acids and iron, but there are so many factors affecting the movement of these substances that we shall not be able to follow them in detail, though we may look at the more important results.

Not all soils are formed by the processes just described, as there may be short cuts or, occasionally, an almost ready-made soil may be deposited naturally. Several kinds of natural deposits provide suitable sites for the growth of vegetation, which may take over very soon after the deposit has been laid. In such cases the soil may develop more quickly than when dependent on the breaking down of solid rock, and the resulting more-or-less thick surface-layers may be of an entirely different nature from the solid underlying rock.

The material in these deposits may have been transported by ice, water, or wind, or thrown out from a volcano, all of which will have left their evidence in either the physical or chemical nature of the residues. Rocks carried by glaciers will have been subjected to enormous battering, resulting in a wide range of particle sizes, from large boulders to fine clay-particles. This mass of transported material is deposited as *boulder clay* when the ice melts. It is interesting to note that the boulders and pebbles in such deposits are generally aligned in the direction of flow of the glacier: that is, the long axes of the more-or-less elongated stones will lie along the direction of the ice-flow. This phenomenon is one of the important methods by which the details of the various glaciations are worked out. The archaeologist should bear this in mind when working in boulder clays, but it is not likely that anyone would interpret the orientation of the stones as the work of man.

Boulder clays will generally cover wide areas and may be of great thickness. On the other hand, glaciers often leave large *mounds* of material. Those along the sides of valleys, formed from rock fragments fallen from the hillsides onto the ice, are *lateral moraines*, whereas those pushed by the advancing face, and left on its retreat, are *end moraines*. *Eskers* are long ridges of sand and gravel, whereas end moraines are very coarse, random mixtures of angular stones. Finally, the boulder clay may have been fashioned, possibly by subsequent ice sheets, into *drumlins*—oval mounds pointing in the direction of the ice-flow.

A further feature of glacial action which may be of importance to the archaeologist is the occurrence of erratics, i.e. rock fragments that are found in alien surroundings, having been carried by the ice a long way from their place of origin. One must take care not to see the hand of man behind the movement of these rocks, which is an entirely natural phenomenon. On the other hand man has sometimes made use of erratics, and one must not overlook the possibility that implements may have been made from erratics rather than carried by man long distances along hypothetical trade routes.

Ice, of course, is much more efficient, though much slower, in transporting material than are water or wind, and it is well known that artifacts found in undisturbed boulder-clay will probably have come to rest a long way from the settlement of their owners.

Water-laid deposits may be of marine or fresh-water origin. The former will be mainly of sand or gravel and will generally contain shells of marine crustacea by which they may be identified and possibly dated. In river valleys there may be *terraces* of sand or gravel at higher levels than the modern flood-plain, and the latter may consist of a flood-loam.

Very small clay particles can be scattered over vast areas from the atmosphere, but silt and sand grains are air-borne only when the wind velocity is adequate, and they tend to keep together more than clay. The heavier sand grains usually move in quite short hops, but even so, whole areas of sand dunes may creep over many miles. Between these extremes are the silt particles, which can be carried great distances but settle readily when the wind-speed falls, producing widespread deposits known as *loess*.

Throughout the world there are soils in all stages of formation, from the raw soil we pictured above to the fully developed soil in which equilibrium has been reached between the numerous and varied processes and known as a *climax soil*. However, the archaeologist is not likely to meet a raw soil in the usual meaning of the term, though he may come across a relatively new and developing soil-profile in an area disturbed by ancient man. In the making of a barrow, for example, the original surface may be left intact, the soil remaining as a *fossil soil*, and the barrow material itself may then begin to form a new soil by the processes of weathering and dissolution, and the formation of a new humus layer. Since the starting material for this new soil may be very different from that of the now fossilized soil, and the climatic conditions may have changed, quite a different type of soil can result.

But the soil is much more than a foundation on which vegetation can anchor itself and from which it can drink in a supply of food. The soil is very much alive. Apart from the more obvious flora and fauna there are countless extremely small plants and animals (*micro-flora* and *micro-fauna*). We shall first look at the inorganic background in which these things live, because the kinds of flora and fauna found in a soil depend very much on the physical and chemical nature of the inorganic constituents.

1. The Physical Nature of Soils

We have seen that the soil is derived from the bedrock by physical and chemical processes, and we must bear in mind that the bedrock, used in this sense, could mean a waterlaid silt or gravel or other non-compacted sediment, besides any kind of solid rock.

The origins of rocks, their classification and composition, will be described later from the point of view of their possible utility to man, but it is our purpose here to form some idea of the variety of soil types that exist by reason of the mineralogical differences in the parent material.

Terms such as clay, sand, gravel, and silt are familiar to all, but like most everyday expressions they are loosely used and often not understood. These words have, in fact, quite definite technical meanings in terms of particle size, although there are differing opinions as to where the dividing lines should be drawn. Table 2 shows what are probably the most convenient size ranges.

TABLE 2

British Standards Institute Scale of Soil Grades

		(mm.)
Stones or cobbles		Greater than 60
Gravel		60 to 2·0
Sand	coarse	2·0 to 0·6
	medium	0·6 to 0·2
	fine	0·2 to 0·06
Silt	coarse	0·06 to 0·02
	medium	0·02 to 0·006
	fine	0·006 to 0·002
Clay		Less than 0·002

Unfortunately, soils never consist entirely of grains of one size-range, so that there is never found, for example, a pure sand or a pure clay. For most purposes it is sufficient to combine the terms to give a rough indication of the proportions of each grade of particle size, using the term *loam* for mixtures containing sand, silt, and clay. For example, a *sandy loam* would suggest a soil which is mainly sand but contains also perhaps from 20 per cent to 50 per cent of silt and clay grades. A simple method of measuring the relative proportions of the various grain sizes is given in Part Three, but it will often be quite adequate to make a rough estimate from the feel of the soil when rubbed between finger and thumb, by associating the properties of grittiness, silkiness, and stickiness with sand, silt, and clay respectively. Note particularly that colour is an independent property of soils; it bears no relation to particle size, but is important as an indication of the chemical composition of the soil, a topic which will be discussed later.

Particles much larger than sand grains are often found in soils, tending to give a more open structure and improve drainage. Boulders are of little interest to us here, but the gravel grades, ranging in diameter from about 60 mm. to 2 mm., may be important. The various grades and size ranges are shown in Table 3.

TABLE 3

Gravel Grades

(*mm.*)

Cobbles	250 to 60
Coarse gravel	60 to 20
Medium gravel	20 to 6
Fine gravel	6 to 2

The particle sizes listed are those that are found by the usual methods of analysis, which involves washing the soil with water in a series of sieves, or shaking it up with water and measuring the settling rate. In either case any natural aggregated structures will be broken down into individual particles, and the method does not reveal the natural *structure* of the soil. The latter may be studied only in horizontal or vertical sections of the soil *in situ*.

Structure is a term used to indicate the arrangement of the particles in the soil, which is not usually perfectly random, except in horizons (layers) which have been extensively leached. This suggests that the material washed out of such horizons is responsible for binding together the soil particles into aggregates of various sizes, and this, in fact, can be shown to be so. The leached materials are mainly lime, iron salts, humus (or other organic matter), and clay. These are all capable, under suitable conditions, of cementing together numbers of small soil particles, as is clearly seen when thin sections of undisturbed soil are viewed under the microscope. The names applied to the various soil structures generally indicate clearly the nature of the aggregates; for example, *crumb*, *granular*, *shot*, and *nut*.

Organic cementing material may be produced by the soil flora and fauna, such as bacteria, fungi, and earth-worms, but also by the roots of the surface vegetation. Grasses in particular seem to have the property of forming stable soil structures, and in this way they are capable of considerably improving heavy clay soils of agricultural land.

Besides structures based on aggregation there are a few produced by the shrinkage of dispersed clay minerals on drying out. The familiar surface cracks in such parched soils may extend to considerable depths, and will close up on wetting and re-open in the same places on drying out again. They may be seen in section and may be described as either *prismatic* or *columnar* according to their appearance. Often the structure does not extend to the surface but forms in some deeper layer or layers, as, for example, in the alkaline soils of western North Dakota.

The most important physical properties of soils are their water-holding powers and drainage characteristics. These are directly related to particle size. It is true to say that the spaces between the soil particles are just as important as the particles themselves, because it is in the interstices that soil-water is held or moves, upwards, downwards, or laterally, carrying the products of decaying humus and soluble extracts of the soil minerals, of which iron salts and lime are generally the most important.

When the interstices are completely filled with water the soil is *waterlogged*, a condition that is quite common after heavy rain in temperate climates, but usually lasts only a short time if the soil is well drained. In such circumstances the soil water is still well aerated, and the soil is not changed chemically as it is when waterlogged for relatively long periods of time. Generally speaking, the larger the soil particles the better the drainage, which is why clay soils are usually badly drained. A nearly pure clay may be almost impermeable to water and so cause waterlogging of the upper soil layers. Waterlogging and the consequent exclusion of air produce the chemical changes described below.

One kind of *water-table* is formed whenever ground water reaches a more or less impermeable rock layer. If the soil above the impermeable layer is relatively open, consisting of gravel, sand, silt, or loam, then the soil-water may be able to move laterally and find its way to lower levels, or emerge again on a hill-side as a spring or series of springs. On the other hand, some rocks of rather open structure, such as some sandstones and limestones, will hold considerable amounts of water that may be prevented from descending further by impermeable rocks, and will not move appreciably laterally. This forms another kind of permanent water-table. The depth of the water-table varies with the rainfall, but the average depth depends on many factors, including climate and vegetation as well as the nature of the soil and bedrock. It is generally found, in developed countries, that present-day levels of water-tables are much lower than in prehistoric or early historic times, largely owing to the better drainage of lower-lying land.

2. The Chemical Nature of Soils

We shall discuss later the more important kinds of minerals that are found in rocks, but it is clear that those minerals that are not easily dissolved out of the parent rocks by rain and surface water will remain as constituents of the soil. In temperate regions these will be mainly silica (quartz), the numerous silicates, and lime-stones; in moist tropical climates some silica will remain but there will be larger proportions of ferric oxide and alumina, the former being responsible for the typical red colour of many tropical soils. The 'red podsolic soils' of the south-eastern U.S.A. are of this type.

The most important chemical property of these minerals from the point of view of soil type is their acidity or basicity. In a simplified way we may picture many inorganic substances as consisting of an acidic part and a basic part chemically combined together. Generally a metal, such as sodium, potassium, calcium, or iron will form the basic part, and a non-metal will be found in the acidic part. For example, in common salt (sodium chloride) the sodium ion is the basic part (derived from the *base* sodium hydroxide) and the chloride ion is the acidic part (the corresponding acid being hydrochloric acid).

In siliceous rocks the basic component of the minerals is silica (forming silicates), sometimes with alumina also, as in felspars. The igneous rocks are therefore classified in the following way;

Acid rocks: with more than 65 per cent silica (e.g. granite)
Intermediate rocks: with from 55 per cent to 65 per cent silica (e.g. diorite)
Basic rocks: with from 45 per cent to 55 per cent silica (e.g. dolerite)
Ultra-basic rocks: with less than 45 per cent silica (e.g. minerals containing iron and magnesium)

But soils are rarely formed directly from igneous rocks in cool temperate regions, although this does occur in certain mountain areas of Australia, Africa, South America, and the south-eastern U.S.A. Sedimentary rocks resulting from the weathering of igneous rocks form the commonest parent materials of soils, and here the acidity may be considerably affected by the nature of any cementing material. When the sedimented particles are cemented together by siliceous substances, or material containing a lot of iron salts, the rock is more resistant to weathering and hence soil formation may be slow. On the other hand, calcium carbonate (limestone), which is the binding material of many sedimentary rocks, is slowly soluble in rain-water, and this leads to relatively rapid weathering of the bedrock and soil formation. Breakdown of the limestone, with loss of the carbonate (acidic) part of the molecules, leaves a surplus of the basic component either as lime or calcium salts. Thus there may be several factors determining the final chemical nature of the 'raw' soil.

Subsequent changes in the soil may produce more-or-less distinct zones of different chemical nature, and often of different colours, known as *soil horizons*, the whole constituting the *soil profile*. Before briefly surveying the types of soil profile and their modes of formation we may conveniently consider the biological content of the soil, which has a profound effect on these.

3. Soil Flora and Fauna

Once vegetation has become established on a soil there is a constant circulation of material, which causes many changes in both the physical and chemical nature of the soil and is a major factor in the production of a soil profile. When the plants die they leave large amounts of organic matter, which feeds the huge population of micro-fauna and is thereby broken down into simpler substances. Some of these residues are soluble in the soil-water and may be absorbed by other plants, so completing one cycle of processes. There are, in fact, several cycles of this kind operating in the soil, some of them very complex. The materials essential for plant and animal life are used over and over again, but much of the soil material does not enter into these changes, and some of it remains unaffected, while other substances are washed out by the movement of the soil-water.

The chief agents of destruction of the plant remains are bacteria, actinomycetes, protozoa, fungi, arthropods, and worms.

Many bacteria live on organic matter, each species having its preferred food and conditions of temperature, atmosphere, and acidity, but in any reasonable soil there are likely to be several thousand million bacteria per gramme of soil. Protozoa are animals, slightly more complex than the bacteria, and, in fact, they feed on the latter; there may be more than fifty thousand of them in one gramme of soil. Fungi (e.g. moulds and mildews) convert some of the carbon of dead vegetation to carbon dioxide, thrive in moist surroundings, and tolerate acidic conditions.

There are other kinds of micro-flora and micro-fauna helping in the destruction of dead vegetation, and it has been estimated that they may account for from 2 per cent to 3 per cent of the total weight of all *organic* matter in the soil.

Among macro-fauna of the soil we may mention spiders, beetles, grubs, mites, slugs, snails, and wood-lice, among many others, and, of course, the extremely important earth-worm. All these help in the comminution and decay of vegetable debris, but the effect of earth-worms far outweighs that of all the others. Although one earth-worm might not appear to make any great difference to the soil, it will be appreciated that a population of something like three million per acre will cause a considerable up-heaval. This is the sort of worm population calculated as occupying a rich New Zealand pasture, and is said to be equal in weight to all the sheep on the same pasture. The casts from these worms amount to over ten tons per acre each year, a valuable contribution to the fertility of the land, because they consist of intimately mixed humus and soil minerals.

The first scientific study of earth-worm activity was made by Charles Darwin and described in *The Formation of Vegetable Mould through the action of Worms* (London, 1881). Worms prefer less acid soils and are rarely found in soils of pH less than 4·5, or in sandy or peaty soils. They burrow by passing the soil right through their bodies, at the same time extracting food from the organic constituents of the soil, particularly in the upper humus layers. It is often necessary for them to come to the surface to dis-gorge the soil in the form of a *cast*. This has the effect not only of mixing the top layers of soil but also of allowing small articles, such as stones or small artifacts, to sink, often producing a stony layer below an almost stoneless upper layer. Here is yet another example of a natural phenomenon which the inexperienced might interpret as the work of man. In fact, human occupation is likely to destroy the effect by re-mixing the stones and soil during cultivation, especially by deep-ploughing.

By the same kind of earth-worm activity the stratification on an archaeological site may be made much less sharp and distinct than it would otherwise be, but the effect will only cause inconvenience in the upper few inches of a rich soil. Earth-worm activity decreases at greater depths and is usually negligible below three or four feet. This also means that the sinking of small artifacts is significant only near the surface, and, since all artifacts originally at the same level will have moved roughly the same distance, the worms will not affect the sequence of the artifact stratification.

Larger animals make larger tunnels and have more serious effects on archaeological sites, but the burrows are generally readily recognized and allowance made for their effects. They are fortunately much less common than worm-holes. Here we have in mind such animals as rabbits, moles, foxes, and badgers.

4. Soil Profiles

Beginners in excavation work are often surprised to find that the side of a trench may show several apparent 'layers' which are not due to human occupation but result from entirely natural processes occurring within an initially uniform layer. The changes are all the result of the movement of soil-water, and may have involved the transport of iron salts, calcium salts, clay, and humus. These, at least, are the important transported materials, which have been most studied, but there is no doubt that other salts are also affected.

Soil-water may move in any direction according to circumstances, but the vertical movement is the greatest and the most effective in profile formation. When rain is falling and entering the ground there will clearly be a general downward movement of soil-water, but during dry periods when water is evaporating from the surface a certain amount of soil-water is drawn upwards to replace that lost. This movement is much less important, however, in profile formation except in arid regions. There are circumstances, none the less, in which the alternating upward and downward movement of a high water-table makes the whole depth of the soil periodically waterlogged, and the soil profile will indicate this very clearly.

The changes in the soil profile, and particularly the visible changes, are brought about by the movement of substances *dissolved* in the soil-water or carried in the form of a colloidal suspension. They will therefore depend on the amount of water falling on the soil and on the solubilities of the substances concerned. The latter, in turn, depend on several factors, mainly the temperature and the acidity of the soil. Rainfall and temperature are climatic factors, and soil acidity is controlled by the nature of the parent rock and of the overlying humus. The two latter are closely related because the rock type largely determines (with the climate) the type of vegetation cover, and the properties of the humus depend on the kinds of plants that produce it.

Freshly fallen leaves and other parts of plants are known as plant *litter*, but, as we have seen, decay will begin very soon and result in the formation of a layer of humus, which may be of one of three types. In their order of decreasing acidity these are known as *mor*, *moder*, and *mull* humus. *Mor* humus is raw humus, decaying very slowly because it is extremely acidic. It is commonly found on heathland and under pine forests. *Moder*, or *Duff*, is an acid humus rich in minerals, rather loose and crumbly with a mouldy smell, found on acid soils under deciduous forest. *Mull* humus occurs on basic soils in moist, mild climates, and is aggregated and friable. The decay products of any form of humus which become finely dispersed in the soil-water and interact with the soil minerals form the *mobile humus* (or endohumus).

The movement of iron and calcium salts depends almost entirely on the acidity of the soil-water, and hence on the soil type and humus type. Generally speaking iron salts are moved in acid soil water (pH less than 5·5) and calcium salts in alkaline (basic) solutions (pH greater than 8·4), but in hot climates iron may be transported at higher pH by a slightly different mechanism, and in cool climates calcium salts are more easily transported.

For one reason or another the acidity of the soil water may change at a particular level in the profile, resulting in a reversal of conditions for the transport of salts or humus. Iron, for example, may be carried down by the mobile humus if it is sufficiently acid, but if the solution reaches a zone of lower acidity (bringing the pH above 5·5) the iron will be precipitated as the hydroxide, a red-brown substance. This is the normal mechanism for the formation of an '*iron-pan*', a hard red-brown layer of variable thickness. It has been said that iron-pan may be formed on an occupation surface that has been well trampled, but it is difficult to see why mere compression of the soil should cause the precipitation of iron; there may be some other explanation, perhaps involving the presence of organic debris and the impairment of drainage. Iron-pan may also be formed on the surface of timber that has been covered by a fairly thick layer of soil. This has been noted, for example, in the timber-laced ramparts of Roman forts, where the iron-pan appears to reproduce the surface texture of the long-decayed timbers. Iron-pan has sometimes been reported as 'iron slag', the waste product of the extraction of iron from its ores, and it has frequently been excavated because at first sight it looks very like the remains of completely decayed iron objects. Chemically the iron of iron-pan may be in the same state as that in the rust to which iron objects decay, but iron-pan is readily distinguished by the fact that it consists of soil particles coated with iron oxide, and the presence of soil particles right through the iron-pan is easily seen (though it may contain much humus). The same observation will also demonstrate the absence of a slag, together with the absence of any signs of vitrifaction.

The calcium salts also may be thrown out of solution by changes in the soil acidity, usually in the form of white, powdery, calcium carbonate, but this also may form hard concretions. Calcium carbonate is held in solution only when there is a surplus of carbon dioxide available, as there is in most soil waters and in the air spaces in the soil. Some of this gas comes from the decomposition of organic matter, and since most of this decomposition will occur in the upper layers of the soil it may happen that lower down there is less carbon dioxide and so the calcium carbonate will be deposited. But there are other processes at work here, and the effect depends also on the acidity of the soil-water. Humic acids (from humus) combine with calcium salts to form *calcium humates*— probably mixtures of various complex salts. These will also be transported, and may be decomposed at lower levels by changes in acidity.

Clay particles are readily dispersed in water as a colloidal suspension and may be transported in this form through the soil, but the presence of salts in the soil-water will generally cause flocculation (coagulation) of the clay particles. Hence the movement of clay in a soil profile is of much less importance than that of iron or calcium salts.

Having now formed a general, simplified, picture of the reasons for, and methods of, the movement of various substances in the soil we may look at the results of these movements in the form of some of the more common soil profiles. But first we must outline the methods used by the pedologist to describe a profile.

The most completely developed soil profile may be described by first dividing it broadly into zones A, B, and C (the D zone does not concern the archaeologist). These represent, respectively, an *eluvial* zone (from which substances have been washed *out*), an *illuvial* zone (*into* which the substances have been transported), and the chemically unchanged bedrock.

The main zones, A, B, and C, may then be subdivided as required to record all the horizons in the profile. Some soils will not have all the three main zones, but many soils will show more than three. A very new soil, only just starting to form, will be described as an (A)C soil, pronounced 'A-bracket C', because it has a humus layer, (A), and the unchanged bedrock, C. The brackets show that the humus, although forming the uppermost layer, is not an eluvial horizon. We may have, similarly, a (B) horizon, i.e. one which occupies the position of a B horizon but is not an illuvial zone. Also, between any two main horizons there may be an intermediate zone, e.g. between an A and a B horizon there may be an A/B horizon, showing some of the properties of each or being an overlapping region.

Subdivisions may be of many kinds, and it will be convenient to illustrate some of these in a diagrammatic representation of a common type of profile known as a *podsol* (or podzol—Russian: ash-coloured soil), Figure 1.

It will be seen that the A-zone consists of three horizons, the raw humus A_0, the dark layer containing mobile humus A_1, and the so-called bleached horizon A_2. The 'bleaching' is not actually chemical bleaching but merely loss of colour owing to the removal of iron. All the three A-horizons have lost some iron but most has been taken from A_2 by the action of the mobile humus. The illuvial zone, B, shows two horizons because there has been a separation of humus and iron, the upper, B_1, horizon has received humus and so appears darkened, and the B_2 horizon has received iron and will probably be red to brown in colour. These two horizons will overlap, but they both belong to the B-zone, so that it is not usual to indicate the overlap in the form of a B_1/B_2 horizon. Below these there is another overlap. Some iron and/or humus have been deposited within the C horizon, i.e. in the chemically unaltered bedrock. So here we have an intermediate horizon, B/C. The C-horizon itself may be divided into C_1, the physically altered (comminuted), and C_2, the unaltered bedrock. This is the kind of profile often found in moist temperate climates on sand or gravel carrying coniferous forest or heathland. The very pale A_2-horizon is very clearly marked, and it will be noted that all the horizons vary in thickness from place to place. It is interesting to see how the horizons change with the presence of larger stones or boulders and with variations in the plant coverage. All these points can be studied quite easily on roads cut through some coniferous forests, such as those of the Forestry Commission in Great Britain.

The nature of the vegetation cover has a very great effect on the type of soil profile developed, and it seems that certain kinds of

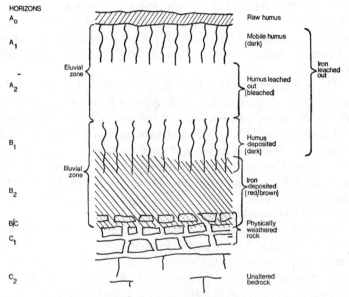

Figure 1   A typical podsol profile.

trees are particularly effective in forming podsols, probably because they produce the appropriate kinds of polyphenolic compounds (tannins). The more important podsol-forming trees and shrubs include pine, heather, oak and beech, and of non-woody plants the most effective is bracken. The complex relationship between soil type and vegetation type appears to be such that the kind of soil that favours the production of a podsol profile also encourages the growth of the podsol-forming vegetation.

Podsols are the predominating soil types over the greater part of northern Europe (including the western half of the British Isles), and Asia (south of the tundra zones), and across large areas of the northern U.S.A. and Canada. In Europe closely related soils, including brown forest soils, generally lie to the south of the podsols, but to the east of them in England. In the U.S.A. the situation is more complex. In the eastern States the north–south sequence is podsols, brown forest soils (etc.), and lateritic soils (red and yellow soils), but then the dividing lines are more north–south, so that from east to west the successive zones consist mainly of prairie soils, 'chestnut' and brown soils, and desert soils, with some complex types in the mountains and mountain valleys. The division between the leached (podsolic) soils of the east and the unleached of the west runs roughly through Western Minnesota, Eastern Nebraska, Eastern Kansas, Mid-Oklahoma, and Mid-Texas.

The soil types here listed are the *zonal* types, i.e. characteristic of the zones indicated, but each type includes several varieties. The zonal soils depend mainly on the nature of the parent rocks and the climate of the region, but variations in either of these will produce more or less important changes in soil type within the zone. If local variations are large then a soil of a distinct type may be produced (an *azonal* soil), but with relatively small variations of climate or rock type the soils will be fairly closely related to the zonal soil (*intrazonal* soils).

We have seen under what conditions the podsols are formed; another common type of profile in cool temperate climates is the *braunerde* (German: brown earth). There are several varieties of braunerde, according to the nature of the parent rock, all being formed on nearly neutral soils, and the different horizons are frequently very difficult to distinguish. The profile is described as A(B)C because there is no transport of iron from the A- to the B-horizons (Figure 2).

Other distinct soil types are found in the arid or desert regions of the world. In the north-western U.S.A. the desert soils are grey and salty, but in the south they are red or reddish brown, with little vegetation apart from cacti and sagebrush. The sandy nature of many desert soils makes them very susceptible to erosion by wind or water, the former often leaving areas of 'desert pavement' which consist of irregular stones left behind when the finer material has been blown away. The stones often show a 'desert gloss'. Desert soils also often contain *pans* or *crusts*. Pans are hard layers below the surface formed by the deposition of calcium carbonate, gypsum, or iron salts by descending water. Although the annual rainfall may be low in such regions, it often consists of very heavy downpours and its effect may be quite pronounced. Deposits left on or near the surface by *ascending* solution during dry periods are called *crusts*.

In southern California, for example, there are soils consisting of more or less reddish-brown layers, the upper ones having lost some iron and calcium, which has been deposited as a red hardpan of iron salts and calcium carbonate on top of the porous brown, unweathered bedrock.

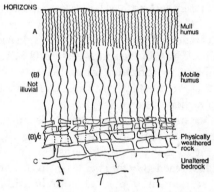

Figure 2   A braunerde profile, with indistinct horizons.

There are so many soil types and profiles that the archaeologist might encounter that we must be content with the very brief summary given above. Furthermore, the nomenclature of soil types, orders, sub-orders, etc., is still in a very confused state, making the study of soils even in one locality quite a difficult matter for the layman. Even so, it is suggested that such a study might be well worth while for the practical prehistoric archaeologist. For workers in Europe the classification devised by Kubiena (*The Soils of Europe*, Murby, London 1953) is the accepted authority (see also I. W. Cornwall), but a more comprehensive scheme, known as '7A', is in use by the U.S. Department of Agriculture (*Soil Classification, A Comprehensive System, Seventh Approximation*, USDA 1960). The most important requirement for most excavators remains to understand the broad principles of the soil-forming processes, the causes of 'horizonation', and not to be misled into seeing the work of man where it does not exist.

Complications may arise where, following a change of climate, a new profile develops on an old one. This is particularly significant when the old profile was of a tropical or sub-tropical type in which considerable chemical change has taken place, because then the new profile, which may develop in a temperate climate, will retain some of the features of the old soil. The latter might be in its original position or it might consist of the soil material (i.e. no longer a profile) as a sediment a great distance from its place of formation. Such soils are called *relict* soils.

At any stage in the development of a soil profile external influences might remove surface layers or deposit fresh material on the surface. Loss of upper layers of soil by erosion has often followed the clearance of vegetation by settlers, leaving a soil with a *truncated profile*. Thus, in the south-eastern U.S.A. deforestation in a region subject to torrential rains led to extensive surface erosion, so that the present-day cultivated soil consists of the *lower* horizons of the earlier soil.

If, on the other hand, deposited material is sufficiently thick it will isolate the developing soil profile, stopping the transport of material within it so that the profile remains fixed at the stage of development it had reached before being covered. The soil-forming processes will subsequently operate entirely within the newly deposited material, and the earlier profile is referred to as a *fossil soil* or a *buried soil*. This can occur by natural processes, but the archaeologist will be more interested in fossil soils beneath man-made structures such as burial mounds, dykes, banks, roads, and earthen ramparts.

In such circumstances the excavator tries to identify the earlier surface. If this was not disturbed before being covered over there is the possibility that the humus from the decayed vegetation will not have been appreciably washed out, and a dark stain will then be seen in the section (Plate II), but even when this is not clear it may still be possible to fix the position of the ancient surface by means of chemical tests for iron and humus in the various horizons. It frequently happens that the ancient surface beneath a structure is at a different level from that remaining uncovered, outside the structure. This has been explained as the effect of the compression of the soil under the weight of the structure, or by the erosion of the uncovered surface, but before accepting such interpretations one should ensure, by means of chemical tests, that the ancient buried surface has been correctly located. On chalk soils dissolution of the subsoil may lower the uncovered surface, leaving the buried surface some inches higher.

Often an ancient 'turf-line' shows very clearly under a structure but disappears abruptly at its edge. The reasons for this are not always appreciated. An example is shown in Plate II, where a section of a Roman road in Staffordshire illustrates the effect. The thick layer of sandstones and clay adequately isolates the old soil, and the decayed vegetation (turf) remains recognizable. Beyond the edge of the road, however, leaching has taken place, so that, as the old surface has become covered by a *slowly* increasing thickness of soil, traces of the old humus have been completely washed out. The work of earth-worms should be remembered when interpreting such phenomena as we have just discussed, but this will be negligible under stonework or several feet of added soil.

It is interesting to note that processes similar to those of soil-profile formation may occur *within* rocks. In particular, during excavation one often finds small stones, especially of porous rocks such as some sandstones, which when broken show two or three 'horizons'. These are usually dark horizontal streaks, and result from the deposition of iron or humus just as in the soil. Pale, leached layers may also be found. Small stones may be completely blackened by humus so as to suggest the presence of charcoal or decayed organic matter, and these can be very misleading if the phenomenon is not understood.

5. Turf

Turf is grass together with the matted roots and a certain amount of the soil in which it is or was growing, although the term is used in some places (notably Ireland) for the thick peat cut from the bogs for use as fuel. It is clear from what has already been said that turf will also incorporate humus, and the soil part of the turf may be saturated with mobile humus. We have also seen that there are three possible consequences of covering growing turf. If the turf is only slowly covered by blown soil, dust, and other air-borne debris, as on abandoned sites on level surfaces, the grass continues to grow normally but the soil surface gradually rises. As humus is being washed downwards by rain-water, old roots are decaying, and earth-worms are at work, the net effect is simply a very slow upward movement of the turf and an increase in thickness of the 'humus layer'.

On the other hand, if a sudden or rapid accumulation of material appears on the surface of the turf the grass may be killed. Then there can be no upward movement. Either the decaying turf remains in its original position, becoming dark grey with accumulating humus, or, if water seepage is appreciable, the humus may be washed down the soil profile, leaving no *visible* trace. There may or may not be detectable remains.

But turf also appears on archaeological sites under other conditions, since it is a useful constructional material under certain circumstances. In many parts of the world turf has been cut for building walls for houses, town walls, or defensive earthworks. The Roman army developed the use of turf for the revetment of earthen ramparts, probably cutting them to a standard size, and inventing the crescentic iron turf-cutter of virtually the same shape as those in use today. They are said to have preferred to stack the turves grass-to-grass, though the reason for this is not now clear. The decayed grass often leaves a black line around the more or less leached turves. If the turves have to carry much weight they become very much compressed vertically and, where possible, slightly squeezed out horizontally.

It is often very difficult to recognize ancient turf-work in an archaeological section. If some humus remains the individual turves may be seen as grey rectangles, but sometimes the humus tends to accumulate at the bottom of the turves, giving thin layers of grey alternating with, usually, paler layers. So much depends on the nature of the soil on which the grass grew; if this was a clayey soil, then the turves will retain the clayey texture, and turves from sandy soil remain of a sandy texture and tend to crumble readily, so that there is no simple rule for the recognition of turf after all the humus has been leached out.

In most parts of the world any area stripped of its vegetation will soon become colonized by various plants and in a very few years will be completely covered again with vegetation, possibly of a quite different type from the original cover. This means that a new soil-profile may be developing with a new 'turf-layer', which need not be merely grass. But very little is definitely known about the time-scale for the formation of turf on a cleared surface; it is bound to vary greatly with the soil and vegetation types. It would certainly be useful to be able to calculate the period of abandonment of a site from the thickness of turf or soil formation, but there are very few sites where this can be attempted at the present time.

6. Cave Earths

The stratification found on the floor of a cave is generally quite different from a soil-profile; it consists essentially of *successive* deposits and is not the result of chemical action. As it is not strictly a soil at all it is better referred to as a *cave earth.*

Most caves are found in limestone rocks and are formed by the dissolution of calcium carbonate by acid rain-water or river-water. The processes of cave formation are complex and not archaeologically significant. The importance of caves to the archaeologist lies in the fact that the large amounts of calcium carbonate in the deposits creates an alkaline environment in which bones, shells, and flint artifacts are well preserved.

Caves are amongst the most difficult of sites to excavate and interpret. Apart from human occupation layers several other kinds of deposit are commonly found, including layers of rodent bones and bat-dung in many cases. Fragments of limestone broken from the roof or sides of the cave by large temperature changes or by the action of freezing and thawing of water will be found, with a certain amount of fine mineral deposits. The latter consist of the small proportion of non-carbonate (insoluble) minerals in the limestone, but over long periods of time can amount to quite thick deposits. There will also be other materials washed in by seeping water or wind-borne dusts drifting in through the entrance and through cracks and fissures in the rocks.

B. The Materials of Antiquity

ONE

INTRODUCTION

In order to reach some understanding of the nature of the materials used by man since his earliest times, and to acquire some insight into the reasons for the wide variations in their properties, it is necessary for us to know something of the fundamental structure of matter.

For hundreds of years the alchemists studied the properties of materials, struggling for some understanding of their origins, mainly for selfish reasons—the search for the Philosopher's Stone, or the Elixir, which would change common metals into gold. There followed a period in which pharmaceutical chemistry predominated, and then, for less than two hundred years, up to the present time, modern chemistry has been developing. Gradually the details were discovered of how different materials are built up, and the amazing fact emerged that everything, from common salt to precious gold, from solid granite to the gases of the atmosphere, is built from precisely the same few fundamental particles.

Yet even with this knowledge and the skills acquired over hundreds of years the chemist is still unable to transmute lead into gold. But he has produced whole new families of materials, and can make complex drugs that are possibly worth much more than their weight in gold. And he could, with the help of the physicist and the politician, transmute a whole world into a sterile mass of grey dust.

The objectives of the science of materials, then, are changing from the investigation of properties towards the production of new materials with pre-determined properties. This aim is as yet only partly realized, but a necessary preliminary has been to relate the structure of a substance to its properties. The subject is intrinsically complex, but it is possible for the non-scientist to appreciate some of the broader aspects of the subject and make use of them in archaeological investigations.

It is convenient to discuss some of these points here, and in particular the structures of atoms and crystals, as we shall need these ideas for many purposes later.

All solids are probably crystalline, though sometimes the crystals may be of microscopic size, and each substance forms crystals of a definite shape, or *habit*, by which it may be recognized. In fact minerals are generally identified from their crystal forms and the optical properties which accompany them, but this procedure is a highly specialized study, which must be left to the mineralogist, petrologist, or geologist. It is important for us to note that the regular external forms of crystals are closely related to the regular internal arrangement of the constituent particles.

All substances are built up from the same fundamental particles in definite stages. It is the numbers *and* arrangements of these particles that determine the nature of the substance formed. A very much simplified scheme illustrating this idea is given as Figure 3.

Only three fundamental particles need be considered for our present purposes. *Protons* and *neutrons* are the heavy particles from which the *nucleus* of an atom is formed. Since protons have a positive electrical charge and neutrons are so called because they are electrically neutral, atomic nuclei are positive. This positive charge is balanced by negative electrons to form neutral atoms. The electrons are much smaller than the other particles and of negligible weight, and they may be considered to be orbiting around the nucleus, by analogy with the movement of the planets around the sun.

It is at this stage in the building process that we can begin to speak of a definite chemical substance, an *element* in fact, since the chemical behaviour of an element depends on the number and arrangement of the electrons around the nucleus. We can imagine starting with the lightest and simplest element, hydrogen, and building up all the others from it. Thus a hydrogen atom consists of only one proton in the nucleus and one electron in orbit around it. By adding one proton (and neutrons also) to the nucleus, and one orbital electron, we produce the next element, *helium*. Proceeding in this way, which is purely hypothetical, we should finally arrive at the heaviest and largest natural atom, that of *uranium*, which is about 238 times as heavy as the hydrogen atom.

We need not go into more details of atomic structure; the point to be emphasized at the moment is that every kind of atom is made

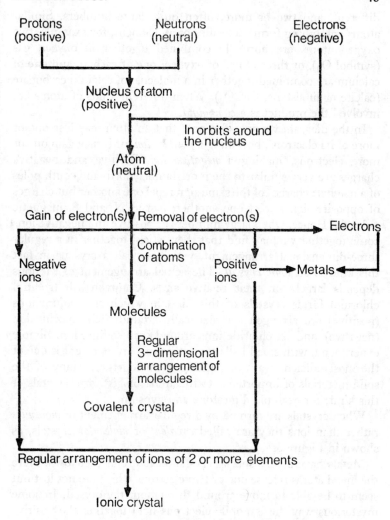

Figure 3   The structure of atoms, molecules, and crystals.

up of the three fundamental particles, but that their numbers and arrangement in the atom determine the nature of the resulting element.

The figure next shows that atoms may combine together to form molecules. This is one of the possible second stages in building up different substances. The atoms combining here may be alike or different, and two or more, often quite large numbers. Similar atoms combining form molecules of an element, for example, two oxygen atoms are normally combined together in oxygen gas (symbol O_2), or three atoms of oxygen, one of carbon, and one of calcium are combined together in a molecule of calcium carbonate (calcite or limestone, $CaCO_3$). When different kinds of atoms are involved the product is a *compound*.

In the diagram we may also note that an atom may lose one or more of its electrons, becoming a *positive ion*, or it may gain one or more electrons, making a *negative ion*. Positive and negative charges are very similar to the more familar north and south poles of a magnet; charges of the same sign repel one another but charges of opposite sign attract one another, just as N. and S. magnetic poles do. Hence, when large numbers of positive and negative ions come together we may find that they 'stick' together in a regular three-dimensional arrangement, which we call a crystal; in fact this kind is an *ionic crystal*. The actual arrangement of the ions depends largely on their relative sizes. Common salt (sodium chloride) forms crystals of this kind in which six sodium ions (positive) are arranged symmetrically around each chloride ion (negative), and six chloride ions around each sodium ion. Simple experiments with small balls show that this arrangement is one of the most efficient ways of packing them together. Many of the solid materials of importance to the archaeologist form crystals of this kind; for example, limestone and gypsum.

When crystals are formed by a regular arrangement of *molecules* rather than ions they are called *covalent* or *molecular* crystals, as shown in Figure 3.

Metals have a very special crystal structure of their own. Here the metal atoms release one or two electrons which are not lost but seem to be able to move around throughout the crystal. In some mysterious way these mobile electrons hold together the positive ions of the metal, and it is these same electrons that are responsible for the high electrical conductance of metals. The passage of an electric current through a metal such as a copper wire is, in fact, the movement of electrons in the metal.

Summarizing, we may say that the arrangement of the particles in an atom determines its nature, and the way that atoms, ions, or molecules are arranged in a crystal determines the nature of the crystal. In particular, *atomic* structures determine the *chemical* properties of the substance, such as how and when substances will react together chemically, and crystal structures determine the physical properties of solids, for example, their densities, hardness, etc. All this should be subject to many qualifications, but it is hoped that it will be adequate for our present purposes.

Chemically, *compounds* are classed as either *organic* or *inorganic*. The former are essentially those produced by living organisms, and this definition will serve us now, but, since there are now far more synthetic organic compounds than naturally occurring ones, organic compounds are generally defined as those compounds containing carbon (except carbonates and a few other simple compounds). *Inorganic* materials, then, must be those found in the earth or atmosphere and not forming part of plant or animal.

In general, organic materials are more perishable than inorganic materials, as is only too familiar to the archaeologist. Wood, leather, and textiles, for example, are preserved only in special circumstances. On the other hand, copper, bronze, and iron often corrode rapidly and may leave little trace on many sites. Special mention must be made of charcoal, although we shall return to it later. Charcoal is carbon produced by the incomplete burning of any (chemically) organic material. It can *not* be formed by any other natural process, and it is virtually indestructible except by further burning in an adequate supply of air.

The materials available to ancient man were very numerous, but it appears that he only very slowly extended his range of tools and his adoption of the various materials. If one considers these two factors as measures of 'progress', a very superficial survey will suggest that the rate of progress of man has shown a steady increase through the ages. This should not be surprising, since it is assumed that the world population has shown, in general, a similar steady increase, with a correspondingly increasing probability of new developments appearing.

Little if any progress was made by the earliest tool-users for a million years, during which time pebble tools were used, but the possibility of a quite extensive use of other implements made of perishable materials cannot be ruled out. At a much later stage one sees a far greater rate of progress, as, for example, from the Neolithic Age through the Bronze Ages to the Iron Age in Britain in less than three thousand years. Conquest has, of course, frequently produced rapid changes in a relatively small area, as when Mexico was suddenly translated from a Bronze Age type of culture into the late Medieval world.

The division of prehistory into Ages of Stone, Bronze, and Iron, can be misleading, if it suggests a preoccupation with these materials and more or less rapid replacement of tools and weapons of one type with those of the new materials. This is very far from the truth. At the very least there would be quite extensive over-lapping, old and new-style tools being in contemporary use perhaps for long periods. Furthermore, it seems that in the early Bronze Age the possession of bronze objects was the prerogative of the wealthy or the powerful, and it may well be that a similar situation was prevalent in the early Iron Age. Again, even when the new materials came into general use there would still be circumstances in which the older tools would be at least as satisfactory as the new. Stone tools, for example, continued in use through Bronze and Iron Ages, and very much later if querns, whetstones, and the like are included.

Perhaps we have here a clue to the paths of progress. Each advance may be the result of necessity, or of some chance discovery, but in either case the requisite technology would have to be available before the forward step could be taken. All the materials were in existence from the earliest times, but the need and the technology developed very slowly.

It is not our purpose here to review the history of technology, but merely to consider the nature of the raw materials in relation to their uses, and how they may have been changed by man before being abandoned in an archaeological environment.

TWO

INORGANIC MATERIALS

1. Rocks and Minerals

In our discussion of the archaeological environment we have seen
how the weathering of rocks can lead to soil formation, possibly by
way of intermediate stages such as loose boulders, scree, etc.
Weathering, i.e. atmospheric effects, and erosion by the action of
glaciers, rivers or the sea, may cause the more soluble constituents
of a rock to be dissolved out, leaving only the harder and more
resistant parts, often in the form of pebbles, which formed the
earliest tools of man.

There are hundreds of varieties of rocks, but, fortunately, only
a small fraction of these was in general and widespread use by man
in antiquity. It will be useful first to see how the different kinds of
rocks were produced, and this we can do very simply, as illustrated
in Figure 4.

All the rocks originated from masses of molten material that may
be present below the earth's crust, or material that became molten
when the extreme pressure on it was released. This is *magma*,
which finds its way from time to time to the surface, where it cools
and solidifies, producing what we know as the igneous rocks.
Other rocks reach the surface through volcanic action, and the
material ranging in size from large boulders to fine dust which is
thrown out during the violent phases of a volcano forms the *pyroclastic* rocks. These are, in fact, igneous rocks, and may be compacted and cemented by the percolation of solutions between the
particles, forming fine-grained *tuff* or coarse *agglomerate*.

When rocks become exposed they are immediately subjected to
weathering, but if they become strained by huge forces such as
occur in folding, quite different changes may take place, particularly if the temperature is high. We can distinguish physical and
chemical changes. For present purposes physical changes are
changes in the large-scale or microscopic form, and chemical
changes involve rearrangements of atoms. That is, in physical

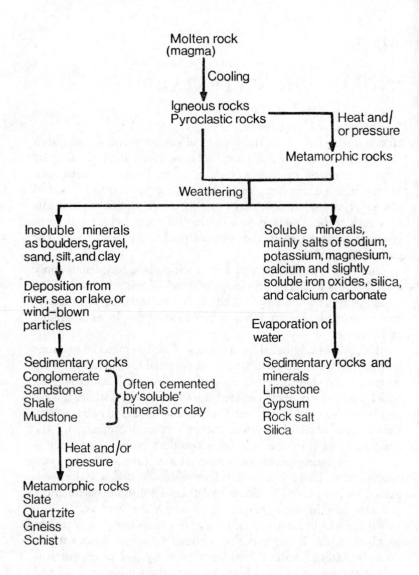

Figure 4   The formation of rocks.

changes the *same substances* are re-organized, as when intimately mixed materials separate and perhaps form large crystals. But in chemical changes the resulting minerals will be different chemical entities from the original constituents. In a simple case this may be by the exchange of oxygen such as that which leads from one oxide of iron to another, a change which is extremely important in other archaeological contexts also.

Weathering involves only physical changes such as breaking down into smaller pieces and dissolution of soluble constituents of the rocks. The most effective agent is frost, particularly when there is frequent freezing and thawing. This results from the fact that water, unlike almost all other substances, expands slightly on freezing, and in cracks and fissures the process can result in the exertion of extremely powerful forces. The effects are familiar in our unprotected water pipes, but the result does not *appear* until the ice melts and the water escapes.

Rain-water is next in effectiveness of weathering in temperate climates, but in tropical countries the alternating heat of the sun and cold of the night can have very considerable effects, particularly on vertical rock faces.

The products of weathering are sorted out by the action of water, as will be seen in Figure 4. Soluble minerals will be largely washed away into streams and rivers, and the slightly acid rain-water will dissolve small amounts of many minerals generally considered to be insoluble in water, such as silica, iron oxides, and calcium carbonate (calcite or limestone). Many of the dissolved minerals will be carried to the sea or to lakes, and the subsequent drying up of inland seas or lakes results in the deposition of the dissolved minerals, forming valuable sources of raw materials. Very thick deposits often occur, such as the salt deposits of Cheshire, England, or of Utah, U.S.A., and these may be the result of continuous or repeated evaporation and the sinking of the bed of the lake.

It should be noted that chalk deposits consist of the remains of the skeletons of minute sea creatures, formed almost entirely of calcite. Although this is therefore of organic *origin* it is not considered to be itself organic since it is exactly the same, chemically, as all other forms of calcite or limestone. (*Chemically*, all organic substances contain carbon otherwise than as carbonate or a few other simple compounds.)

The insoluble products of weathering may be classified according to size as boulders, gravel, silt, or clay, and they may all be carried considerable distances by running water. Clearly, the smaller the particles the further they will be carried, and the faster the current the larger the pieces that will be moved. Here again there will be deposition from the water of river, lake, or sea, and other kinds of sedimentary rocks will be formed. After being deposited as loose layers of particles other changes will take place, particularly as the result of the pressures building up as more and more material is deposited on top, but also with the removal of water. The particles then become cemented together, sometimes by clay or by minerals such as silica or calcite coming out of solution.

Sedimentary rocks of this kind are named mainly according to the size of the particles, from *conglomerate*, containing small boulders, pebbles, or large gravel grades, to sandstone (visible sand grains), shale, and mudstone. Shale consists of flat silt and clay grains which are too small to see with the naked eye, and which tend to lie in one direction, parallel to the bed on which they were deposited. This is why shales are easily split into thin sheets, but, being usually soft, the sheets tend to crumble. When cemented with silica or iron oxides shales are much stronger.

Mudstone is similar to shale but the grains are not flat and the rock breaks equally well in any direction.

Both igneous and sedimentary rocks may become metamorphic rocks, which are usually more obviously crystalline. An igneous rock or a conglomerate or sandstone will generally change under the effects of pressure or heat to a *gneiss* or *schist*. These are, respectively, coarsely banded and finely banded rocks, but the actual crystals or grains may be either large or small in each type. Sandstones may also recrystallize to quartzite. Shales and mudstones are metamorphosed to slates.

Metamorphism also occurs in regions of contact between the hot volatile material associated with the magma and the rocks through which it intrudes. Such *contact metamorphism* produces important minerals, including precious and semi-precious stones and metal ores.

It might be expected that the distinction between sedimentary and igneous rocks would be clear, but this is not always so. The grains in sedimentary rocks are separate, since they were individually deposited, but they may have been very much compressed

Plate I   Misleading 'small finds': (a) a pebble showing 'pressure marks'; (b) bone and pottery: a fragment of Romano-British coarse ware compared with a piece of fossilized bone of the cave-bear; (c) fragments of fossilized sea-lily in limestone, which could be mistaken for beads; (d) naturally formed fragments of stone that have the appearance of artifacts.

Plate II   An ancient turf-line preserved below the sandstone metalling of a Roman road.

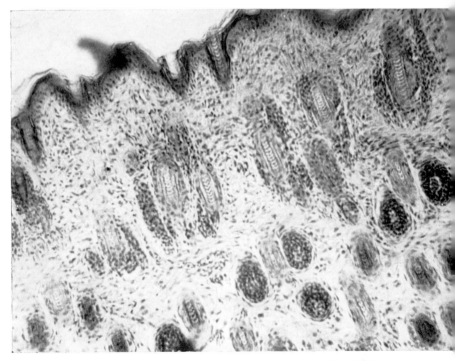

Plate III   Section of the skin of a cat, showing follicles.

and cemented together by other substances. Hence they are often visible to the naked eye or under a lens, but some sediments consist of very small grains, especially those formed from the 'soluble' minerals. The crystals of igneous rocks, on the other hand, are interlocked very tightly, needing no extraneous cementing material. Where a clear stratification is seen in the rock it is probably of sedimentary origin, unless it is a gneiss or schist, in which case the rock will be crystalline. But the apparent absence of stratification must not be relied on as proof of the igneous source of a rock. Also, joints and fissures in igneous rocks are easily mistaken for *bedding* (stratification).

A knowledge of the sources of rocks and the mode of their formation may help towards their identification, but it gives only a superficial, large-scale view, which is none the less useful and important especially from the point of view of selecting suitable rocks for particular purposes. For this one also needs to know about the hardness and brittleness, in which direction the rock can be most readily split or cut, and how it will stand up to weathering or use. These properties depend on both the macroscopic and the microscopic structure of the rock.

In considering, for example, the splitting of rocks, it is clear that some of the less compacted sedimentary rocks will split readily along planes parallel to the bedding plane, that is, by the separation of successive layers of sediment. On the other hand, igneous rocks will split only by breaking innumerable crystals, since, as we have seen, the rock is entirely composed of interlocking crystals. Here there is no preferred direction of splitting; the rock will break equally well, or badly, in any direction. In such cases the factors which determine the strength and other properties of the rock are the properties of the constituent minerals.

The difficulties encountered in classifying and identifying rocks are largely due to their infinite variety. It is not possible to use a simple three-stage scheme of classification such as Family, Genus, and Species, as in botanical nomenclature, since the distinctions are not as clear-cut as between plants. We may see (Figure 5) how *origin* and *structure* may be used as a basis for classification, but it is not often necessary to specify the origin, since this may generally be inferred. For example a *schist* is a finely-banded metamorphic rock; the full expression 'metamorphic schist' is unnecessary.

3*

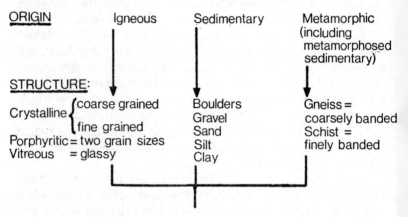

MINERAL COMPOSITION:
Quartz = silica

Silicate minerals:

Felspar = aluminium silicates with sodium, potassium, and/or calcium
Mica = potassium aluminium silicates with fluorine and hydroxyl and sometimes magnesium and iron
Pyroxene = iron magnesium silicates with calcium, sodium and aluminium
Hornblende = iron aluminium silicates with calcium, sodium and hydroxyl
Olivine = iron magnesium silicates
Hydrous silicates (clay minerals) e.g. china clay (kaolin)

Non-silicate minerals:

Corundum (alumina), including emery, sapphire, and ruby
Fluorspar ('Blue John' in Derbyshire) = calcium fluoride
Mineral deposits from soluble products of weathering:

Limestone = calcite (calcium carbonate)
Gypsum = hydrated calcium sulphate
Rock salt = sodium chloride
Silica, including flint and chert

Figure 5   The classification of rocks.

Suppose, then, that we rely on the structure for our first stage of classification. We should then require as our second stage a simple term expressing the mineral composition. Although this may be occasionally possible, as in 'porphyritic quartz', it will not generally be so, as many rocks contain many minerals in varying proportions. Furthermore, the minerals themselves are not always very clearly defined, or, in other words, cannot be given a definite or fixed chemical formula. Felspars provide simple examples. They are aluminium silicates with varying amounts and proportions of sodium, potassium, and calcium, the properties of the mineral varying accordingly.

To illustrate the complexity of rock classification we need refer only to a definition of *granites*; these are coarse-grained (sometimes porphyritic) igneous rocks composed mainly of felspars, quartz, and mica, but some granites contain only felspar and quartz, and others may contain hornblende or mica. In addition, certain precious or semi-precious minerals may occur in granite, such as topaz, tourmaline, or garnet. Thus archaeologists could hardly be expected to master the intricacies of rock classification, let alone the details of mineral identification, but they should try to familiarize themselves with the appearance and properties of those most commonly used by ancient man.

First let us look at the minerals listed in the lower part of Figure 5. Quartz is a crystalline form of *silica*, which is the normal oxide of the element *silicon* (chemical symbol Si). The chemical formula for silica is SiO_2, indicating that there are twice as many oxygen atoms as silicon atoms in the crystals. In a crystal of pure quartz each silicon atom is surrounded symmetrically by four oxygen atoms (an arrangement based on the regular tetrahedron) and each oxygen atom is bound to two silicon atoms, forming a three-dimensional network known as the *crystal lattice*. It is the regularity of this structure in all directions, and the fact that the atoms are strongly held together, that accounts for the hardness of quartz. A very similar arrangement of atoms is found in the crystals of carbon known as *diamond*. Here, in addition to the regular three-dimensional arrangement we have only one kind of atom, and this gives a completely symmetrical and tightly bound crystal, which is the hardest of all minerals. On the *Mohs scale of hardness* diamond is given the value 10, talc, the softest mineral, occupies position 1, and quartz has hardness number 7 (Table 4).

If a mineral is crystallized from magma containing aluminium as well as silicon, then the resulting crystal structures could be very similar to those of quartz, but with aluminium atoms (Al) occupying some of the positions in the lattice normally occupied by silicon atoms. By reason of the difference in structure of these atoms, this substitution upsets the balance of electrical charges,

Table 4

The Mohs Scale of Hardness

10 Diamond
9 Corundum
8 Topaz
7 Quartz
6 Felspar
5 Apatite
4 Fluorspar
3 Calcite
2 Gypsum
1 Talc

which must be redressed by the addition of an appropriate number of other atoms, in particular those of sodium (Na), potassium (K), or calcium (Ca). Without going into further detail it will readily be seen that these changes will also disturb the symmetrical arrangement which we saw in quartz, resulting in reduced hardness. The minerals so produced are the felspars, and one of these (orthoclase) is the standard for hardness number 6 of the Mohs scale of hardness.

As we have already seen, the numerous varieties of felspar arise from the different proportions of the three metals, sodium, potassium, and calcium in the crystals. We can look at these from another point of view. Aluminium occurs as an oxide known as *corundum* (hardness 9 on the Mohs scale), which is chemically called *alumina* and given the formula Al_2O_3 (i.e. three oxygen atoms to two aluminium atoms). Thus we have two extremes of crystal structure, quartz and alumina, and between these are the felspars which contain both silicon and aluminium. Clearly there can be an infinite number of felspars. Then there must be one sodium or potassium atom for each aluminium in the felspar (or one calcium atom for each *two* aluminium atoms) to produce electrical neutrality. The sodium felspars are called *albite*, potassium felspars are *orthoclase*, and calcium felspars are *anorthite*, but many felspars are mixtures of these.

So far we have considered only one type of crystal structure, based on quartz, but silicon has the peculiar property of being able to form numerous crystal types in which silicon and oxygen atoms alternate. In quartz this occurs in all three dimensions, but it may

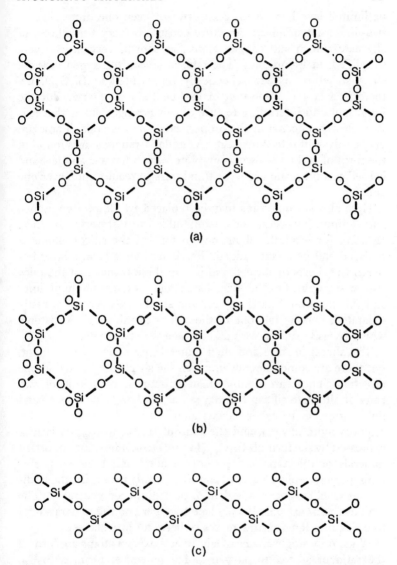

(a)

(b)

(c)

Figure 6   The structures of some silicate minerals. These are only diagrammatic representations; the atoms are not all in the same plane, e.g. the oxygen atoms shown close to silicon atoms actually lie directly above them, and the symbols show the positions of the *centres* of the atoms but not their sizes: (a) a sheet structure; (b) a double chain structure; (c) a single chain structure.

be limited in other substances to two or even one dimension. A two-dimensional silicate structure consists of very thin sheets of alternate silicon and oxygen atoms, as shown, very much over-simplified, in Figure 6(a). The ratio of silicon to oxygen in these sheet structures is 2:5 (chemically represented as Si_4O_{10}), i.e. there is a larger proportion of oxygen than in quartz. But the important and interesting feature of this arrangement is that it is very clearly reflected in the properties of the minerals. These are very easily split into thin sheets. A similar arrangement is found in the form of carbon known as graphite, which has a soapy feel and is used as a lubricant since the thin layers so readily slide over one another.

Here also silicon atoms may be replaced by aluminium atoms, and sodium, potassium, or calcium added to restore the balance. In *mica*, for example, about one in four of the silicon atoms is replaced and potassium added. The latter atoms form a layer be-tween the sheets of silicate, and it is in these planes that the mica is so easily split. On the other hand, *talc* contains no aluminium, and therefore no potassium, and the sheets are even more easily separated, making talc one of the softest of minerals. Soapstone, which is easily carved with a knife, is a variety of talc.

The sheets in mica and such minerals are of indefinite extent, but there are some minerals in which the sheets are limited in one direction. These are double-chain structures, consisting of two rows of alternate silicon and oxygen atoms lying side by side and linked together by other oxygen atoms at regular intervals. This requires more oxygen, and the ratio of silicon to oxygen is now expressed by the formula Si_4O_{11} (Figure 6(b)). The most important minerals of this type are the hornblendes, and here again aluminium may replace some of the silicon, this time with the addition of iron, magnesium, calcium, or sodium for neutrality. The double-chains are only loosely held together and the minerals tend to break into long narrow pieces rather than into sheets.

When only single chains of silicon and oxygen atoms are formed the ratio of silicon to oxygen is 1:3 (chemical formula Si_2O_6) (Figure 6(c)), and again aluminium may replace some of the silicon. The minerals thus formed are known as *pyroxenes*, and contain magnesium, iron, calcium, or sodium. These minerals break relatively easily in two directions at right angles, and they have hardness values of 5 or 6 on the Mohs scale.

A final group of silicate minerals has a silicon to oxygen atom ratio of 1:4 (formula SiO_4). This requires other metals to give it electrical neutrality, and these are usually ions of magnesium and iron, as in *olivine*. As the SiO_4^{4-} ions are almost distinct the minerals will break in any plane with equal ease.

The minerals in silicate rocks may be broken down on weathering into simpler minerals known as *clay minerals*. At the same time the grains are reduced in size until they are generally less than 0·002 mm. in diameter. The term 'clay' is strictly a description of grain size, but it is usually found that these very small particles also differ mineralogically from the larger grains of silts and sands. Clay minerals also contain chemically bound water (i.e. they are *hydrated* aluminium silicates), and clay deposits will generally contain other substances derived from the original rock, not only unaffected minerals such as quartz and mica, but other impurities such as compounds of calcium and iron. It is the latter that gives the characteristic reddish colour to many clays.

A clay that has remained in the position occupied by the parent rock is called a *primary clay* or *residual clay*. These are the purest clays available but are not usually sufficiently plastic for immediate use by the potter. They include the white or very pale yellow *china clays* or *kaolins*, which usually contain at least 5 per cent of impurities such as quartz and felspar.

Secondary clays are those that have been transported either by water or ice from the site of the parent rock, and in the process have become mixed with other substances, including iron oxides, lime, and various soluble salts. The clay particles may also be broken down still further during their journey, giving a finer, but less pure, clay. Some clays must have been moved more than once since their original formation.

Where ice sheets were responsible for the transport of clays it is generally found that they have become mixed with larger-grained material, which is distributed in a random manner throughout the clay. In other words, the material has not been sorted as it would be if deposited from running water or in a lake (lacustrine clays). As glacially transported clays often contain quite large boulders they are known as *boulder clays*. The relative importance of the various clays to the ancient potter will be discussed later, but it should be noted here that the clay particles have the sheet-like structure of aluminium silicates, being flat and often elongated.

Now let us look at the non-silicate minerals. Corundum has already been mentioned, and the precious stones related to it that are coloured by various impurities. Fluorspar (calcium fluoride) also is often coloured by impurities, but the pure mineral is white. In Derbyshire it is frequently tinged with various shades of blue and known as 'Blue John'. It has many modern uses but was apparently not used in antiquity.

Limestone is well known in its many varieties, which all consist mainly of calcite (calcium carbonate), from the very pure chalk to the sandy or clayey marls. When the calcite was deposited around grains of sand or quartz, forming spherical particles, the limestone is said to be *oolitic* (egg-like). Otherwise deposition may have been direct from sea-water, or in the form of minute shells or skeletons of creatures that formerly lived in the sea.

The weight of later deposits compressed limestones to the solid rocks we find today, but this process does not appear to have affected the fossils, which are usually well preserved and very numerous in most limestones. The deposits are often extremely thick and sometimes also contain layers of shale.

Marble is a re-crystallized limestone; it may consist of large calcite crystals or be very fine-grained. The colours of some varieties are due to impurities such as iron oxides or carbonized organic substances, and these may be evenly spread throughout the rock or they may form streaks as though the molten impurities had 'run' during the alteration of the rock.

All limestones, as we have seen, dissolve slowly in slightly acid ground-water or rain-water, and much more rapidly in cold acids, such as acetic acid (vinegar) or hydrochloric acid, which cause effervescence owing to the release of bubbles of carbon dioxide gas. This is a simple test for limestones, but the same reaction occurs with lime mortars, cements, concretes, and wall plaster.

Frequently, some of the calcium in calcite is replaced by magnesium to form a magnesium limestone, or, in extreme cases, the mineral *dolomite*, with equal proportions of calcium and magnesium carbonates.

A few other salt deposits are archaeologically important. Common salt (sodium chloride), *halite* to the mineralogist, is found in large areas, such as Cheshire in England and Utah in the U.S.A. It is still mined as *rock salt* in one mine in Cheshire, in parts of Poland and elsewhere, but many places have now gone over to vacuum processes for the extraction of the salt from brine. This may be a natural brine or one produced by pumping water down drillings to the deep salt deposits. In hot climates salt has been recovered from sea-water from very early times by running the water into shallow salt-pans and allowing it to evaporate. Sometimes the evaporation is assisted by making charcoal or turf fires around the salt-pans or saltings. Many old place-names and road-names provide evidence of the routes by which the salt was distributed in later times.

Often in association with common salt is the mineral salt known as *gypsum*, which is important for its use in ancient wall-plasters. It is a hydrated calcium sulphate, usually white but sometimes discoloured by iron salts. In making plaster gypsum is heated gently so that it loses some of its water of crystallization. It will then absorb water readily, being reconverted to gypsum, which sets hard but is easily softened again by moisture and is therefore not suitable for use as wall-plaster in damp climates. It is now better known as *plaster of Paris*. Since gypsum is often found on or near the surface of deserts, left by evaporating brines, it was commonly used for decorating walls in the Near East.

In our list of 'soluble minerals' in Figure 4 we have included silica. In fact silica is only very slightly soluble in water at ordinary temperatures, but at tropical temperatures it becomes much more soluble. We have already seen that silicon and oxygen can combine together in several ways to form chains, sheets, or three-dimensional structures, all with alternate silicon atoms and oxygen atoms. This peculiar tendency also affects the nature of the silica that comes out of solution, for example by the evaporation of the water from a solution. Most substances start to precipitate as extremely minute particles, which steadily grow into crystals increasing in size until they fall to the bottom of the solution. But silica behaves quite differently. It grows into a shapeless mass consisting of a skeleton or framework of silica in which is trapped or enmeshed quite a large amount of water. The silica is said to be in the *colloidal* state, and this particular kind of colloidal state is called a *gel*, since jellies are of a similar type. When some of the trapped water is expelled by heating, the mixture becomes quite solid, though remaining a gel.

The difference between silica gel and crystalline silica is quite simple but very important. In a crystal the units from which it is built (atoms, ions, or molecules) occupy very definite positions, that is, there is a regular three-dimensional arrangement throughout the crystal, which is reflected in the regular external shape of the crystals. But in a gel, although there is a framework of particles, these are not regularly arranged but completely random. A gel also always contains a second, quite different substance (the water in silica gel).

Silica is often found as a mixture of crystalline silica and silica gel, and the mineralogists use different names according to the relative proportions of each form of silica, as listed below. In all cases the crystals are sub-microscopic, and the minerals are said to be *cryptocrystalline*.

Opal—practically all silica gel
Chalcedony—less gel (*carnelian* is a red variety and *agate* is variegated)
Flint—a little gel remains
Chert—a coarse flint
Jasper—entirely cryptocrystalline.

Silica gel is much more easily leached out of these rocks than is the crystalline silica, especially in alkaline conditions (e.g. in limestone soils). This leaves the rock with a very porous crystalline surface, which appears white unless stained by its absorption of coloured salts from the soil water. This changed surface is called the *cortex*, or, particularly in archaeological contexts, a *patina*. On flaked surfaces of flint such a patina develops more or less slowly, depending on the nature of its surroundings.

A further distinction between crystalline and colloidal minerals is in the fracture or cleavage. The form of fracture is described as rough or smooth, whereas the cleavage describes the directions or planes along which the mineral is most readily broken. Crystals tend to break more easily along planes across which the chemical bonding is weakest. An extreme example is that of mica, which, as we have seen, splits easily into thin sheets. Such a mineral is said to have a good cleavage in one direction. Felspars in general have good cleavage in two directions, and rock salt (halite) in three directions at right angles, forming cubes.

On the other hand the partly colloidal minerals, because their internal structures are not regular, tend to break with *curved* surfaces, and show minute cracks in the form of concentric rings, all centred on the point of impact. Since the curvature and the markings resemble certain sea-shells (conches) the phenomenon is called a *conchoidal fracture*. This is familiar in worked flints and is found in all the partly colloidal silica minerals listed above, and in glass and the vitrified (glassy) rocks such as obsidian. The latter is produced in the rapid cooling of the magma when there is insufficient time for the formation of crystals.

The splintering of manufactured glass to produce very sharp edges and points is all too familiar today, but perhaps we do not realize that cutting tools of various kinds were made by Palaeolithic man from very similar, naturally occurring materials, particularly obsidian. Although the latter does not splinter quite so easily as window glass it is very brittle and the more homogeneous forms have a conchoidal fracture, giving good, smooth, sharp edges. Obsidian is found in Europe only in Hungary, the Lipari Islands (off Sicily), and in the Caucasus mountains. There are also deposits in Mexico, New Zealand, and Ascension Island.

Almost as good as obsidian for making sharp-edged flakes are the chalcedonic forms of silica already discussed. They are not as brittle as obsidian and are probably a little easier to work to the desired shapes. In the past there has been a tendency for all implements and weapons made from any of the five minerals listed above to be called *flint* artifacts. The minerals occur mainly in chalk and limestones, and occasionally in sandstones and shales, in the form of nodules or bands. Nodules from the chalk are usually called *flints* and those from limestone *chert*, but these are not necessarily correct descriptions.

Tools such as hammers, axes, and adzes have to be much more resilient, or less brittle, than rocks used for small cutting tools. They must be able to withstand heavy blows, much heavier than those used in flaking flint, though a few flint axes are known. The choice of rock is fairly wide, the commonest being *greenstones*, which are *hornblende schists*. These are hard, but not as hard as most granites or flints, and can be ground and polished comparatively easily, usually on sandstone polishing stones. The igneous rocks dolerite and basalt were also often used for axes and other 'heavy' tools.

For saddle-querns and rotary-querns a moderately hard rock is required, one which will not become polished by use but that will remain always rough on the grinding surfaces. Many fine-grained sandstones are suitable and were frequently used in antiquity and for later, water-powered, millstones. Stones were often imported specially for such purposes and a particular basalt from Germany was in great demand in the European Iron Ages.

Stone vessels were quite common in Egypt from very early times, and it may be somewhat surprising to find that many of these were made from quite hard igneous rocks such as granites and basalt. Just how these were worked is not fully known, especially the methods for hollowing-out narrow-necked jars. On the other hand, vessels from the very soft rocks such as soapstone (steatite) and serpentine were easily made by the use of stone tools before the age of metals, and the North American Indians used soapstone pots quite extensively.

Between these extremes there are moderately soft rocks such as limestones and alabaster (a form of gypsum) which have also been used for making vessels of various kinds, and, in fact, alabaster continued in use for small vessels such as unguentaria, vases, and perfume jars until quite recently. Even shales have been used in this way, in particular a very soft shale from the south of England known as Kimmeridge shale, which has the added advantage that it is impregnated with a bituminous substance that makes the products virtually water-tight.

The essential or desirable properties of building stone include a crushing strength sufficiently high to withstand the weight of the building to be erected on it, a hardness suitable for being worked with the tools available, durability or resistance to weathering, and a pleasing appearance. The soft sedimentary rocks such as mud-stones and shales are obviously unsuitable, and, at the other extreme, some of the hard igneous rocks might be unworkable, or suitable only for the most expensive buildings. Therefore, before medieval times at least, it is generally found that masonry is composed of some of the more compact and well-cemented sedimentary rocks such as sandstones and limestones, although granites and other igneous rocks have been used.

In building terminology walls of dressed and coursed stonework are known as *ashlar*, whereas walls made of irregular stones of various shapes and sizes are called *rubble* walls, whether coursed or uncoursed. Many ancient buildings had rubble walls, in some cases the rubble consisting of flint nodules set in a large quantity of mortar.

There are several important considerations in using sedimentary rocks for substantial structures. If the rock can be cut equally well in any direction it is known as *freestone* and it may also be laid in any position. On the other hand, if the bedding or jointing is pronounced, then it is better *base-bedded*, i.e. laid in the same position as that in which the layers of sediment were deposited. When *face-bedded*, i.e. when the successive layers of sediment are vertical, there is a great tendency for the rock to flake away, especially if it is also porous.

Where a rock is required to span a gap, as for a lintel, it is necessary to ensure that it will not readily crack or fracture. There must be no jointing or weak areas in such rocks, and usually a hard igneous rock or a well-cemented sedimentary rock (e.g. a siliceous sandstone) would be selected. On the other hand, for roofing, such as barrel vaulting, a light-weight material is necessary, such as tufa, a form of limestone deposited around springs in which the water contains a large amount of lime.

Different considerations apply in the choice of rocks for decorative purposes on buildings or for sculpture. These must be hard but not too brittle; and the hardness must not be too great for the available tools. Before iron chisels were used hard rocks could only be carved by hammering or 'pecking' with harder stones, or by drilling. The difficulty of shaping hard rocks may partly explain the Egyptian practice of producing reliefs rather than three-dimensional sculpture. For the latter the Greeks found an almost ideal material in the crystalline marbles of Greece and Italy. These homogeneous, fine-grained rocks enable fine features to be produced, which will also take a high polish.

2. Metals

The earth contains very few *native* metals, that is, metals not chemically combined with other substances. Archaeology seems to show that of these gold was the first to be used by man, and copper and silver much later, though the reasons for this are not entirely clear. It is apparent, however, that native gold and copper must have been much more widespread and common than they are today, and, indeed, many anciently exhausted sources of gold are known.

Gold occurs mainly in veins in quartz rocks or in the sedimentary products of the weathering of these, and a large proportion of the native gold used in antiquity was probably obtained from such deposits in river beds, i.e. by intercepting it on its way from the igneous rocks to the areas of formation of new sedimentary rocks. The gold found in mountain streams in most parts of the world would be in the form of small nuggets or fine dust, which, because of its high specific gravity, would settle rapidly, whereas the unwanted lighter particles could be washed away in the *panning* process.

Native gold practically always contains appreciable amounts of silver or copper, or both, and smaller quantities of other metals. These affect not only the colour but also the physical properties of the native gold, small amounts of copper giving it a deeper colour and making it less soft. Silver, on the other hand, makes gold paler, and if the proportion of silver approaches 25 per cent the alloy is almost white and is called *electrum*. Some gold was used directly for making jewellery and other articles, but the silver was removed if a purer gold was required.

Gold is the most malleable of all metals; i.e. it can be beaten out into extremely thin sheets, called *gold-leaf*, which was wrapped around glass or other metals for decorative purposes.

Silver was almost invariably obtained in antiquity either from electrum or by the desilverization of lead—produced mainly from the ore *galena*.

Native copper is less widespread than gold and was not widely used in antiquity, possibly because it would appear black or green owing to the corrosion of its surface, whereas gold does not corrode and would always appear bright and attractive. It is clear that copper would have been used just as extracted from its ores before man learnt how to harden it by adding tin. Archaeologists have sometimes tried to distinguish a Chalcolithic Age preceding the early Bronze Age, but its extent would appear to be very vaguely defined.

It is becoming clear from several recent analyses that many so-called bronzes are really brasses. Strictly speaking, bronze is an alloy of copper and tin, containing about 90 per cent copper, and brass is an alloy of copper with zinc in which the proportions may vary considerably. The proportion of zinc in many 'bronzes' has been found to be quite high, and other metals, particularly lead, are often also present. It is not possible at the present time to say whether lead and other metals were deliberately added to the copper or if, as seems more likely, they happened to be present in the ores from which the copper or the tin were extracted.

An alloy known to numismatists as *orichalcum* (or aurichalcum = 'golden copper') was used extensively for Roman coinage from late Republican times. It was a copper alloy whose composition did not remain constant over long periods, but it generally appears to have contained a small percentage of tin, lead, and iron, with, at first, about 22 per cent zinc. From the time of Nero the proportion of zinc was gradually reduced and occasionally we find an increase in the lead content.

Alloys of this kind were made from about the fourth century B.C., but its use in coinage dates from 45 B.C. It appears, from various ancient literary sources, that the alloy was made by heating the crushed *calamine* (zinc carbonate) with powdered charcoal and small lumps of copper. The product is really a brass, being essentially an alloy of copper and zinc; modern brasses contain from 30 to 40 per cent zinc.

Analyses of 'bronzes' from Nigeria suggest that the early examples consist mainly of brass and later ones of bronze, but all contain both zinc and tin to some extent.

There is little evidence of the use of tin alone in antiquity, but the metal was extracted from *tinstone* or *cassiterite* (tin oxide) and used in making various alloys besides bronze. Pewter, for example, was an alloy of lead (about 20 per cent) with tin and possibly other metals, though again these may have been accidentally present. Lead is not permitted in modern pewter because lead compounds are cumulative poisons. Its place is taken partly by antimony, which, it should be noted, is also extremely poisonous, being very similar to arsenic in many ways. However, the antimony is not so readily dissolved out of pewter as lead would be.

The most important lead ore is galena (lead sulphide), which forms grey cubic crystals, which may appear very highly polished on fresh fractures. Galena nearly always contains some silver, which was recovered by the process of *cupellation* of the extracted metal. The cupel was a porous stone on which the impure metal was heated in air, some of the products, generally the oxides of the metals, being absorbed by the cupel, or blown away by the strong current of air used. Silver remains on the cupel as a shining globule.

Lead also is a soft metal with many uses besides the making of the alloys already mentioned. One of its advantages is its low melting point (327°C), so that it could easily be cast into almost any desired shape. It was used for roof covering, making water-pipes, sealing tanks, keying stonework, and many other purposes.

The metals other than gold and silver were first extracted from their oxide or carbonate ores. The removal of the chemically combined oxygen or carbon dioxide from these ores is an example of the process known as *reduction*, which is essentially the reverse of *oxidation*. The various elements have different *affinities* for oxygen, that is, some will combine with it more easily than others, so that if two elements are heated together in a limited supply of oxygen the one with the greater affinity will be oxidized (converted to its oxide). In other words, there will be a competition for the available oxygen, and the element with the greater affinity for oxygen will win the contest. A similar result is found when one heats an oxide of a metal with a substance which has a greater affinity for oxygen than has the metal concerned. Such a substance may be carbon. In fact carbon will remove the oxygen from any metal oxide above an appropriate temperature, but for many metals this temperature is higher than was available to prehistoric man. It is mainly for this reason that metals such as aluminium and magnesium, which are so familiar today, were not extracted in antiquity.

It is not surprising to find that the metal first extracted from its ores, copper, is the most easily obtained. One can imagine that the accidental heating of a piece of malachite or azurite, both highly coloured and attractive ores, in a wood fire, oven, or pottery kiln could have produced the first extracted copper seen by man.

Zinc metal was not known in prehistory because it *boils* at 927°C and would have volatilized and been lost in the smoke from the furnace. Iron was not produced until much later than copper and tin, for quite opposite reasons. When the oxides of copper, lead, and tin are reduced by heating with carbon (i.e. charcoal) the temperature is such that the metals produced are liquid and they run to the bottom of the furnace. The various impurities, such as silica from various rocks, float on top of the metal and on cooling form a *slag* which is easily removed. But iron melts at about 1,500°C, which is above the temperature normally available to prehistoric man, so that the iron and the slag would remain intimately mixed as a spongy mass called *bloom*. There must have been a considerable lapse of time before man discovered that the bloom could be *forged* in order to separate the iron from the slag. Forging is the process of repeatedly heating and hammering, during which the iron particles are consolidated and the slag is squeezed out. But, inevitably, some pockets of slag remain in forged iron, their shape showing the method and direction of working the bloom. Areas of slag or iron oxide in wrought iron are regions of weakness.

The majority of ores now used for the extraction of the common metals are sulphide ores. Some of these are quite complex compounds, but simple sulphides are compounds of a metal and sulphur. However, sulphide ores do not generally yield to the same treatment as oxide ores, and, in fact, it is usually necessary to roast sulphide ores to convert them to oxides. Roasting is simply heating in an adequate air supply so that the sulphur is removed as the gas sulphur dioxide and the oxide of the metal remains. The necessity for the additional process no doubt delayed the use of sulphide ores.

This brief review of the metals of antiquity illustrates the great variety of their properties and gives some guidance as to the choice of suitable metals for any particular application, though, as always, economic reasons were usually decisive. Thus, gold and silver were always rare and therefore 'expensive', so that only the wealthy and powerful could be expected to own any quantity of gold or silver ornaments. Tin was not much more plentiful in any prehistoric or protohistoric period, workable deposits being limited to relatively few areas.

The need either to find new sources of tin or to control mines already in production has been suggested as an important reason for various migrations and conquests which took place after the beginnings of the Bronze Ages of Asian and European regions, extending even as far as the Roman invasion of Britain. Whereas this might have been so for events in early Bronze Ages it could only have been of very minor importance for Mediterranean peoples in later times when iron had replaced bronze in many of its applications. Bronze was still important, not only for ornaments but also in coinage, but adequate supplies were probably available from Spain and Brittany, and, after all, there was a flourishing trade in tin with Britain which could be maintained without the dangers and expense of conquest.

In the selection of suitable metals for a particular purpose the most important properties to be considered would be hardness, melting point, malleability, and durability. Hardness would be a particularly important consideration for tools, especially where cutting edges were required, and the soft metals tin, zinc, and lead would be ruled out. Pure copper is also too soft, but bronze or brass are much harder and were the most satisfactory until iron could be extracted. A serious disadvantage of bronze is that in use, especially if repeatedly bent, it becomes 'work-hardened'; i.e. there are changes in the crystal structure which make the alloy hard but brittle, so that it is liable to break under strain.

For early coinage gold and bronze were the obvious choices in times when face-value and intrinsic value were identical. Both are sufficiently malleable and durable in normal use. But when the habit of debasing the coinage started (i.e. of reducing the intrinsic value below the face-value) various metals were added to both kinds of coin. It is not always possible to tell whether some of these contaminants were deliberately added or appeared as impurities in the original ores. Copper and lead were added to gold coins, the copper giving them a deeper colour and the lead compensating for the loss of weight produced by replacing some gold by copper. Lead was also added to bronze coins and a little zinc is also often found in both bronze and gold coins.

Apart from tin, which was not extracted directly from its ores to any great extent, lead has the lowest melting point (327°C) and we have already noted some of its uses. Copper, on the other hand, melts at 1,083°C, but by adding tin or zinc the melting point can be brought down below 1,000°C, depending on the proportions of the added metals. Thus bronze was much more conveniently cast than was copper. These alloys also are malleable, but they, and copper itself, become hard when hammered in the cold because the crystals are distorted, and if hammering is continued too long the metal will crack as the crystals break apart. This is prevented by reheating the metal and allowing it to cool before continuing the hammering. A final cold hammering produces a hard copper or bronze object or part of an object such as a blade.

Just as many so-called bronzes are really brasses, so many examples of ancient iron have been found, in fact, to be steel. The difference may appear slight but it is important. Steel is iron that contains a small proportion of carbon, and, since early methods of extraction of iron involved heating the ore with a large amount of charcoal, the product would always be a steel, though a very impure one. However, we often call these materials *wrought iron*, or *low-carbon steel* if they contain less than 0·5 per cent carbon. Generally speaking, the effect of the carbon is to increase the hardness of the metal, but it also makes it brittle. A maximum of 5 per cent carbon is added today to produce *cast-iron*, which is extremely brittle, and other metals, including chromium, manganese, and nickel, are added to increase the strength or give other desirable properties to the steel. But steels of this kind are modern developments, though similar alloys were occasionally produced by chance in Iron Age times, the alloying metals being present in the iron ore used. Carbon also was deliberately added at a very much later date by covering the iron with charcoal and keeping it red hot for quite a long time.

3. Pottery

Pottery may be defined as any utensil or vessel made from baked clay. We need not go into great detail as to the various stages of pottery making, but it is instructive to consider what happens during firing to convert a rather moist, soft clay into a dry, hard and perhaps rather brittle object.

Apart from the obvious loss of water, other more subtle changes occur as the temperature of the kiln is raised and other conditions varied.

Let us consider first the effect of heating a fabric or body of clay alone, without glaze or any of the numerous possible additives. We have seen that clay consists of extremely small particles, usually elongated and flattened, and that when mixed with water it forms a colloidal system in which there is a framework of overlapping clay particles with water trapped between them. If excessive water is added the framework breaks down and the mixture becomes liquid; in fact a suspension of clay in water, and partly a colloidal *sol*. In ceramic technology such a suspension is known as a *slip*, and may be used to give a very fine, smooth surface to the pottery, or, in a different colour from the body, applied as decoration. The latter process was the basis of the popular medieval *slipware*.

Clays are hydrated aluminium silicates, which means that they contain chemically bound water, which is quite different from water loosely held between the silicate sheets. Water molecules form part of the crystal structure, i.e. they occupy definite places in the crystal lattice. Therefore it is called *water of crystallization*. Water that is only loosely held or trapped between clay particles is easily removed by warming, when it will practically all be removed at 100°C, since at this temperature it is converted to steam. But water of crystallization is removed only at higher temperatures, and its loss means that the remaining atoms must rearrange themselves to give a different kind of crystal structure. In this way there is a shrinkage of the clay on heating, and this must be carefully controlled if cracking is to be prevented.

At even higher temperatures *sintering* occurs. This is a well-known phenomenon in many substances, including glasses and metals, in which the surfaces of small particles start to soften at a temperature well below the normal melting point of the substance. On cooling, the particles will then stick together. Sintering of clay can begin at fairly low temperatures, perhaps below 800°C, depending on the nature of the clay, its mineral content, and the presence of impurities or additives. The normal melting point of clay is over 1,700°C. Sintering also causes shrinking of the clay.

It is possible to estimate the original firing temperature of a sherd owing to the sintering process. If the sherd is steadily heated in a special piece of apparatus in which its length is continuously measured it is found that normal expansion first occurs. But when the original firing temperature is reached the process of sintering is continued from the point where it originally finished, and the sherd begins to shrink. It has been found that some very early pottery was fired at only 800°C, but that later prehistoric potters were able to attain temperatures of well over 1,000°C.

Pots fired at low temperatures remain porous, but the porosity decreases as sintering increases. If a pot is heated to too high a temperature it will become soft and lose its shape, or, in extreme cases, actually start to melt.

The *plasticity* of a clay usually requires adjusting before use; if it is too plastic it will shrink too much on drying, and if not sufficiently plastic it will be difficult to work and liable to crumble. The numerous additives found in prehistoric pottery were almost all used for reducing the plasticity of the clay. They are mainly fine sands or finely ground material that will not shrink on drying and will not otherwise spoil the body on heating. Powdered fired clay was often used, or old pottery, burnt ('calcined') flint, shells, straw, or various kinds of rock. Attempts are being made to determine the place of manufacture of ancient pottery from an analysis of the minerals in the sand additives, and there would seem to be some prospect of success for certain types, but the method is not likely to be universally applicable.

Strictly speaking, pottery fired at low temperatures, that is, when sintering is only slight, should be called *terracotta*, and that fired between 1,000°C and 1,200°C, to produce the most satisfactory amount of sintering, is *earthenware*. *Stoneware* is made from clay which sinters at even higher temperatures.

No clays are absolutely pure. *China clays* may contain up to 95 per cent kaolinite, with 5 per cent felspar, but these are unusual. Apart from mineralogical differences, most clays also contain various impurities taken up as ions from the soil-water, partly by the process of *ion-exchange* in which positive ions dissolved in the soil-water may exchange places with the aluminium ions of the clay minerals.

This process is reversible and is precisely the same phenomenon as is utilized in water-softening, where the magnesium and calcium ions of *hard* water exchange places with sodium ions in the exchanger through which the water flows. The unpleasant and wasteful scum formed in hard water by the use of soap results from the production of insoluble salts of calcium and magnesium, but sodium does not form insoluble salts, so the replacement of the former metal ions by sodium ions *softens* the water. When the water-softener has exchanged most of its sodium ions for others it becomes exhausted, but can be regenerated by passing a salt (sodium chloride) solution through it, because the ion-exchange process is reversible and the exchanger will be re-converted to its 'sodium form'.

The most important impurity ions in clays are those that colour them, and the pottery produced from them, the commonest of which is iron. Other coloured ions include copper, cobalt, nickel, and manganese, but these are rarely present in sufficient quantities to give any depth of colour to pottery, though they were used in glazes, and they are, in any case, far less widespread than iron.

Organic matter in pottery may also affect its colour. For example, straw added to reduce the plasticity of the clay will burn in the kiln and only the carbon may remain, giving a grey tinge to the pot. The presence of such carbon may also modify the colours produced by other substances.

Ancient pottery is rarely white, being usually either pale grey to black, or pale buff to brown or red, depending, as we have seen, on the amounts of organic matter and of iron present in the clay body, but partly determined by the conditions of firing.

From what has been said elsewhere concerning the building-up of molecules and crystals it will be appreciated that atoms of different elements combine together in *definite* proportions. In simple compounds, such as the oxides of the metals, the proportions can be represented by small numbers, as indicated by the chemical formulae. For example, in calcium oxide (lime), formula CaO, there are equal numbers of calcium and oxygen ions, and in sodium oxide, Na_2O, there are twice as many sodium ions as oxide ions. But some metals can form two (or more) different ions, by means of very slight re-arrangements of their electrons, and hence two (or more) series of compounds. All the coloured ions mentioned above belong to elements of this kind. Iron is the only one of importance in connection with pottery production.

An atom of iron may form a stable ion by losing either two or three electrons. In the former event the ion has two positive charges (Fe^{2+}) and is known as a *ferrous* ion, and the alternative (Fe^{3+}) is the *ferric* ion. When these ions combine with oxide ions (O^{2-}) they form *ferrous oxide* (FeO) and *ferric oxide* (Fe_2O_3), respectively, that is, there may be equal numbers of iron and oxide ions, or these may be in the proportions of two ferric ions to every three oxide ions. There is also a third oxide of iron of interest to us here, Fe_3O_4, known as *magnetic iron oxide*, *magnetite*, or *ferrosoferric oxide*. It receives the last name because it appears to be a compound of the other two oxides ($FeO + Fe_2O_3 = Fe_3O_4$), and, as the other names indicate, it is magnetic.

Ferrous oxide and magnetite are both black, but most other *ferrous* compounds are greenish. On the other hand, ferric oxide is red ('jeweller's rouge', haematite) and other ferric compounds generally red or brown. Here we have the basis of practically all the colours found in ancient pottery bodies. Blacks and greys are almost certainly due to the presence of magnetite, ferrous oxide, or ferrous salts, whereas ferric oxide or ferric salts are responsible for the buffs, browns, and reds.

The addition of more oxygen to ferrous oxide to convert it to ferric oxide is an example of the process of *oxidation*, and the reverse change is known as *reduction*. Pottery containing iron when fired in a good draught of air will have a buff to red colour, but if the air supply is inadequate the red oxide will be reduced, though mostly only as far as magnetite, with a resulting grey or black-coloured product. Reduction may have been either deliberately or accidentally produced, often by using damp wood for firing the kiln, particularly in the later stages, so that the pottery is in a reducing atmosphere caused by the excessive smoke, steam, and lack of oxygen.

Experiments have shown that the 'sandwich' appearance of the edges of many sherds is a result of incomplete oxidation. The outer regions of a pot will be readily oxidized in an adequate air supply, but it will take some time for all the water to diffuse out from the innermost parts, and for the removal of the products of the combustion of any organic additives. Similarly, the passage of oxygen into the centre of the fabric is a relatively slow process, and all these factors tend to delay the oxidation of deep-seated clay. If the firing was at a rather low temperature or not held at the correct temperature for sufficient time, then a normally red or buff pot will be found to have a greyish central region.

Other additives may be found in pottery, particularly in such specialized vessels as mortaria. The inside of a mortarium must be rough if it is to be effective in breaking down the various kinds of foodstuffs that are to be ground in it by means of a pestle. The roughness may be produced by a coarse sand or many kinds of crushed rocks. Crushed shells have sometimes been reported in mortars, but at the temperature of the kiln it is unlikely that any of the shell would avoid loss of carbon dioxide, forming lime and losing its shape and hardness. If shell, limestone, or calcite are shown to be present it suggests a very low firing temperature, probably below 850°C.

Bricks and tiles are essentially the same as pottery, although it is often apparent that less trouble was taken in the preparation of the clay for these products. The air-drying of large numbers of bricks or tiles before firing must have presented quite a problem, and it is not really surprising to note how frequently the imprint of paw or hoof of a domestic animal is found on tiles and bricks.

4. Glass, Glazes, and Enamels

Since these three kinds of materials are essentially of the same basic composition they will be considered together. They are not always clearly defined, but the correct terminology is that glasses are made and formed to stand alone, glazes are applied to pottery bodies, and enamels are *fused* to a metal surface. Any form of vitreous decoration attached to a metal background by means other than fusing together of the materials is commonly, but incorrectly, referred to as enamel.

Several substances can be obtained in a vitreous (glassy) state, but by far the most important of these is silica. The various forms of crystalline silica have been described in connection with the composition of rocks and minerals, where we have seen that the crystal shape and the properties of the minerals result from the regular arrangement of the units (atoms or ions) throughout the crystals. Also, crystals tend to break more easily along planes of atoms or ions, forming flat fracture surfaces, whereas in the absence of the regularity of structure, fractures are usually conchoidal. Glasses fracture in the latter manner, showing that they are not crystalline materials; they are, in fact, generally called *super-cooled liquids*.

In liquids the particles (molecules or ions) are more or less randomly distributed, and move around very much more than in solids, but, on cooling, a molten substance will generally crystallize. In order to form the crystals it is clearly necessary for the atoms or ions to move through the liquid to their correct places in the crystal lattice, but in a vitreous substance this is largely prevented by the very high viscosity of the liquid. Hence, a glass is a substance that should have crystallized before becoming cold, but which has been prevented from doing so and retains the liquid form although in fact it is solid. This is the meaning of the expression 'super-cooled liquid'.

Obsidian is a natural silica glass, which may be almost pure silica, but the melting point of silica (1,710°C) is far too high to have been attained artificially by prehistoric man. Only in very recent times has pure silica been used to any extent, for example for small laboratory wares such as crucibles and furnace tubes, but these are not *glass* objects; they are known as *fused silica* vessels. Glass consists mainly of silica, known as the *glass former*, but also contains some substance, called a *modifier*, which changes the structure and considerably lowers the melting point of the silica. The product is then a three-dimensional, but irregular, network of alternating silicon and oxygen atoms with the modifier atoms or ions trapped within the network. In addition a colourant or a decolorizer may be present in a similar way.

The silica for glass, glaze, or enamel may be used in the form of quartz, sand, or crushed flint. For glazes the silica of the pot itself may be involved, but if flint is used it is generally first calcined (burnt). Most sands contain some iron salts, a rough idea of the amount present being given by the depth of red colour of the sand. So, for colourless or very pale-coloured glazes a white sand is necessary in the absence of quartz or flint.

Glass modifiers are usually the oxides of sodium, potassium, calcium, or lead (and perhaps of magnesium, zinc, and aluminium in glazes and enamels). Lime, in fact, is necessary in glass to prevent devitrification, i.e. the change from the vitreous to the crystalline state. This change is usually extremely slow and depends on various factors, particularly the composition of the glass. Even modern glass has been known to become appreciably devitrified in twenty to thirty years.

Potassium glass has a lower melting point than sodium glass and would be easier to make and work. In antiquity the potash was provided by plant ash, especially from bracken. Potash is an old and popular name for potassium carbonate and originates from the practice of evaporating solutions of plant ashes in pots. Fortuitously the ashes also contain some calcium salts, so that lime was probably not deliberately added in making ancient glass.

Recent work has shown that changes in the composition of glass took place at approximately the same time over practically the whole of Europe, North Africa, and the Near and Middle East. There appear to have been three main periods; from the beginning of glass manufacture to about the middle of the first millennium B.C. glasses have a high magnesium and potassium content, but from that time until the late first millennium A.D. there is a much lower proportion of magnesium and potassium in samples, except possibly in one or two areas such as Mesopotamia and India. During the subsequent period the magnesium content was again high, though this regression did not appear in some Middle Eastern countries until the tenth century. The dating can be only approximate and does not indicate a sudden change but rather a gradual spreading of new methods of manufacture. It seems likely that new sources of the alkalis used as modifiers were found around the times mentioned. For example, in Egypt before 800 B.C. it is possible that the natural deposits of *natron* (sodium carbonate with a little magnesium and potassium carbonates) were used in glass-making, but that subsequently, and elsewhere, plant ashes were used, including bracken, seaweed, and various trees. Seaweed would give a glass with a high sodium content but low potassium and magnesium, whereas it has been suggested that the change to high magnesium content resulted from the use of beech-wood. We may be sure that such explanations are over-simplified as it is difficult to believe, for example, that beech-wood was readily available over the whole of the vast areas concerned.

In making glass it helps to add a certain amount of scrap glass, known as cullet, to the molten *metal* (i.e. glass). This appears to facilitate the start of the vitrifying process.

Very many colourants have been used from time to time in glasses, glazes, and enamels, so that it is quite impossible to consider these in any detail. Iron oxides, present as impurities in so many minerals, including sand and clay, give yellow, red, or brown colours in oxidizing conditions, or greenish colours in reducing conditions, but even these colours may be drastically changed when certain other substances are also present.

There are almost as many ways of applying glazes and decoration to pottery as there are different colouring matters, but we are concerned only with the nature of the materials and not the techniques themselves. One particular glazing method must be mentioned, however, since it produces side-effects. This is salt-glazing. Here the salt is not applied directly to the pot but is thrown into the fire beneath the kiln, where it is vaporized, giving a bright yellow flame. The sodium ions produced then react with the steam from moisture in the fuel to give sodium hydroxide (caustic soda). As this is a glass modifier it converts the surface of the clay body into a glaze, which is usually rather rough. A fairly high temperature is required for this process and every clay surface within the kiln is indiscriminately glazed at the same time.

Slip glazes are applied as suspensions of fine clay particles in water to pots already fired. Re-firing at above 1,200°C then vitrifies the slip. A red clay was frequently used in this way, but the result must be clearly distinguished from *glosses* such as those found on the so-called 'samian' ware. Glosses are formed by slip, but this is applied to the wet clay body and the firing temperature is not high enough to cause vitrification. The slip used for samian ware contained a large proportion of *illite*, a clay mineral with particularly thin, flat particles. The glossiness is produced by the layer of illite particles flat on the surface, almost like fish scales, but very much smaller.

A material which resembles in many ways both clay and glass is *faience*, a paste of powdered quartz with some form of alkali. In desert regions, such as Egypt, the mineral *natron*, sodium carbonate ('washing soda') was used. The mixture, with a little water, is more or less plastic and can be formed in a similar way to clay, but if larger quantities of natron are used the melting point is lowered so much that the product is a sodium glass.

5. Pigments

There are many techniques available for colouring all kinds of objects. Excluding the very specialized methods used in making coloured glasses and glazes, we may describe all other colouring methods as either painting or dyeing.

A paint consists of a pigment (the colouring matter) and a *medium*, which is essentially an adhesive to hold the pigment in place, but might also improve the consistency or help to preserve the pigment. On the other hand, many media, especially those of organic origin, decay rather quickly, and rarely remain on archaeological sites.

Paints are applied, usually by brush, to the surface of an object. Modern paints contain drying oils, which oxidize on exposure to the air, forming very tough, thin films. Ancient paints had to rely on the medium holding the paint securely to the object.

In contrast to paints, dyes actually penetrate the material being coloured, and often combine chemically with it. One normally thinks of dyeing in relation to textiles, but dyes may be applied to other materials, such as wood, paper, and leather. On the other hand, applying a water-soluble colour to wood is commonly called staining.

The practice, popular with the Romans, of applying a pigment directly to new, moist wall-plaster should strictly be called *fresco* work. Such colours are firmly fixed and very hard-wearing, probably because the pigment takes part in the chemical changes that plasters undergo during drying and setting.

Pigments may be either organic or inorganic in origin. The former will be referred to later. The earliest inorganic pigments were simply powdered coloured rocks, but not all coloured rocks are suitable. Geologists use a *streak test* in identifying or describing rocks, which is simply carried out by rubbing the rock on a piece of unglazed porcelain. If there is sufficient depth of colour the streak will be coloured, but many coloured minerals, e.g. hornblendes, give a white, or nearly white, streak.

Yellows and browns, known as *ochres* (from the Greek for yellow), are usually varieties of iron oxides with various impurities; for example, limonite is yellow and haematite is red. There are so many possible inorganic pigments that it is quite impossible, and unnecessary, to list them here, especially as the colours of the minerals vary from place to place, and further changes were made by heating, roasting, or burning. The two 'non-colours', white and black, were made from china clay, chalk or lime, and charcoal or soot, respectively.

Paint (tempera) media were very similar to glues, being mainly proteins derived from egg-yolk or egg-white, bones, or fish. Some of these may persist, but they may become very brittle and often blackened, for which reason they are frequently referred to rather vaguely (and incorrectly) as bituminous materials. They are, of course, *organic* substances, but it is convenient to mention them here.

6. Plaster, Mortar, Cement, and Concrete

Mud and clay were used from very early times both for setting stonework and for giving a crude finish to walls. It is customary to distinguish mortar, which contains sand and is used mainly for binding together the bricks or stones of walls, from *plaster*, used for facing walls. The binding medium in each case is either lime or gypsum, one of these alone being used in fine plaster, but mixed with sand for mortar. In fact walls were often coated first with a mortar and finished with a thin coat of fine plaster.

Both gypsum and lime plasters work on the same principle. Gypsum, hydrated calcium sulphate, is heated to drive off *some* of the water of crystallization, giving a white powder known today as plaster of Paris. When this is mixed to a paste with water it is slowly reconverted into gypsum and sets hard in the process. If the gypsum is heated too strongly it loses all its chemically bound water, becoming *anhydrite*, which does not behave in the same way as plaster of Paris. Then the gypsum is said to be *dead-burnt*.

Lime is produced by heating limestone or chalk to drive off carbon dioxide and leave *quicklime*, calcium oxide (CaO). This is *slaked* with water, during which it becomes very hot and is converted into *slaked lime*, calcium hydroxide, a fine white powder when properly made. On exposure to the atmosphere the slaked lime absorbs carbon dioxide and is re-converted to calcium carbonate while setting hard. But pure lime makes a poor-quality plaster because only the surfaces harden completely, the inside remaining soft and moist so that it is easily damaged by frost. The plaster is much more efficient if it contains a small amount of clay, because it then sets by combining with a small amount of water besides the carbon dioxide. Such limes are called *hydraulic limes* because they set with water, and with larger amounts (up to 25 per cent) of clay they will set rock-hard even under water.

The raw materials of ancient plasters and mortars always contained impurities, probably small amounts of clay and some residues from the fuel used in lime and gypsum burning. Limestone was often burnt by mixing it with the fuel, so the resulting plaster or mortar would contain a certain amount of charcoal. Other materials such as straw or hair were often added to give greater strength to a plaster.

Cements are made by heating clay and limestone together. Complex chemical changes occur so that the atoms are regrouped to form calcium silicates and aluminates. When water is added the cement sets by the formation of long, interlocking crystals. Hydraulic lime plasters and cements, then, differ in that the clay in the former is not burnt, whilst for cements it is burnt with the lime. It will also be noted that, since the two are mixtures of chemically different substances, the setting processes are different.

In making *lime mortar* sand was added to quicklime before slaking, so that the sand grains are held together by the cementing action of the lime. *Pozzolanic mortars*, which are waterproof, included other materials such as tufa or crushed brick. The Roman *opus signinum* was of the latter type and so had a distinct pink colour.

Concrete is a mortar or cement to which has been added a proportion of small stones, gravel, broken bricks, or other hard material, which is known as the *aggregate* or *hard-core*. A thin layer of cement or mortar, with no aggregate, was sometimes laid on a concrete floor to give it a smooth finish if it was not to form the foundation for a tiled or tessellated floor. In that case cement or mortar would be necessary for holding the tiles or tesserae in place. Tesserae themselves were made from either tiles or stone.

THREE

ORGANIC MATERIALS

1. Introduction

Organic materials have been defined as substances that formed part of or were produced by a plant or animal. Thus they may be actual plant or animal structures, consisting of some form of *tissue*, or they may be excretions or secretions of plant or animal, which will show no structural features, such as gums, resins, and coprolites.

Some general characteristics of plant and animal tissues may first be mentioned. The most striking feature is the *cellular* structure of such tissues. Most plants and animals start life as single cells which repeatedly divide into two similar cells, but at later stages cells may develop in different ways to form specialized tissues and organs. Under the microscope the cells of some plant and animal tissues may look very similar, the main difference being that plant cells are enclosed in conspicuous *cell-walls*, whereas animal cells usually have no definite walls at all. The persistent parts of plants that may be recovered during excavation consist almost entirely of the cell-walls, but under normal conditions the only parts of animals likely to be found are bones and teeth, which are not formed of cell-walls but of material deposited between the cells.

The essential, living part of a cell is the *protoplasm*, usually a colourless, jelly-like mass in which are embedded certain vital structures, in particular the *nucleus*, which controls the whole of the life processes of the cell and contains the hereditary factors. In green plants there are also minute bodies containing the green pigment *chlorophyll*, which is essential for the process of photosynthesis. Many cells retain this form for their whole lives, but in plants many also undergo drastic changes of shape, size, and sometimes structure, losing their living contents but maintaining very important functions in the living plant, such as the transport of food and of unwanted or waste materials and the provision of mechanical strength.

Whilst animal cells also show a variety of shapes and sizes most of them still retain their protoplasm and remain living cells as long as they are performing their functions. But since protoplasm is so rapidly attacked on the death of an animal it will not be of any archaeological interest.

The importance of animal remains from archaeological sites is widely recognized, but it is doubtful whether all archaeologists realize the equal significance of plant remains apart from easily recognized timber residues and charcoal, though all will be aware of the occasional use of pollen analysis. A comprehensive review of all the uses to which animal and vegetable materials have been put in the past is quite impossible here. Some of the more important ones will be summarized, but as structure and use are intimately related they will generally be considered together.

2. Materials of Vegetable Origin

2.1. Introduction   The term *vegetable* in this connection covers all forms of plant life from the lowest, such as algae, fungi, and lichens, through 'higher' forms, including mosses and ferns, to the herbs, shrubs, and trees. Botanists divide the whole vegetable kingdom into four large groups, as follows:

> Thallophyta (Greek *thallos*, a young shoot, and *phyton*, a plant): including algae, seaweeds, fungi
>
> Bryophyta (Greek *bryon*, a moss): liverworts and mosses
>
> Pteridophyta (Greek *pteris*, a feather): including ferns, club-mosses, and horse-tails (*Equisetum*)
>
> Spermaphyta (Greek *sperma*, seed); (Flowering plants) divided into (a) Gymnosperms (Greek *gymnos*, naked): cycads, conifers; (b) Angiosperms (Greek *anggeion*, a case): flowering herbs, shrubs, and trees

There can be no doubt that prehistoric man made use of large numbers of plants from all these groups for many purposes. The early food-gathering cultures must have had a very varied menu, at least in temperate regions, since crops of suitable foodstuffs would generally be limited and fruit of small size. In more tropical climates where more productive plants flourish the food-gatherer would tend to have less variety in his diet, but in any case it is extremely difficult to draw any definite conclusions in regard to vegetable dietary in prehistory because the evidence is very sparse.

Plate IV Transverse sections of the stems of (a) oak, showing ring of large vessels, groups of small vessels, and a large medullary ray ($\times 50$); (b) beech, a diffuse-porous wood ($\times 15$); (c) Scots pine, showing resin-ducts but no vessels ($\times 50$);

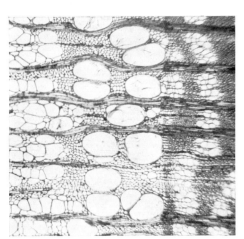

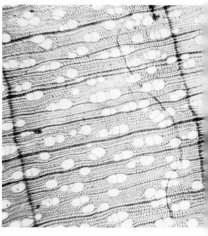

Plate IV (d) elm (× 50); (e) yellow Canadian birch (× 50); (f) ash (× 15).

Whereas shellfish-eaters left ample evidence in their 'kitchen middens', the vegetable-eaters discarded very little, and what they did leave was almost entirely perishable. Much of the evidence here comes from a few examples of carbonized grain and other vegetable fragments, some impressions of the same kind of materials on pottery, and remains from waterlogged sites such as the Swiss lake-dwellings.

Quite recently a vast amount of information on the diets of ancient civilizations, particularly in Peru and Mexico, has been derived from studies of coprolites (fossil dung). It has long been known that the wing-cases of small beetles, shells, fragments of bone, and remains of seed-cases frequently appear in such material, but scientific examination has revealed traces of a large number of plant and animal tissues.

Some idea of the extensive use of vegetable products may be derived from the residual practices of more recently civilized or discovered races or tribes. Work being done in New Guinea should prove useful in this respect, and we already have useful information from studies of the North American Indians. The latter still continue some of their food-gathering practices in the more remote areas, and many tribes are able to produce evidence from their folk-memories and traditions. In addition, we have the reports of the conquerors of Central America and the early settlers in North America. Yarnell has calculated that the North American Indians made use of about a quarter (roughly 500) of all the higher plants (Pteridophyta and Spermaphyta) in their areas, perhaps as many as 200 of them for food. Diet would vary with the seasons, not only as regards the kinds of plants used, but also the particular parts of the plants. In the spring young shoots and buds would provide nourishing fare, and later in the year the seed and fruit of appropriate plants as they matured. Winter food was presumably largely supplied by storing those parts in which the plants had stored food for their own use, such as tubers, rhizomes, bulbs, and corms, and by raiding the supplies laid in by animals such as squirrels and chipmunks.

Then one must not forget the use of plants for producing drinks of many kinds, fermented liquors for common or ritual purposes, and crude medicinal extracts. Flowers (containing useful nectar), seeds, fruits, and leaves of many species were widely used in this way, and, if the North American Indians are typical examples,

4

prehistoric man even learnt how to use poisonous plants for food and drink after suitable treatment to remove the poison.

A similarly large variety of plants provided materials for other uses by prehistoric man. The most obvious are the trees, which produced timber for building houses, making boats and furniture, handles for tools and weapons, and served many other purposes. Quite a number of plants provide fibrous tissues from which ropes, matting, and textile fabrics can be produced. Leaves that are long and narrow may be used directly for some of these purposes, for example grasses, reeds, and sedges. For weaving and other finer work fibres were extracted from many plants by *retting*, that is, soaking in water until the unwanted material had been broken down by bacterial action. Esparto grass, halfa grass, papyrus, and even stinging nettle were treated in this way, besides elm, willow, and birch for the extraction of their *bast* fibres (see below).

It would be quite impossible to detail all the probable uses of plants by prehistoric man, but perhaps enough has been said to illustrate the importance of vegetable materials and to emphasize the significance of any possible piece of archaeological evidence of plant use that might appear. It seems that in the past much evidence of this kind has been discarded, ignored, or merely overlooked because of the smallness and fragility of plant remains in general.

Before we proceed to consider the structure and nature of the various materials of vegetable origin in turn let us look at the most persistent part of most vegetable cells, the cell wall.

Plants take in oxygen and carbon dioxide from the atmosphere and water and numerous mineral salts from the soil. These substances provide the elements from which various complex compounds can be built up, such as proteins, carbohydrates, and fats. The higher animals, including man, cannot manufacture their own supplies of some of these essential substances and so depend for their existence, directly or indirectly, on plants. Carbohydrates consist of carbon, hydrogen, and oxygen, with the last two in the same proportions as in water, that is, two hydrogen atoms to one oxygen atom (hence the suffix '-hydrate'). Sugars are carbohydrates and some of the simple ones, e.g. glucose, contain six carbon atoms per molecule (monosaccharides), and these can be combined together in twos or threes or more (di-, tri-, or polysaccharides). Cane sugar (sucrose) is a disaccharide, and *starch* and *cellulose* are polysaccharides. The last two, of course, have quite different tastes and other properties from the simple sugars, but they are broken down in the body to monosaccharides by appropriate enzymes.

Substances which are built up by the combination of large numbers of identical smaller molecular units are called *polymers*, and the units themselves are *monomers*. Synthetic polymers are now familiar to all, for example polythene and various vinyl polymers such as 'P.V.C.', but there are also many natural polymers such as rubber, starch, and cellulose. We are particularly interested here in the latter. Molecules of cellulose are very long chains which readily bend at many points and so can take up innumerable shapes from the fully extended chain to the tightly coiled arrangement that is almost a sphere.

When first laid down by the protoplasm of a cell the cell walls are only a few molecules thick, consisting of cellulose chains laid side by side or intricately interwoven, giving strength with flexibility. Later such walls may be thickened, by the deposition of more cellulose, but not always uniformly, more or less regular patterns of pits being quite common and spiral bands of thickening not uncommon. These may be seen under the microscope and can help the expert to identify the plants concerned.

Alternatively, the original cellulose may be overlaid with other materials when different properties are required, the most important being *lignin* (Latin *lignum*, wood) which is deposited over the cellulose walls to form woody tissues, giving mechanical strength. Some trees exude gums, which are often produced from the cell walls, sometimes by breaking down the long cellulose chains into shorter molecules that are still chemically cellulose, but in other cases involving further chemical changes, perhaps to form sugars or other simpler carbohydrates.

We may now look at the characteristic structures of the more important plant tissues that were used by prehistoric man and which could possibly be of archaeological importance.

2.2. Wood Archaeologists would find it very useful to be able to identify the more important and commoner kinds of wood on their sites, and probably even more useful to identify the corresponding charcoals. The latter are so important that they will be treated separately below. Before any attempt at identification can be made, or the reasons for the selection of woods for different purposes understood, it is necessary to follow their development from the fragile seedlings to the mature trees. We shall restrict this description as far as possible to the development of those tissues which are particularly useful for identification.

As the apex of a stem or branch grows by the repeated division of a bunch of cells near its tip some of the cells soon become differentiated to form tissues for the transport of food and other substances (*vascular* tissues). The form and arrangement of these specialized cells vary considerably between different plants, but there are some general rules that are helpful in identification. The angiosperms are divided into two classes, *monocotyledons* and *dicotyledons*, according to whether they produce one or two seed-leaves, and there are several other distinguishing features, the most familiar of which is that most monocotyledons have parallel-veined leaves whereas the leaves of dicotyledons have a network of veins. Differences are also seen in the vascular tissues, or *vascular bundles*, which consist mainly of fibres and vessels.

In monocotyledons the bundles are more or less randomly scattered through the stem, but in mature stems of dicotyledons the bundles have fused together to form a complete ring of vascular tissues. In either case, the bundles, or the ring of vascular tissue, consist essentially of two parts known as the *phloem* or *bast* and the *xylem* or *wood*. The phloem of dicotyledons lies just below the bark and is often called the *inner* bark. It may be peeled off some trees in thin layers and may have been used in this form, but only the fibrous parts have been put to general use. An interesting example is the Lace-bark tree of Jamaica, where the thin sheets of inner bark look like lace because they are perforated where the *medullary rays* (see below) passed through.

The bast consists mainly of bast fibres and sieve tubes, the former being long, pointed cells, which carry sap down from the leaves; the sieve tubes are series of cells, one above the other, the walls being very thick and the end-walls perforated like a sieve. Finer details of archaeological interest will be mentioned later (§2.3, p. 89).

Woody tissues consist mainly of wood fibres and vessels, the latter, when mature, being more or less long, dead cells with walls thickened and hardened by the deposit of lignin and giving strength to the tree. The outer layers of woody tissues are the youngest, called the *sap wood*, whereas the dead inner region contains the *heart wood*. The still soft fibres of the sap wood transport sap upwards and provide a useful source of food for food-gathering peoples in the spring, but if a tree is completely ringed, i.e. the inner bark removed from all round the trunk in any one place, the tree will die. Presumably prehistoric man knew that he must avoid doing this.

Vascular bundles in monocotyledons do not grow much once they have been formed, but new bundles are produced as the stem grows, so that the inner bundles are the older ones. In dicotyledons there is a more or less continuous growth of vascular tissues, usually much more vigorous in the spring than in the autumn, with the formation of the familiar *annual* rings. It will be seen that the larger cells of the spring growth are followed by cells of decreasing size in summer and autumn, and a rest period in winter before the next spring's spurt of growth. Clearly, such rings will appear only in seasonal climates. There are relatively large vessels within the annual rings, and the arrangement of these vessels is one of the most useful criteria in the identification of woods.

We have seen that tracheids, vessels, and sieve-tubes move the sap upwards or downwards, but it is also necessary for it to be transported radially, inwards and outwards, in order to feed the inner tissues or to dispose of unwanted materials in the heart wood or pith (medulla). For these purposes chains of cells known as *medullary rays* are formed, radiating from the medulla towards the bark, some covering the whole distance but many only extending over part of the range. These rays usually consist of only a few layers of cells in the vertical plane; in the horizontal plane they may be only one cell thick, when they are called *uniseriate* rays, or several cells thick (multiseriate) (Plate IV). These also are important diagnostic features.

The two kinds of trees so far discussed are deciduous trees, which produce timber known as *hardwoods*. *Softwoods* come from coniferous trees, which belong to the alternative division of the flowering plants, the Gymnosperms. Any classification is to some extent arbitrary and may occasionally separate very similar members. This appears to be the case with the conifers and the deciduous dicotyledenous trees. Nevertheless, there are sound reasons for their separation, from the nature of their reproductive organs, and, furthermore, there are important distinctions in the structure of their woody tissues.

Softwoods show all the characteristics of the dicotyledenous hardwoods, with the exception of vessels. In place of vessels the conifers may have resin-ducts, but these are generally far fewer than the vessels in hardwoods, and serve a different purpose. Resin-ducts run vertically through the woody tissues, and some are found passing radially through the stem within the medullary rays.

Since roots have to perform quite different functions from stems they will clearly have different structures, and the identification of tree roots is often more difficult. The development of a root also follows a different pattern. In young roots the vascular bundles consist of alternate regions of bast and wood, forming an irregular star of from three to six points. Later wood is formed in annual rings as in the stem. Also, the annual rings are often much less conspicuous and more irregular than in the stem, fibre cells may be longer and softer, and the distribution of vessels may appear quite different. It is important for the archaeologist to bear these points in mind, especially if charcoal is to be identified, because one must assume that roots were often used as fuel or were burnt in a general conflagration.

It is not intended to give a guide to the identification of wood as this is really a specialized study, though one that would be invaluable to the archaeologist who has the time and interest to give to it. The two most important diagnostic features are the vessels and the rays. If there are no vessels then it is a softwood (coniferous). If the vessels are arranged in rings the wood is said to be *ring-porous*, if they are scattered then the wood is *diffuse-porous*. The thickness and depth of the rays and the nature of their cells are also important, but beyond this it is necessary to consider microscopic features, often including the pattern of the arrangement of the pits in the cell walls. In the bibliography are given some useful references, but it must be remembered that some of these deal only with woods produced for *timber*, whereas many more kinds of trees, shrubs, or herbs may be found on archaeological sites, including also many immature specimens.

Oak is said to be the most easily recognized wood, and Dimbleby has suggested that many advantages would accrue if the archaeologist could himself identify this wood or its charcoal. Because oak is so commonly found and consequently the least useful for dating or for ecological purposes, it is usually a waste of the botanist's time to send it to him for identification. If the archaeologist would learn to distinguish just this one wood much time could be saved. For this reason cross-sections of some common woods are reproduced as Plate IV.

It will be seen that oak is mainly ring-porous, i.e. there are rings of large vessels, but there are also clusters of smaller vessels. Also, some of the rays are very large (multiseriate). A specimen of wood or charcoal showing *all* these three features is certainly oak, but if any one of them is not clearly seen then the identification should be left to the expert.

Wood was one of man's earliest materials and he must have learnt at a very early date how to select the best wood for a particular purpose. At first he would be able to make use only of twigs and small branches, but he would know, for example, that ash makes the most satisfactory handles or hafts for stone tools. Later, the same tree provided hafts for bronze tools, and forked branches were particularly useful for palstave hafts. The use of birch bark by the North American Indians for canoes is well known, and there can be no doubt that this was also practised in the Old World. The bark is easily stripped from a birch tree in very large pieces, unlike most other trees where the bark is rather brittle and not easily detached. Birch bark was also used for roofing where very large leaves or material for thatching were not available.

The use of 'heart of oak' for ship-building is also well known, and it was a favourite timber for building purposes, though it tends to split lengthwise. Where this was not permissible elm was a suitable substitute, being similarly heavy and hard. Elm was used particularly for such things as wheel hubs and mallets.

For basketry nothing has yet been found to beat hazel and willow, particularly the young growths of the willow known as *osier* (*Salix viminalis*). The best bows have probably always been made from yew, which, as a conifer, is classed as a softwood but is in fact quite hard.

2.3. Vegetable Fibres   In spite of the rapid increase in the production of synthetic ('man-made') fibres in recent years it is interesting to note that two of the oldest natural fibres, cotton and wool, are still produced in greater quantities than all the synthetics together. Of possibly greater interest is the fact that more than *forty* different natural fibres are produced *commercially*, and in addition to these many others are used locally in different places because of their availability and cheapness (Cook, 1968).

Fibres may be taken from three parts of a plant; the stem or trunk, the leaf, and the seed or fruit. Those from the stems or trunks of dicotyledonous plants or trees are the *bast fibres*, sometimes called the 'soft fibres'. Leaf fibres (also called 'hard fibres') are from the veins of the leaves of monocotyledonous plants. The third type of fibre grows from the walls of the seeds of plants such as the cotton plants.

Not all these fibres have been used for making textile fabrics; some, according to their particular properties, have been used for matting, ropes, and cords. Also, the long thin leaves of many plants have been used directly, by plaiting or weaving, for many purposes; plants such as grasses, sedges, and reeds. In arid regions of Egypt and North America such materials were also used for making sandals. But for most purposes it was necessary to separate the fibres from the rest of the plant material, usually by the process known as *retting*, which consists of soaking in water until the unwanted parts have partly rotted by the action of bacteria. Beating with sticks will then remove the partly decayed soft tissues and the remains of the wood, leaving the long fibres.

The fibres associated with the wood of trees are generally too strongly attached to the vessels and much more difficult to separate than the bast fibres, which are associated with the sieve-tubes and soft connective tissues of the inner bark. The cells of bast fibres are relatively long and pointed, and the overlapping points are cemented together by gums, resins, or lignin to form very long fibres, often running the full length of the stem. After being separated from the other tissues by retting, the fibres will usually be found to be thicker at the joints (nodes) than along the lengths of the individual cells, and this swelling helps in the identification of bast fibres.

In Europe the most important tree for fibre production was the lime, with elm, birch, and willow also popular. Lime bast fibres can be quite fine, but in general tree fibres are coarser than bast fibres from herbaceous plants. Of the latter the best known and longest used are flax, jute, hemp, ramie, and nettle. In Egypt ramie has been identified in material from the fifth millennium and flax from the third millennium B.C., and ramie was also used by the earliest peoples of America, but there can be no doubt that many other local products were used concurrently: for example, in pre-historic Egypt, the leaves of *ensete*, which until quite recently had been confused with flax.

Leaf fibres are produced commercially at the present time from some twenty species of monocotyledons, but many more have been used in the past, some of them only locally in various parts of the world. Commercial production on a large scale is economic only from the very large leafy plants indigenous to tropical or semi-tropical regions, though many of the plants are now cultivated far from their native areas. Central and South America, particularly Mexico and Brazil, produce and export several kinds of leaf fibres, and others come from the Philippines, Africa, India, Pakistan, the West Indies, and New Zealand.

Sisal is now the most important leaf fibre, produced from a plant indigenous to Central America and named after the port of Sisal on the Gulf of Mexico. It was used by the Aztecs and possibly earlier cultures of Central America. Leaves are not usually retted but the soft tissues are scraped off the fibres, which are then washed and dried and bleached in the sun. It seems most probable that smaller leaves were used in a similar way in other areas, and in fact it is known that many grasses (e.g. esparto), reeds (e.g. papyrus), and sedges were used in ancient Egypt. Papyrus was used not so much for textile fibres, ropes, and cords as for the well-known writing material. For this the fibres were not extracted, but thin strips of pith from the flower stalks were laid side by side with alternate layers in different directions, and then beaten with sticks until the whole securely stuck together by the natural gums from between the fibres.

Seed fibres are single-celled outgrowths from the seed cases of certain plants, presumably developed to assist in the dispersal of the seed but also perhaps to absorb moisture to enable the seed to germinate. Cotton is by far the most important seed fibre both commercially and archaeologically. It has been suggested that cotton was used in Egypt as early as 12,000 B.C., but the evidence is slight. It is certain, however, that it has been found in very early Chinese cultures, on Indian sites dating from the third millennium B.C., and in pre-Inca Peru where the advanced techniques and intricate designs suggest a late stage of development.

Many seeds produce fibrous outgrowths, but only the longer and more copiously produced fibres would be worth extracting, which again means that plants suitable for large-scale commercial production would be indigenous to tropical or sub-tropical regions. This obviously does not indicate the areas where seed fibres of one kind or another were used in prehistory.

Cotton plants are perennials which may reach twenty feet in height, though the modern method of production treats the plants as annuals limited to from four to six feet tall. No doubt the wild ancestors of these plants were smaller and produced fewer fibres, but seeds of cultivated varieties may have 20,000 fibres each, and several seeds to each fruit or *boll*. When the seeds are mature the fruit bursts and reveals the mass of white fibres in which the seeds are enmeshed and from which they must be removed before use, formerly by hand. There may be as many as 150,000 fibres in one boll. The cotton is then combed to remove rubbish and very short fibres (linters). Other seed fibres would be similarly treated before spinning and weaving.

Under the microscope cotton fibres show characteristic twists and, when dry, they are rather flattened single cells. In cross-section they are more or less oval, with a central space (lumen) which is large in young or living fibres but becomes narrower in mature fibres by the deposition of more cellulose by the proto-plasmic contents. Cotton fresh from the plant may consist of 94 per cent cellulose, and after treatment, particularly scouring and bleaching, may be 99 per cent cellulose.

Other seed fibres include coir, kapoc, and some species of milk-weeds that are indigenous to America. The last two are too brittle to spin and are used mainly at the present time for matting, cordage, and stuffing life-jackets.

Some fibres have surface markings and peculiarities of cross-section by which they may be recognized, but the identification of fibres from archaeological sites is extremely difficult. It might often be possible to distinguish between vegetable and animal fibres, or between bast and seed fibres, but to proceed even as far as the genus of plant is not usually possible. This depends, of course, on the amount of sample available as well as on its condition. Under suitable conditions the peculiar twists in cotton fibres make them probably the easiest to identify, but cross-sections will generally be necessary also.

2.4. Pollen It is well known that pollen is often well preserved and may sometimes be used for dating a site or to give some indication of the ecology of the site and hence possibly of the climate at the time of occupation. Pollen, then, did not provide a material of use to ancient man, but is nevertheless an important material to the archaeologist.

Pollen is generally produced in great abundance by the male organs (anthers) of flowering plants and dispersed by various agencies, most commonly by the wind or by insects. In most plants which can not be self-pollinated the process is a very hit-and-miss affair, fortunately for the archaeologist, because the vast majority of pollen grains fail to reach the stigmas of appropriate flowers and remain, wasted, on the ground. This may be quite close to the parent plant or, with wind-borne pollen particularly, possibly some miles distant, a factor to be considered in the interpretation of pollen analyses.

Most pollen grains are yellow, but red, blue, black, green, and white pollens are known, and their size ranges from a two-hundredth to a thousandth of an inch. There is a fascinating variety in the shapes and markings of fresh pollen grains as seen under the microscope, many of them being more or less spherical with almost geometrical patterns and often with the casing apparently split in three places. Others are elongated, triangular, or even cubic (like *Basella*), some smooth, and some hairy or prickly in appearance. With so much variety one might expect identification to be a comparatively simple matter, but it is not often that the particular species can be determined, usually only the genus. The process clearly becomes much more difficult with ancient specimens, which may be partly decayed or crushed.

In place of pollen flowerless plants produce *spores*, which also are quite often preserved on archaeological sites. That they do not perform quite the same function as pollen grains is not important here. Identification is not often possible in the case of fungal spores or fern spores, but some important types are recognizable, for example spores of sphagnum mosses, bracken, and club mosses. Fungal spores from the wheat-rust fungus and from the ergot of rye have been recognized in archaeological contexts, but under unusually good conditions for preservation.

2.5. Fruit and Seeds Botanically the fruit of a flowering plant is the ripened ovary, but often some other part of the flower also forms part of what is commonly known as the fruit. The functions of the fruit may be to support or protect the seed or to assist in its dispersal. In some plants (e.g. poppy) the fruit remains on the plant but bursts open in one of many special ways when the seeds are ripe, scattering the seeds or allowing them to be blown away. Other plants release the whole fruit (e.g. apple, strawberry), which may be eaten by animals and the indigestible seeds thus disseminated. But some fruits consist merely of one small seed, which may be dispersed by the wind.

Once again, then, we see an almost infinite variety in the structures, sizes, and dispersal mechanisms of fruit and seeds, so that it is usually possible for the botanist to identify the species of plant from which they came. This applies also to specimens from archaeological sites, whether they have been preserved by burning or otherwise.

One can generally recognize the seeds of fruits that are widely eaten today, especially the larger kinds such as plum or cherry stones, but it is clearly impossible in a book of this type to review even the commoner varieties. Some of the seeds of greatest interest to the archaeologist are very small, such as those of the grasses and plants we now think of as weeds but which at one time provided rich sources of food. It is, in fact, in relation to food that the recognition of seed and fruit remains is important. Not only do these remains provide evidence for the nature of the diet of the peoples concerned, but they may also be important in unravelling the long processes in the development of cultivated plants, in particular the cereals. For example, the study of remains of corn cobs on sites in Central America has revealed the origins and evolutionary course of maize to the varieties known today. Similar work on wheat has shown the relationships between the wild and early cultivated varieties of *einkorn*, *emmer*, and *spelt* in the Near East, and the more recent varieties of wheat. Some of the evidence here comes from impressions of the grains on pottery.

2.6. *Miscellaneous Plant Tissues*   Under suitable conditions practically any part of a plant may be preserved and appear as archaeological evidence, more especially in charcoal samples. One tends to think of charcoal as the carbonized remains of wood, used either as timber or as fuel, but there is no apparent reason why small whole plants should not be similarly preserved, or individual leaves apart from fruit and seeds.

Impressions of plant tissues are also found on pottery and tiles, and those of leaves are particularly useful as their identification is relatively straightforward.

2.7. Gums and Resins Gums are produced in some plants by chemical changes in certain cell walls which convert the cellulose to simpler carbohydrates that will dissolve in water. When the water evaporates the gum remains, first as a sticky *sol* and then as a *gel*. Gums are obtained either by tapping appropriate trees (such as acacia for *gum arabic*), or extracted from seeds by soaking them in water. Very dilute solutions of gums are known as *mucilages*, and these are found in seaweeds and some lichens, though there is no proof that they were extracted in antiquity.

Being soluble in water, gums are not likely to survive in most archaeological contexts, but traces have been found in paintings and written documents where they were used as bases for the pigments or inks.

Resins occur mainly in coniferous trees, from which they may be obtained by *tapping* as solutions in volatile oils known as terpenes (e.g. turpentine oil). When the oil is removed the solid resin (or rosin) remains. Resins are used for waterproofing, adhesives, bases for varnishes, and cosmetics (e.g. frankincense, myrrh), among other things.

Latex is a milky sap tapped from many plants and consisting of a suspension of fine particles in water. The particles may be of rubber, starch, or proteins. Trees with appreciable amounts of rubber latex are indigenous to the New World, and rubber was extracted by the early civilizations of Central America for waterproofing and for making rubber balls for their games.

Amber is, strictly speaking, the resin of an extinct coniferous tree (*Pinus succinifera*), but the name is often applied to other species of resin. It is often called a *fossil resin* and classed as of mineral origin as it is mined in several places, notably around the Baltic coasts. But it is clearly of vegetable origin and is not fossilized in the sense of being a mineral replica, as are fossilized trees and animals. Chemically it is probably little changed since it was first exuded from the tree in Tertiary times, but the precise composition of amber is variable and very complex.

Until about a hundred years ago it was thought that all the amber artifacts found in the Mediterranean regions had been made from Baltic amber, and the ancient routes by which this amber was transported have been very carefully established. But it is quite possible that local amber or amber-like resins were often used, or that it was exported from other areas, including France and Britain. Amber was sufficiently plentiful to be used in parts of south-eastern France as fuel until the last century, and a dark variety (copaline) is found in London Clay.

Attempts have been made to determine the source of amber by chemical analysis, in particular from the proportion of succinic acid which it contains, but so far with little success. Amber was used mainly for making beads and other small objects, and it is well known that it occasionally includes insects and other materials; they would have been trapped in the resin as it oozed from the tree.

Jet is a black substance which is probably an intermediate stage between peat and coal, i.e. it was formed from wood under very high pressures and temperatures but has not been chemically changed as much as coal has. It may be considered as a mineral as it occurs in isolated fragments in shales and mudstones.

2.8. Other Vegetable Products In addition to gums and resins numerous substances have been extracted from plants for various purposes, including dyeing and painting. The latter technique requires a pigment and a *medium*, which is mainly an adhesive. In prehistoric times pigments were almost exclusively mineral products (see §2.5, p. 77), and adhesives were gums and resins.

Dyes impart colour to textile materials by being directly attached to the fibres, either chemically or physically. A few dyes were extracted from animals, but the vast majority came from one part or another of a plant. In either case the method of use was simply to soak the material in the solution of the dye. The solution penetrates between the individual fibres, and even into the cellulose or lignin of the fibres, carrying the coloured substance with it, so that the colour of the dyed fabric is not only on the surfaces of the fibres but well inside them. Sometimes the solution is heated or the fabric actually boiled in it.

Different fibres have different dyeing properties such as fastness to washing or to light, but many of the dyes used in antiquity were not very persistent. One way of improving fastness that was apparently used at a quite early date is by *mordanting*. If the dye itself does not adhere very well to the fibres to be dyed then it may first be attached to a white powder (the *mordant*) to form a *lake*, and the lake will then adhere better, or it may be that the fine particles are simply trapped between the fibres in some cases. Modern mordants include aluminium salts, and it seems that potash alum was used in prehistory when it was available locally, but chalk and kaolin were more common.

One might expect useful green dyes to be abundant, but in fact they quickly fade. Perhaps this was why greens were commonly produced in Europe by the use of a yellow dye from the plant Dyer's Greenweed (*Genista tinctoria*) and the well-known blue dye *woad* (*Isatis tinctoria*).

The whole plant of Dyer's Greenweed was used, but generally only one part is suitable. Those who have picked the fruit of the wild bilberry and similar plants will appreciate the value of these berries as a blue dye. Often the root was the source of the dye, as with the red dye *madder* (*Rubia tinctorum*), or the leaves, as with the yellow dye from Dyer's Thistle in Asia and southern Europe. Some idea of the numbers of plants involved may be gathered from the statement made by Dimbleby that about one hundred wild plants are still used in Britain as a source of dyes for handicraft purposes.

Another, quite different, use of plant extracts is in the tanning of leather. One of the most active tannins was extracted from the *galls* of oak trees, and this was also used as an ink, similar substances having been used in Egypt from the fourth century B.C. The wood of oak also provides tannin, as do chestnut, mimosa, and mangrove, the bark of the larch, sumac leaves, and the North American hemlock.

3. Materials of Animal Origin

3.1. Introduction Animals have been defined as having powers of locomotion, ability to assimilate organic substances, and containing no chlorophyll or cellulose. These are the factors that broadly distinguish them from plants, though some animals do not satisfy *all* these conditions. For example, some animals (especially molluscs) are permanently attached to a particular spot, and some plants can absorb organic compounds, as the

Sundew digests captured insects, mainly for their nitrogen. But no doubt the Sundew can manage without insects, since it contains chlorophyll and so can build up its tissues from inorganic substances. The essential difference between the two kingdoms lies here. Animals *must* get their proteins and carbohydrates from plants (or other animals).

The essential, living part of all animals, as with plants, is protoplasm, but when this has gone we are left with a large number of possible materials, in contrast to the very few in plants. Correspondingly, the classification of animals is more complex, but broadly they are divided into *Vertebrates* and *Invertebrates*, animals with and without backbones, respectively. But practically all the animal materials likely to interest the archaeologist are from vertebrates, important exceptions being the shells of molluscs, including sea creatures, fresh-water shellfish, slugs, and snails.

3.2. Skins, Hides, and Leather   These three terms are often loosely used and may be thought to be identical, but the expert distinguishes the untreated *skin* from the other two. *Hides* are skins that have had all hair and fatty tissues removed, and leather is produced by tanning hides. Frequently the hides or pelts of small animals are called skins.

Most of the skins used by man are from mammals (an exception is crocodile hide), and these consist of three layers, the *epidermis* (or outer skin), the *corium* (inner skin), and the hypodermis ('below the skin') or subcutaneous fatty tissue. The corium is the thickest and most important part of the skin since this provides the required strength and elasticity and contains the sweat glands, hair roots, blood vessels, and nerves. The epidermis is thin and serves to protect the corium, consisting of thin, flat cells, which die and peel off, being replaced by others from below. The fatty layer keeps the animal warm and provides a reserve food-supply, but as soon as the skin is removed from the animal the fatty tissue begins to decay, and unless it is very soon removed it will contaminate the whole hide.

The fatty layer is removed from a skin by scraping, originally by means of the familiar stone scrapers but later with iron implements, precursors of the much later double-handled fleshing knives used on a skin thrown over a half-cylindrical support called a *beam*.

Hides prepared in this way could be used directly for clothing, but they would have to be rubbed with fats or oils if they were to be kept soft and flexible. Dubbin is still used for this purpose (it was originally a mixture of cod-liver oil and tallow), but similar effects can be obtained by dressing the hide with suitable salts. Common salt is the oldest of all preservatives and might have been rubbed into the skins for this purpose, when it would be found to soften the leather also. Alum was used in a similar way (this process was called *tawing*), but all these methods produced only short-lived effects, which could easily be washed out.

Both the fatty layer and the hair or wool were removed together, probably from very early times, by soaking the skin in urine, or some other strongly alkaline solution such as quicklime or *fresh* wood ash. Another ancient practice was *puering*. The puer used for this soaking was a fermented mixture of dog dung and water, used hot, and this allowed the remains of hair roots, epidermis, and fatty layer to be easily scraped off.

Tanning is a chemical treatment of skins or hides, which serves to preserve them almost indefinitely, because the tannins are not merely absorbed, as salt dressings are, but actually combine chemically with the fibres of the hide. In this respect tanning is somewhat similar to dyeing, since in each case a solution must penetrate between and into the fibres. To facilitate the penetration of tannins it is preferable to make the hide swell by puering (or plumping).

If the hair or wool was to remain on the skin it was still necessary to remove the fatty tissue, but more care was needed to avoid damage to the hair roots. After fleshing or scudding with scrapers the skin could be preserved by tawing, but the inside may have been chewed, as it is by some primitive tribes today, to remove final traces of fat, make the hide supple, and help to preserve it.

Since we are to look at animal *fibres* in the next section we shall consider here the structure of the leather only.

Leather consists of several layers of *collagen* fibres arranged in characteristic ways, so that the expert can identify the different leathers under the microscope. The arrangement of fibres also produces the *grain* of a leather, which is often clearly visible, though also produced artificially in modern leathers or leather substitutes. The form and arrangement of the hair roots (follicles) is also of diagnostic importance; they may be single follicles in irregular wavy lines, or groups or clusters of follicles in a more open pattern (Plate III).

Collagen is a protein, which can be broken down by prolonged boiling in water into gelatinous substances, which have been used as glues.

When leather is swollen by soaking it may be split into several layers if a thinner material is required. In this way parchment or vellum was prepared from calf skin, followed by tawing and chalking to prepare a writing surface. Alternatively, when oiled, a sheet of parchment was often used in a window in place of glass.

3.3. Animal Fibres   Here again nomenclature is confusing. In the textile industry fibres from the coats of all animals except sheep are known as *hair*, the term *wool* being reserved for the sheep's coat. On the other hand, it is sometimes useful to distinguish the long, coarse fibres from any animal as hair and the shorter, softer fibres of the undercoat as wool. Whatever the preferred nomenclature, this confusion merely demonstrates the fact that all animal-skin fibres consist of the same material: the protein *keratin*.

Animal hair is now removed by shearing. Before the invention of shears it was probably shaved off, first by means of flint instruments and later with metal razors. It is possible to pluck the hairs off the skin, but the roots come away with the hairs and no further growth can occur. The method could be used on the skins of dead animals, but much easier ways were available, such as soaking the skin or applying a paste of lime to the underside, when the hair is loosened without damaging it.

Trade in wool has very ancient origins. It is reputed to have started between Britain and the Near East before the seventh century B.C., probably involving wool from the indigenous wild sheep, which would be rather coarse and a mixture of long hair and short fine wool. The long, coarser hairs have been almost completely removed from the coats of modern sheep by hundreds of years of careful breeding.

The fine structure of wool has been very extensively studied, since it is the most important commercial animal fibre, and the reasons for all its important properties revealed. Starting with the individual molecules of keratin, it is believed that these are more or less spherical and are strung together in long chains to form *fibrils*, and large numbers of fibrils laid together side-by-side form the walls of a cell of the central part of the wool fibre, the *cortex*. Millions of these long spindle-shaped cells form the cortex, and all are twisted in such a way that the whole fibre is given a characteristic waviness. Covering the cortex is a scale-cell layer, the flat cells overlapping like roof-tiles, with from 700 to 2,000 scales to the inch according to the variety of the wool. Finally, the whole fibre is enclosed in an extremely thin water-repelling membrane, which is the only part of the wool not made of protein.

Water will not pass through the outer membrane in bulk, but there are many very fine holes through which water vapour may pass and become absorbed in the cortex. This is why woollen fabrics will absorb moisture from the body without feeling damp, and will slowly release it again when placed in a drier atmosphere.

The unique twist of wool fibres, not found in any other natural fibre, and the nature and number of the scales are important features in its identification. Mohair, from the Angora goat, has only about half as many scales to the inch as wool, and they are flatter on the surface, whereas those of camel hair are hardly visible under the microscope. In llama and alpaca hairs also the scales are rather indistinct. The last two animals are natives of the high Andes and their hair may be found on sites of early Central American cultures. Many other species may have provided hair or wool in the past, including smaller animals such as rabbit and beaver.

Some other features of the structure of wool are of interest. It may be stretched by about a quarter to one-third of its length and will then return almost to its original length when released. This elasticity is a result of the arrangement of the keratin molecules in the fibrils of the cortex. All proteins consist of many amino-acid molecules joined together in long chains, the specific amino-acids involved and their precise order in the chain being characteristic of the protein concerned. Keratin is a little unusual in that the protein chains are not simply lying side-by-side but are chemically linked together (cross-linked) at regular intervals along their length, and, in addition, the chains themselves are *folded* or zig-zagged. When a wool fibre is stretched all the fibrils are gradually unfolded until they become fully extended. Any further stretching will break the fibre, but, otherwise, when the fibre is released it will tend to return, perhaps slowly, to its original folded condition.

Another interesting point about the cross-linking of wool and hair fibres is that it can be re-arranged by suitable treatment. When wool or hair is carefully heated the cross-links are broken, and they re-form on cooling. If, in the meantime, the shape of the fibre has been changed then the new cross-links will be in different places and will tend to retain the new shape of the fibres. This is the basis of the original method of waving the hair by the use of curling-tongs; modern 'permanent' waving methods use chemicals to break the cross-linking, and these are neutralized when the new waves have been set.

If heated too strongly wool or hair will decompose completely, first changing colour, then charring and giving off a familiar smell. Wool can be identified by burning because the fibres shrivel to a black blob of carbon just outside the flame; they do not inflame.

When wool is spun and woven it may become stretched, and the fibres will tend to return to their original shapes afterwards. This is not possible when dry, but in rain or during washing, when the fibres are 'lubricated' and softened by the water, they will recover and the yarn or fabric will shrink. This is called *relaxation shrinkage*, in contrast to *felting shrinkage*, which is not fully understood but is related to the scaly nature of the fibres. The scales all 'face' in the same direction, i.e. the free ends of the scales all point one way so that the fibre feels rough in one direction and smooth in the other. It is easy to see that in a mass of fibres each will move more easily in one direction (with the projecting free ends of the scales pointing backwards) than the other. Consequently, if wet woollen yarn or fabric is pulled about, or squeezed, the intertwining fibres become firmly entangled or knotted, causing shrinkage. In extreme cases the whole becomes a formless mass of felted fibres.

Silk is the only animal fibre produced as one very long continuous strand. It is not a skin fibre but is produced by the so-called *silk-worm* as a cocoon. The silk-worm is in fact the caterpillar of a moth and, as everyone knows, lives on mulberry leaves. When hatched it is about one-eighth of an inch long, but it grows to about three inches in some thirty-six days, during which time it moults four times, and also consumes vast quantities of leaves. At this stage the grub is ready for its metamorphosis into a chrysalis (pupa) and begins to form its protective cocoon in which to undergo this change. The cocoon consists of a continuous double fibre up to one mile long, produced from two glands in the insect's head and extruded through the spinneret. The cocoon is complete in two or three days.

After the chrysalis comes the moth, which emerges from the cocoon and lays its eggs, and so the life cycle continues. But in escaping the moth dissolves away part of the cocoon and so breaks the silk thread into hundreds of shorter pieces. To prevent this, silk producers kill the chrysalis before it becomes a moth.

There are many other kinds of silk-worms, which have not been so intensively cultivated but live more or less wild and from which a lot of silk is still produced commercially. No doubt this has gone on for thousands of years. The Tussah silk-worm, for example, feeds on oak leaves and is much larger than the cultivated species. There is another found in America and Asia, which lives on the castor-oil plant, and an African species that prefers fig leaves and builds nests of silk in addition to cocoons.

Silk is another protein, called *fibroin*, covered with the gummy protein *sericin*, which can make up almost a quarter of the weight of raw silk. As we have seen, there are two fibres stuck together, and they are not usually separated until after weaving. The sericin gum gives the fibres (called *hard silk*) a rough feel, but after its removal by boiling in soapy water the soft shininess of the silk fibres themselves becomes apparent. *Soft silk* was made in China long ago, but it is not clear just how the gum was removed.

Chinese legend dates the start of silk culture to 2,640 B.C., but it did not spread appreciably for three or four millennia, and reached Europe under the Roman Emperor Justinian in A.D. 555. Long before this time, of course, there was a trade in silk between China, India, and the Mediterranean civilizations.

In cross-section silk fibres appear more or less triangular, with rounded corners, and in the raw state two fibres are held by the gum with two flat faces together. Wild silk is rougher and less regular than cultivated silk, and under the microscope the ends of the fibrils can often be seen (in section) in the walls of the fibres. In each case the fibres are smooth and semi-transparent.

Chemically, silk protein (fibroin) differs from the keratin of wool and hair in not being cross-linked. The molecules are not folded as in wool and therefore silk does not have the elasticity of wool; it stretches only a little and recovers very slowly. Also, the threads of silk are not twisted, nor can they be 'waved' in the same way as wool. These properties are demonstrated in the well-known tendency of silk fabrics to spring back after being crushed in the hand.

3.4. *Bones* We shall distinguish between *bones*, which form the skeletons of vertebrate animals, and *shells*, which constitute the external skeletons of some invertebrate animals. Shells, which are formed completely of inorganic materials, will be discussed in §3.6, p. 113.

The main purposes of the skeleton of a vertebrate animal are to give support to the body, to protect some of the internal organs, and to produce the red and white corpuscles of the blood. The latter is not a function of all bones throughout their life, but whether or not they are producing corpuscles they need a supply of blood and nerves, so that minute holes for the passage of blood vessels and nerves will be found in all bones. In addition there will be specially placed projections for the attachment of muscles, and these can be useful in the identification of bones.

All the points so far mentioned go to emphasize the essential *living* nature of bones. Under the microscope (Plate V) one can see that the apparently solid parts of a bone actually consist of narrow channels ('canals' and 'canaliculi') through which the blood vessels run and around which the bony material has been deposited in many layers. The outer parts of a bone are always more compact than the inner portions, which may be spongy (cancellous), or there may be a cavity through the middle, particularly in long bones. Finally, on the outside of all bones there is a very thin adhering membrane, the periosteum, though this will certainly not be found in archaeological contexts.

Chemically, bone consists of both mineral and organic materials in the approximate ratio of two to one by weight. The mineral part is mainly *calcium phosphate* with a little calcium carbonate, and the organic materials are largely proteins and fats, the most important protein being *ossein*. The bone marrow, blood vessels, and nerves account for most of the organic matter present in living bone.

Bones are said to be 'stronger than oak', and may be specially strengthened in areas where extra strain is to be borne. They are very resistant to crushing and very elastic, the ribs of large animals having been used as bows in some prehistoric cultures.

In the adult human skeleton there are two hundred and six bones, each one specially constructed for its particular purpose and all distinguishable to the expert. If this number were multiplied by the number of animal species likely to be found on any archaeological site, including birds and fish, the result would be a truly formidable total of different kinds of bones, and very few archaeologists could be expected to become familiar with a majority of them or adept in their identification. But by limiting the field, say to one's own country or archaeological period, or by concentrating on the more useful types of bone, such as those of the feet, and having some knowledge of the skeleton in general, many archaeologists could readily learn sufficient to enable them to identify the commoner animals and to sort out large finds, so as to save the time of the expert should his opinion be deemed necessary.

Collections of bones of various origins may appear during an excavation. If there is any possibility of the bones belonging to one person or animal and lying more or less in their original relative positions then very careful excavation is necessary in order to preserve as much of the whole skeleton as is present. It is usually considered necessary to uncover and photograph such skeletons before removing any of the bones. On the other hand, collections of human bones not so arranged may be seen, for example, in mass graves or where the old skeletons have been removed from a burial mound, or pushed to one side within the mound, before new burials were introduced, as occurred in some Neolithic cultures.

Of great importance also are the collections of animal bones found on or near prehistoric sites and providing evidence of the eating habits and general economic background of the peoples concerned. There are also bones of domesticated animals to be found, which must be studied not only from the point of view of the domestic economy but also in relation to the development of the domestication of animals and their breeding for particular purposes. But such investigations must of necessity be left to professional zoologists and palaeontologists, and the archaeologist must be able to assess the importance of a find, decide whether expert investigation is necessary, sort the bones into convenient groups, carry out essential *in situ* measurements, and clean, repair, and preserve them as required. Clearly these processes require a good knowledge of anatomy and osteology, and it is only possible within the scope of this book to mention some of the broad principles involved.

First we note that the skeletons of all mammals, which includes the vast majority of animals of interest to the archaeologist, conform to the same general pattern, modified in some species by the fusion of adjacent bones or the virtual disappearance of others. This is particularly true of the bones of the feet. Animals, including man, that walk on the sole of the foot (*plantigrade* animals) generally have the full complement of foot bones, but those that walk on the toes (*digitigrade*) usually have some modifications, depending on the walking habit. Dogs, for example, have long narrow feet and an extremely small first toe. The heel bone also differs from man's for reasons connected with the fact that the heel does not touch the ground. In hoofed animals (*ungulates*) there is more variation; the pig walks on four toes, the rhinoceros on three, the ox on two, and the horse on only one, although there was once a three-toed horse (*Hipparion*) which is now extinct. The feet of some of these animals contain remnants of other toes, sometimes separate and sometimes as two bones fused together. The main long bone of the foot of these animals, the *cannon-bone*, is very useful for identification. In the horse it consists of only the third digit, whereas in the ox and red deer it clearly shows as a fusion of two bones. The pig has four separate foot-bones, the middle two much stronger than the others, which do not reach the ground.

Similar comparisons may be made between corresponding bones in different species of animal, possibly leading to their identification, but two other factors are usually considered first. The *symmetry* of a bone gives some idea of its position in the body. Bones with bilateral symmetry, where one-half is the mirror image of the other half, generally lie on the main axis of the body, since the body itself is bilaterally symmetrical. The obvious examples are the vertebrae that make up the spine, and the skull, although the latter actually consists of several bones fused together.

Other bones are usually found in pairs, one on each side of the body, and mirror images of each other. These are asymmetrical bones such as the ribs, or the femurs of the legs.

For identification purposes, as also for making tools and other artifacts in antiquity, the *long bones* are the most important, i.e. the main bones of the arms and legs. They contain marrow in the living animal, but old long bones will be found to be hollow-shafted and the swollen ends (epiphyses) consist of cancellous (spongy) bone shaped to form joints with other bones. The remaining bones are either short, as those of the toes, irregular like most bones, or flat, like the bones of the skull. The latter were also used in antiquity for making flat artifacts.

The main difference between mammal bones and bird bones is that the latter are thinner and lighter and the central cavities are filled with air. Although the various bones of the bird skeleton correspond more or less to those of the mammals there is more variation in shape, and other important differences. Altogether the identification of bird species from their bones is more difficult; the beak and feet are the most useful parts, but are not often likely to be found intact.

Fish bones may appear in middens or other parts of a site. The bones of a fish skull are easily separated, and complete skulls are rare. All fish bones are rather rough and flat, except the vertebrae, which have concave ends and are thinner in the middle. Some fish (e.g. sharks and skate) have skeletons of cartilage instead of bone, which, being softer, is not preserved, but they have pointed scales, called denticles, which may be quite well preserved as they are in some ways intermediate in character between bone and teeth. Some denticles (e.g. in skate) are about half an inch long, with quite sharp spines topped with enamel and with a core of dentine (see *teeth*).

Where large numbers of bones of any kind are found it is important to estimate the numbers of each kind of animal concerned. This can be a very complex statistical exercise because it very rarely happens that all the bones, or even all the long bones, of all the animals have been found. For example, one might have thirty sheep femurs, but they would not necessarily be from fifteen sheep, even if half of them were left femurs and half right. Perhaps careful measurement might pair off the femurs, but experience shows that complete pairing-off is not likely to be achieved, and one might be left, say, with ten pairs (twenty femurs) and ten 'odd' femurs. Would it then be correct to deduce that the bones represented the remains of twenty sheep? Again, a similar process with a different bone, say the humerus, would most probably give a different result. Nevertheless, accurate counting of bones must be done and lists drawn up, preferably in the form of tables showing the numbers of each kind of bone from each species of animal, divided as far as possible into left and right bones where applicable.

Broken bones present further difficulties in counting, since it is quite impossible to relate, say, proximal (near) ends of femurs to their appropriate distal (far) ends. In such cases special statistical methods may be used if care is taken in the choice of method. The advice of a statistician should be sought.

In some circumstances it is necessary to carry out such counts for different strata on one site with the hope of tracing any changes in eating habits or in farming practices during the occupation periods concerned. Careful measurement of bones can often give information on the size of the animals, and their sex and age at death, but this is a very specialized field best left to the expert. The incidence of diseases in man and animals often leaves evidence in the bones, and here the non-specialist can generally sort out those bones that appear to have become distorted or are otherwise abnormal and pass them on for detailed examination.

It is said that *antlers* are outgrowths of the skull *bones* and that *horns* are outgrowths of the *skin*, but essentially both horns and antlers have both skin and bone. On the one hand antlers have a skin covering known as *velvet* until they are fully grown, when the skin is shed, and on the other hand horns have inner *cores* of cancellous bone with outer layers of *keratin*, with the exception of rhinocerus horn, which is skin alone. Keratin is the main constituent of hair and hoof and also forms part of the skin, so that in fact only the outer layers of horns consist of 'skin'. Horn cores are outgrowths of the skull but are not shed annually as antlers are, and they are much lighter than antlers because they are hollow. It is the outer, fibrous layers of 'horn' which are used for making various artifacts.

A further distinction between horns and antlers is that when the latter are shed they leave a bony protrusion called a *pedicle*, and the base of the discarded antler carries a swelling called a *burr*. But when an antler is removed from a dead animal the burr and pedicle will remain intact, and part of the skull bone may also be attached to the pedicle. The shapes and sizes of antlers differ from one species of deer to another, but when only part of an antler has been used in making an artifact it is very difficult to identify the species.

There also seem to be wide differences of opinion concerning the cross-sectional appearance of sheep and goat horns. Perhaps the reason for this is that the shape may vary with both sex and age of the animal, but in any case there is no simple guide to the identification of these animals from cross-sections of their horns. The general shape of a horn is probably a reliable guide, since goat horns are much straighter and more erect than sheep horns, and both kinds grow upwards from the head, whereas ox horns project in an almost horizontal direction.

It is interesting to note that if horn is boiled in water after soaking, the various layers (laid down annually, like tree rings) can be separated, and were in fact used in place of glass for windows or for inlaid decoration of wooden articles.

3.5. Teeth   Teeth are extremely important to the practical archaeologist because they are by far the most persistent part of the mammalian body under most environmental conditions. This would be of little value, however, were it not for the fact that even a single tooth, in the hands of the expert, can be made to tell almost the whole of the life history of its owner. In fact teeth carry so much information that some extinct animals are known from only a few specimens of their teeth, from which a fair picture may be formed of the probable size and nature of the animal together with its place in the family tree, i.e. its relationships to known species. For the more familiar species teeth provide probably one of the most satisfactory means of identification, besides giving information on the animal's diet and age at death, which in its turn is important in relation to the ecology of an area, and possibly in studies of the development of the domestication of animals or methods of husbandry.

Of non-mammalian animals of interest to the archaeologist, birds do not have teeth, and the teeth of fish are really *denticles* that have become enlarged and specialized. Fish teeth can be distinguished from mammalian teeth by the fact that the point is usually bent sharply backwards, but those of skates and rays are flattened for use in crushing shellfish.

The living part of a tooth is the *pulp* in its centre, to which blood vessels and nerves enter through holes in the tips of the roots. All the hard non-living material, except the enamel, is laid down in turn by the living pulp, and in most mammals this work is complete by the time the tooth reaches its normal height above the gum. There are, however, some animals, such as rodents, in which some of the teeth continue to grow so as to compensate for heavy wear of the crown of the tooth. In such teeth the roots are wide open, in contrast to the more usual almost closed root-tips.

The main part of a tooth consists of *dentine*, which is chemically very similar to bone but contains much more calcium phosphate and calcium carbonate (about 72 per cent). Also there are no canals in dentine, but only many very small tubes (tubules) communicating with the pulp cavity. These two differences account for the greater hardness of dentine compared with bone. Covering the exposed part of a tooth is a thin layer of enamel, the hardest substance in the body, which contains only 2 or 3 per cent of organic material. In contrast, the part of the tooth below the gum is covered with a thin layer of *cement*, which is softer than dentine and very similar to bone. This region is also covered with a very fine membrane, the periosteum, which lines the socket and helps to fix the tooth. Cement is also laid down on top of enamel in depressions in the crowns of the teeth of some animals where rough grinding surfaces are required.

It is generally considered that primitive mammals had a full set of forty-four teeth, but most of the mammals now extant have fewer. The full complement consists of eleven teeth in each side of both the upper and the lower jaws, and they are named partly according to their main purposes: *incisors* (cutters), *canines* (as in the dog), premolars, and molars (grinders or chewers, from Latin *mola*, a millstone). In some animals the premolars are similar to molars, but in others they are more like incisors or canines, the actual form depending on the normal diet of the animal concerned. Species having a general diet tend to have a full or nearly full set of teeth. For example, the pig has

$$\left. \begin{array}{l} 3 \text{ incisors} \\ 1 \text{ canine} \\ 4 \text{ premolars} \\ 3 \text{ molars} \end{array} \right\} = 11 \times 4 = 44$$

The arrangement of the teeth in an animal is called its *dentition*, and for various reasons the actual dentition may differ from the normal dentition of the species. Although such differences are believed to be uncommon in most animals, the human animal tends to have a reduced dentition when there has been intensive inbreeding.

When recording the dentition of an animal it is not necessary to note the full set, since the jaws are symmetrical. The teeth of one side of the upper jaw and one side of the lower jaw must be noted, since these often differ, and the full dentition of the pig may be written

$$I\frac{3}{3}C\frac{1}{1}P\frac{4}{4}M\frac{3}{3}$$

But since the four groups are recognized in all mammals it is not essential to use the letters I, C, P, and M; we may write

$$\frac{3.1.4.3}{3.1.4.3}$$

This shows twenty-two teeth on one side of the skull, and therefore a total of forty-four. The mole also has the full complement, and hence the same *dental formula* as the pig, though its diet is probably not so general as that of the pig. In the pig, also, the canines are specialized, growing much longer than the other teeth to form sharp *tusks*.

Ruminants (cud-chewers) are vegetarians, or herbivores, which *tear* or break off the grass rather than bite through it. They have no use for strong, sharp incisors, nor for canines, since most of the work of their teeth is in grinding the grass after it has been regurgitated from the first stomach. So we find that animals of this Order, including cattle, sheep, goats, and deer, have no upper incisors or canines and only three premolars. The dental formula for all these animals is

$$\frac{0.0.3.3}{3.1.3.3} \quad (= 32)$$

Flesh-eating animals, the *carnivores*, on the other hand, use sharp incisors for tearing the flesh and large, strong canines for holding their prey, and the molars are less important. So we find that the dog has

$$\frac{3.1.4.2}{3.1.4.3} \quad (= 42)$$

and the cat

$$\frac{3.1.3.1}{3.1.2.1} \quad (= 30)$$

Rodents (Latin, *rodo*, I gnaw) have specialized incisors which, as we have seen, continue growing to replace the worn crowns. The dental formula of a rat or mouse is

$$\frac{1.0.0.3}{1.0.0.3} \ (= 16)$$

Hares and rabbits also have very strong, continuously growing incisors; their dental formula is

$$\frac{2.0.3.3}{1.0.2.3} \ (= 28)$$

but insectivores have almost a full set, the hedgehog, for example, having

$$\frac{3.1.3.3}{2.1.2.3} \ (= 36)$$

There is more variation in the dentition of horses, particularly in the canines, which are often missing in the female horse. Hence, the dental formula is written

$$\frac{3.(1).3.3}{3.(1).3.3} \ (= 36 \text{ or } 40)$$

Sometimes, also, horses have the fourth premolars required to give the full set of forty-four teeth, the additional premolars being known as 'wolf teeth'.

Dietary factors also help to determine the shape of teeth and the nature of their attrition, though the latter may be affected by the shape and arrangement of the teeth themselves. For example, when the canines are large and interlock, any appreciable grinding action is prevented, so that the teeth become worn only in irregular localized areas, unlike human teeth, which all tend to wear down to the same level. Even so, it is possible to make certain deductions about diet from the type and extent of attrition of the teeth.

It should be noted that the dentition of the milk teeth, or deciduous teeth, of many animals differs from that of the permanent teeth, being fewer in number. A full set consists of only twenty-eight teeth, which are usually less specialized. The main difference is that there are no premolar milk teeth.

For many animals the average ages at which the permanent teeth erupt are known, so that it is often possible to determine the approximate age at death of a young animal. For older animals one must estimate age from the condition of the teeth, particularly the amount of wear, which may be estimated from the appearance of the marks and depressions in the crown of the tooth. But ages determined in these ways can not be at all accurate, owing to the great variations in all the factors concerned amongst members of the same species, possibly resulting from sex-linked characteristics, differences in diet, and other causes. Conversely, if the age at death is known from some alternative source the condition of the teeth may provide useful information concerning diet, which is especially important in the case of human remains.

3.6. Shells Shells of various kinds are often found on archaeological sites, either as a product of human occupation or resulting from entirely natural causes. The latter may be of interest to the palaeontologist, who may be able to deduce useful information concerning climatic changes and ecology on the site, particularly from the species of molluscs (*mollusca*) present. For such purposes it is the almost invisible shells which are the most important, and these must be found and identified under the microscope by the expert. The same applies to the remains of the marine species known as *foraminifera*. Analysis of the species of molluscs from a buried surface may be used in a similar way to pollen analysis.

Larger shells were used by man from very early times for personal adornment, and for such purposes holes may have been bored through them, though they were rarely worked in any other way. Buttons, which may have been decorative or utilitarian, were made from *mother-of-pearl*, the pearl-like lining found in the oyster shell, and, in fact, this use of mother-of-pearl has continued into the present century.

It seems that the only egg-shells used for making beads, were those of the ostrich; other egg-shells would be much too fragile.

Some ancient peoples of hunting and food-gathering cultures, living near the sea coasts, included shell-fish in their diets and have left evidence of this in deposits of discarded shells often referred to as *kitchen middens*. These have been found around the coasts of Europe, North and South America, Japan, and Australia, and some of them cover large areas to considerable depths. For example, in Florida there are some kitchen middens reaching a height of forty feet, but about ten feet or less is more common, though some of these may cover as much as four acres of ground. On later sites much smaller collections of shells may be found, and these also are interesting as indications of the occupants. In Europe, Africa, and the near East deposits of oyster shells are a feature of many Roman sites, since oysters were very popular and were, in fact, cultivated in many places.

All the shells mentioned above consist almost entirely of calcium carbonate. We shall discuss the effects of environments on this substance later (§3.6, p. 149), but it is worth noting here that when heated fairly strongly calcium carbonate decomposes, losing carbon dioxide and leaving a residue of lime. There is some doubt as to whether the so-called 'shell-gritted' pottery contains deliberately added shells, because it would have had to be fired at the very low temperature of about 850°C. Otherwise (above 900°C) the shell would decompose and the escaping gas would cause the disintegration of the pottery. At the lower firing temperature the pottery would be rather soft and not at all suitable for mortaria or similar vessels.

The skeletons of minute animals called *diatoms* may be found on microscopic examination of the soil and may be useful in the study of buried surfaces, but they consist of *silica* and not calcium carbonate.

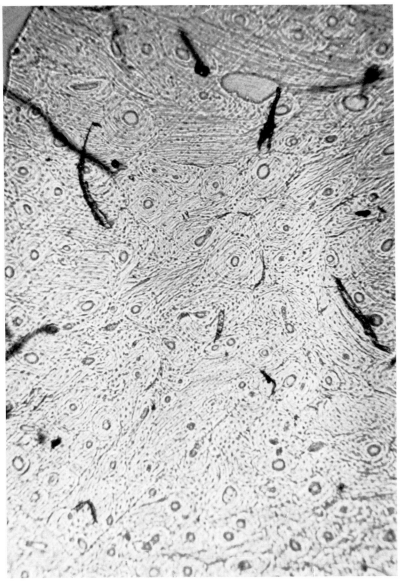

Plate V   Transverse section of fresh human bone.

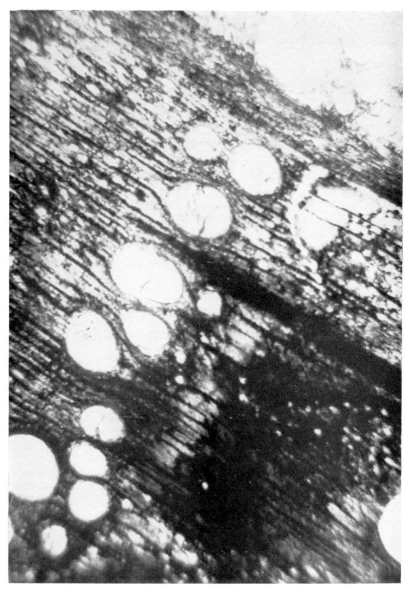

Plate VI   Transverse section of oak charcoal (× 50)
(Cf. Plate IV (a)).

C. The Interaction of Materials with their Surroundings

ONE

INTRODUCTION

In Section A we have reviewed the general nature of the archaeological environment and some of the more common variations of this, and in Section B we tried to get a picture of the nature of the numerous materials that the practical archaeologist may meet in his excavations or his study of artifacts. It is now time to bring these two lines of thought together, to put the artifact in its archaeological context, and to follow the changes that may occur in the material from its pristine freshness until, perhaps, all trace of the artifact finally disappears.

It may be that we are being unduly ambitious in attempting this task, and certainly it would be true to say that in the present state of knowledge the precise fate of some buried materials remains something of a mystery. Not that it is beyond the ability of modern science to unravel some of these mysteries, but that up to the present time the vast amount of work that would be required has not been considered justifiable. Archaeology has always had to depend almost entirely on the by-products of industrial research for its scientific methods and for interpretations of observed phenomena. But this is not entirely a one-way process; industry has occasionally benefited from the results of archaeological observations, as exemplified by the effects of certain plant extracts in preventing the rusting of iron—a story told in fascinating detail by Biek.

A complete description of all the known effects will certainly not be possible, nor will it be attempted. The main objective is to stimulate the reader's interest in the study of artifacts and other materials, not from the aesthetic or typological points of view, but from the broadly scientific standpoint. It is hoped that this will enable the archaeologist to appreciate the position of the archaeological scientist, to be able to recognize materials in almost any condition, and by understanding the decay processes to appreciate the kind of treatment that may preserve them from further loss, and the care with which they must be handled.

One other fact must be kept in mind. New evidence of the effects of different environments on decay processes is continually being produced, and there is always the possibility of hitherto unknown effects appearing, either to complicate the theories or even to overthrow accepted ideas. It is this process of continuous development of theories and the investigation of new evidence that makes the study of archaeological materials so fascinating to the scientist. But it also makes it more difficult for the layman to follow, and consequently more important for the scientist to attend to the lines of communication from time to time and become an interpreter. It cannot be too frequently stated that everyone, from every walk of life, has something to offer to archaeology. Few can be experts in any branch, but all should aim at some understanding of all aspects, including the scientific approach; and it is just as vital for healthy progress in archaeology for the scientist not to become isolated but to keep in touch with developments along other lines, such as typological dating and the interpretation of excavation results.

It will have become apparent that for any one material, decay may follow one or more of several possible paths, so that the number of possible permutations is enormous. It would be useful and convenient to classify the decay processes themselves and then review the results of these processes when applied to various materials. For example, one might first outline the ways in which abrasion, dissolution, oxidation, reduction, etc., occur, and then show the effects of each of these on appropriate materials. But this approach would tend to over-emphasize the mechanistic point of view, whereas the archaeologist's first question on seeing an artifact is 'what is this material'. In this section we shall therefore follow more or less the same order of presentation as in Section B, starting with inorganic materials, and making cross-references where necessary in order to avoid undue repetition.

TWO

INORGANIC MATERIALS

1. Stone

The changes that take place in stone, used either as building material or for the manufacture of artifacts, are precisely the same as the changes produced in the natural rocks by weathering. They will therefore depend on the environment of the stone throughout its lifetime and on the physical and chemical nature of the rock and its minerals.

Stone structures exposed to the atmosphere will be subjected to changes of temperature, soaking with slightly acid rain-water, and, particularly in arid regions, bombardment by sand grains. The effects of the latter are obvious on many Egyptian monuments. These various effects have already been discussed, but we may here consider whether man's use of the materials has in any way affected the decay processes or accelerated or delayed them. Generally we may assume that this is not so, but there are some exceptions. When, for example, building stone is face-bedded it presents a different surface to the elements from when it was in its natural position. In the case of sedimentary rocks, especially the more porous kinds, this means that more water will be able to penetrate the stonework and dissolve out some of the minerals, thus loosening the structure and resulting in the peeling-off of surface layers, or, in extreme cases, the complete crumbling of the surface.

In dry weather the evaporation of water from the stone-work causes the dissolved salts to be re-deposited. This occurs near the surface because the solution must move outwards before the water can escape from the stone. Crystals forming in this way can exert considerable pressures and rapidly crumble the surface layers, besides leaving a white incrustation of precipitated salts. This phenomenon is often called *salt-infestation*. If these processes continue over a long period of time they may result in the collapse of the building. Some very porous sandstones cemented with limestone can completely disintegrate and leave only a fine sand. The process is accelerated where there is appreciable freezing and thawing.

On the other hand, stonework below ground level is usually protected from the extremes of climate and less liable to decay, except possibly in very acid soils. Again, porous stone will become saturated with soil-water in wet seasons, but the movement of this water will be mainly upwards or downwards, carrying with it the numerous substances dissolved out of the soil or the humus layers above. In this way underground stonework may come to contain large amounts of salts or humic substances, the latter often causing dark stains through the stones. This effect is also often seen in separate small stones or pebbles during excavation, a broken surface sometimes giving the appearance of stratification, but in fact representing merely the concentrated effects of the transport of soil materials, particularly humic acids, iron salts, and calcium salts, such as we have seen taking place during the development of a soil profile.

It should not be surprising to note that by the time man came to make use of stone for building dwellings he had a deep understanding of the properties of the various rocks. He had known probably for over a million years how to select the most suitable stones for his implements and weapons, and for thousands of years had used stones for tombs and ceremonial circles. No doubt the choice often had some mystical significance, as, for example, in the use of the blue stones from Wales for one phase of the construction of Stonehenge in southern England, but nevertheless the exercise would add considerably to the knowledge of stone-working.

With the growth of civilization came the desire and the opportunity for the artistic use of stone, not only in sculpture but also in the decoration of buildings and the production of many new kinds of artifacts. The survival of so many examples over several millennia pays tribute to the skill of their creators in the choice of suitable materials, quite apart from their craftsmanship in the execution of the work. But, of course, we can know very little of their failures; how many early attempts resulted in complete decay in much shorter periods of time?

The decay of stonework which is completely submerged under water will follow a similar pattern to that exposed to the atmosphere in moist climates. One might expect the dissolution of minerals from the stone to be much more rapid, and this may be so in some cases, but where the building was designed to stand in water, or to be washed with water on one side, the use of a harder, more compact rock could mean a greater resistance to decay. Also one must note that under such conditions the stone would not be subjected to great temperature changes nor to the effects of salt infestation, at least below water level. Sea water, especially when heavily polluted, would be expected to be more destructive; the critical condition of much of the city of Venice is evidence of this.

Small stone artifacts found on sites of all periods may appear to be in very good condition. Two kinds of decay may be distinguished: dissolution of minerals and abrasive action. Artifacts that have lain undisturbed since they were abandoned will show no signs of abrasion except that produced on the working surfaces during use, but implements are frequently found at great distances from the places where they were abandoned. This applies especially to Palaeolithic stone tools, since settlements of these times were mainly on river gravels and changes of river courses resulted in artifacts being washed away. On their journeys downstream, possibly in many stages, stone tools became heavily abraded, largely by their continual bombardment by fine sands or gravels. In this way all corners are rounded off but internal angles and holes may be much less affected.

The effects of dissolution of minerals from stone are universal but the speeds at which the changes occur will differ vastly from one specimen to another. The most obvious effect is the formation of a *patina*, a change in the surface layers of the stone that is usually made apparent by a difference in colour or texture. A newly broken pebble will usually show this quite clearly. It is said that many semi-precious stones lie undetected on open beaches because they are disguised by their patinas.

The process starts from the outside and slowly moves inwards, soluble minerals being gradually removed, leaving only a skeleton of the less soluble or insoluble minerals. In temperate climates the latter will be mainly quartz and some silicates, but sodium and potassium salts are readily soluble and quickly removed, and the slight acidity of rain-water will cause limestone to dissolve. Buried stones are subject to additional attack when the soil is an acid one, which generally means when it is not calcareous nor lacking in humus. In such circumstances magnesium and iron salts may also be removed from rocks, and since these are frequently responsible for the colour of a stone the result is a much paler patina, although a whitish patina may be entirely due to the textural change. In hot climates silica is much more soluble and the decay of buried stones more rapid.

On the other hand, it frequently happens that the patinated surface of a stone, being much more porous than the unaffected rock beneath it, will absorb iron salts and so become coloured yellow, brown, or red, or, if humic acids are absorbed, the colour may be almost black.

Apart from the colour and textural changes in the patina there will, of course, be a weakening of the stone. In addition, water can easily penetrate as far as the interface between patina and unchanged rock, with the result that freezing and thawing may cause disintegration. By some such process it often happens that large curved layers, of a few millimetres' thickness, become detached from the surface of a pebble, and on archaeological sites these fragments have been momentarily mistaken for potsherds.

Patination is probably more commonly recognized on flint than elsewhere. It has been shown that flint is one of a group of rocks in which some of the silica is in the colloidal state. This form of silica is more soluble than the normal, crystalline, form and so is dissolved out first from the surface of flint, leaving a porous skeleton of crypto-crystalline silica, which appears white because of the way it scatters light. As with other rocks, the porous patina may absorb coloured salts or very dark humic material.

Under desert conditions flint is sometimes found with very highly polished surfaces known as *desert gloss*. This has been variously attributed to the natural polishing action of desert sands, or to a thin layer of pure colloidal silica, which was dissolved out of the flint by hot water in a wet period and redeposited on drying. It is probable that both these mechanisms are at work. *Sickle-gloss* or *corn-gloss* is a similar polish often found on surfaces on or near the working edge of sickles or other flint cutting-blades, and produced by the repeated polishing action that occurs during the cutting of corn or other grasses, which contain much silica.

Finally, flint and other partly non-crystalline rocks often show evidence of *pot-lid fractures*. These are well-named from the shape of the small fragments that split off under the effect of frost or large temperature changes. The loss of pot-lid-shaped fragments leaves a more-or-less circular shallow depression which is quite characteristic of this kind of fracture and distinct from man-made flaking scars. The latter are always formed by striking on one edge of the scar, and a *bulb of percussion* and series of ripple-marks are usually clearly seen.

The effect of fire on all kinds of stone is to cause cracking and disintegration, often with discoloration also. Rocks containing an appreciable amount of iron, such as many sandstones, may become deep red when heated.

Pot-boilers are recognized by the masses of small cracks all over the surface that are produced when heated stones are thrown into water in order to boil it in a vessel that cannot be directly heated over the fire.

2. Plaster, Mortar, Cement, and Concrete

Since these man-made materials are closely related to rocks and minerals we shall consider their decay now, and leave the quite different processes involving metals to the end of this section.

The main constituents of pure wall-plasters are gypsum or lime (calcium carbonate), both of which will dissolve in acid rain-water or soil-water, the lime much more quickly, but the effect on most lime plasters is much less because of the natural, accidental presence of small amounts of clay and sometimes of other, deliberate, additives. Consequently, most lime plasters are much more persistent than pure lime would be; as for gypsum plasters, these were rarely used in other than arid climates, where they have often survived for long periods on internal walls or when buried in the mainly dry soil.

Disintegration of plaster would result from dissolution of its main constituents, but this could also arise in temperate regions, especially very humid areas, from the effects of salt infestation (as in stones) or of freezing and thawing. In either case buried plaster would be partially protected.

Mortar, which contains sand in addition to lime, will be subject to the same decay processes, the sand sometimes remaining as the only evidence of its final decay. On the other hand, decayed lime concrete will be represented by the residue of hard-core and sand, whilst *opus signinum* residues will contain the crushed brick or tile fragments.

Cements are extremely resistant to weathering, but will be liable to cracking where large temperature changes occur, and to frost damage, leading to disintegration, but with very little loss of material by dissolution.

The effects of fire on these materials are interesting. Whereas heat may cause disintegration it is possible that, with lime-containing materials, intense heat might reconvert the calcium carbonate to quicklime. Subsequent rain or high humidity would then slake the lime and it would re-set as a new plaster or mortar.

3. Pottery

The persistence of potsherds under virtually all circumstances is a well-known fact. When fired at a sufficiently high temperature clay becomes practically indestructible, but some ancient pottery was inadequately fired, probably to only 800°C or even less, so that very little sintering occurred, and in wet surroundings such pots will slowly soften and disintegrate. In fact any pottery is liable to suffer in this way when wet and dry conditions have alternated over a long period of time. Otherwise, apart from mechanical damage, including abrasion, salt infestation is probably the greatest enemy of abandoned pottery.

In a very mild form salt infestation might merely make the pottery soft and fragile, but on careful drying it becomes hard again. However, the permanent effect is that edges and decoration have become rounded-off or very much softened so that original designs or figures may be hardly recognizable.

Really serious salt infestation of pottery is rarely found otherwise than in specimens recovered from waterlogged sites or, in particular, from the sea bed. With the rapid growth of underwater archaeology in recent years and the recovery of large quantities of pottery from ancient wrecks the problem of salt infestation has received considerable attention. In bad cases the cure can be a very long process since it involves soaking in good-quality fresh water, preferably flowing, and finally in distilled water until all the soluble salts have been removed.

Much information that would otherwise have become available from potsherds may be lost during or after excavation by rough or careless handling. When removing a sherd from the ground, for example, it is very tempting to rub off the adhering soil in order to attempt a rapid identification and make an inspired guess at the date, but the serious excavator will never allow himself this luxury. Such a procedure might destroy very important evidence, not merely traces of figures or designs necessary for typological dating, but details of surface treatment such as remnants of glaze or colour, effects of burnishing, gloss (as on samian ware), and traces of material remains of the contents of a pot which might give important clues concerning the nature of the site or the technology or feeding habits of the inhabitants. On professionally organized sites well-tried routines are established for the handling of small finds, but in the final analysis the information gained, or lost, depends on one person. Directors should ensure that this person is well acquainted with the kinds of information that might be available from small finds, especially potsherds, on the site, and also what further tests are possible and practicable in specialist laboratories.

4. Glasses, Glazes, and Enamels

Very little ancient glass was exposed to atmospheric weathering except that used in windows, and this would last almost indefinitely under such conditions, if it were not broken. Even in the heavily polluted atmospheres of modern cities glass windows are virtually unaffected. However, when glass has finished its useful life or is abandoned and becomes buried in the ground decay is a little faster, though still relatively slow. The worst conditions for the preservation of glass are found in alkaline soils because the silica skeleton of the glass is attacked and soluble salts are gradually removed.

The most soluble salts are those of sodium and potassium, which were used as glass modifiers. Calcium salts dissolve more slowly and will delay the decay process, but it is said that too much lime tends to increase the danger of devitrification. When this occurs very small crystals are formed, so that the final result is the complete collapse of the glassy structure as a fine powder, which would not be likely to be observed during excavation.

Removal of the modifiers from thin layers of the glass surface leaves a porous and fragile layer of silica, which easily peels off. Several such layers may become slightly separated, with extremely thin spaces between them which, by their irregular thicknesses, diffract light in different ways, producing the colour effects which we know as iridescence. The effect is similar to that of very thin oil-films on water. There is no way of restoring such glass to its original condition, but one might consider that in many cases the iridescence enhances the appearance of ancient glass vessels. In fact, the effect has been artificially produced by forgers wishing to make worthless glassware appear ancient and valuable.

Lead glasses are more resistant to weathering than other glasses owing to the much lower solubility of lead salts in general.

In acid soils glass is often quite well preserved, broken pieces even retaining very sharp edges after burial for one or two millennia.

What has been said about glass also applies to glazes, but since these were originally applied as only very thin layers to pottery surfaces they will disappear relatively quickly in alkaline soils. Their loss will be assisted by any changes in the pot itself that alter its size or shape, such as repeated wetting and drying or large temperature changes. These will all crack and chip off the glaze and increase decay by allowing the soil-water to penetrate between the glaze and the pot. Salt glaze will not be so susceptible to this kind of attack because it is formed from silica in the clay itself, and there is no clear demarcation between glaze and body.

Enamels also are subject to damage by dissolution of their soluble salts, but they usually contain more lead and other less soluble salts added as colourants as well as glass modifiers, so that enamels are generally better preserved than glass. But further considerations apply here because of the different properties of the enamel and its metal backing. Large temperature changes, particularly if recurrent, would tend to strip the enamel from the metal, possibly also cracking or otherwise damaging the enamel itself.

5. Pigments

Very little can be said concerning the decay of inorganic pigments. Since most of these consisted of naturally occurring minerals, such as iron salts, they would be expected to persist for long periods, but their preservation would be closely related to the nature of the materials on which they were used. Dyes, for example, would disappear with the decay of the textile materials, and fresco work with the crumbling of wall plaster.

There is, however, one aspect of pigments that appears to have received very little attention. Excavation reports almost invariably seem to assume that the colours of pigments as found were in fact their original colours. No doubt this is very often true, but one must expect that in many cases changes have occurred, often to a much greater extent than by mere fading. Pigments exposed to the atmosphere will generally suffer little change except fading (which may involve oxidation) unless they have soluble constituents, but burial in the soil may cause other changes by oxidation or reduction or the effects of acidity or alkalinity. Colour changes under such circumstances may not be very great, but there is little evidence available.

Much more drastic effects may be found when pigments have been strongly heated or burnt. In the rare event of the survival of a pigment after a fire we might expect to see the same effects as in pottery, i.e. the reddening of iron compounds by oxidation if the air supply was adequate, or blackening if heated in a limited air supply. Other effects may be seen with organic pigments, which are dealt with later.

Bacterial action and the acid solutions secreted by fungi, algae, and lichens can rapidly destroy many pigments. It is indeed fortunate that the presence of such growths on the rock walls of the Lascaux caves was discovered before the famous paintings were attacked, and steps have now been taken to remove the growths and preserve the paintings. The appearance of such growths more than twenty years after the discovery of the paintings raises interesting questions. The paintings had existed, apparently in their original forms, for about eighteen thousand years when found in 1940, and so the threat to their future must have been caused by changes which have been made by modern man. Two such changes are apparent: the fixing of doors to the cave entrances, and the passage of thousands of visitors through the caves each year. No doubt detailed reports will show exactly how the contamination came about, but it is clear that the movement of crowds of visitors will have completely changed the atmospheric conditions in the caves, introducing bacteria, fungal spores and such, the doors will have prevented the free circulation of the air, and the access of light will have encouraged the growth of algae.

6. Metals

The corrosion of metals is most familiar in the rusting of iron. The precise mechanism by which iron is converted to the reddish oxide which we know as rust is extremely complicated and has been, and is being, studied extensively because of its industrial importance. Most other metals corrode under appropriate conditions, but the products may be quite different, and the processes concerned are usually considered to be much more straight-forward. We shall therefore consider separately each of the metals used by man before the industrial revolution.

6.1. Gold Gold is one of the few metals which are resistant to corrosion, which explains its use in early coinage and its continued use to the present day as a standard of international finance. It is this corrosion-resistance which allows gold to remain free and un-combined (but not pure) in nature, being found as nuggets or dust in rivers and streams. Hence, gold articles are found unchanged and easily recognizable after long periods of burial, apart from possible physical damage.

Alloys containing gold may corrode, but only the alloying metals will be affected. Electrum, for example, contains about 25 per cent of silver and would be expected to show signs of the corrosion products of silver after burial or exposure for any appreciable time. Similarly, copper-gold alloys will be subject to corrosion of the copper. In fact, the presence of gold actually increases or acceler-ates the corrosion of other metals alloyed with it or in contact with it. The whole question of alloys and metals in contact will be discussed below.

6.2. Silver The corrosion of silver does not lead to the forma-tion of silver oxide but to the chloride or sulphide, depending on the environment. The chloride is particularly interesting. It is formed on silver in soils containing relatively large amounts of chloride ions (perhaps as sodium chloride, common salt), or in sea-water. When freshly formed silver chloride is white and it will remain so until exposed to light, when important changes take place. Silver chloride is very similar to silver bromide, which is vital to the photographic process. When these salts are exposed to light they decompose, releasing chlorine or bromine and depositing metallic silver. In photography it is this silver that forms the 'latent image' that is subsequently developed to give the negative (that is, in black and white photography).

By the same process it will be found that a white-coated piece of silver removed from the soil or the sea-bed will soon begin to darken as minute grains of silver form by decomposition of the chloride. The colour changes through grey to a pale purple, unless it is contaminated by other coloured materials.

Silver chloride forms as a dense layer, which protects the underlying silver from further corrosion unless it becomes scratched or the chloride layer otherwise detached. Thus silver artifacts are generally quite easily cleaned and retain their original form, since the corrosion layer is thin.

When exposed to the atmosphere silver will tarnish slightly except in polluted areas, where a thin layer of silver sulphide will form. This will also occur in the sea and in some soils, more particularly when decaying organic matter is present, since the latter releases sulphur compounds such as hydrogen sulphide with its familiar smell of bad eggs. Silver from rubbish pits or wells will usually be particularly badly affected.

Silver also was used in early coinage, but it is very soft when pure. Alloying with copper gives strength to silver, and this was also done at certain times to produce a debased coinage. The effect on corrosion is that a 'silver' coin will become coated with greenish copper-corrosion products.

6.3. Copper   The most striking thing about the corrosion of pure copper is the wide range of colours that can arise, commonly red, green, blue, and black, with mixtures or patches of these under appropriate conditions.

Red colours come from copper oxide, which may be formed by simple atmospheric oxidation of the copper surface. But under normal conditions further changes take place, so that the red oxide is usually found only between the metal surface and an outer layer of other corrosion products, or in fine cracks, fissures, and joints.

In the atmosphere copper generally becomes coated with the green *copper carbonate* by combining with carbon dioxide, probably after oxidation, or, in wet climates, with a layer of *basic* copper carbonate (malachite to the mineralogist), which is intermediate between the normal carbonate and the hydroxide. These compounds give the familiar green colour to copper-covered domes and minarets. But in coastal areas the green colour on copper may be at least partly due to copper chloride formed by the reaction of the copper with sea spray. Under dry conditions the basic copper carbonate formed will contain less water and more carbon dioxide, being then identical with the mineral *azurite* and having a blue or greenish-blue colour. Polluted atmospheres containing large amounts of sulphur compounds may produce the blue copper sulphate or black copper sulphide on exposed copper surfaces.

Buried copper corrodes in similar ways, most commonly to the green carbonate or chloride. The latter is particularly important and interesting since the presence of chloride on copper causes the corrosion to continue after excavation, and, as it appears to eat into copper or bronze, the process has become known as 'bronze disease'. If an object is to be preserved it is important to check the disease as soon as possible by immersing the copper or bronze object in a silver nitrate solution, or by painting the solution onto a large object. This breaks down the copper chloride and leaves a white deposit of insoluble silver chloride, which protects the metal from further corrosion.

Copper artifacts from water-logged ground may be quite well preserved if air has been virtually excluded from the time of their abandonment. A slight tarnishing might be the only effect. Similar conditions are often found in wells or other fresh-water environments, but clearly sea-water will be disastrous for copper owing to its very high chloride content, bronze disease rapidly destroying the whole object.

No appreciable differences have been noted between the corrosion of copper and bronze, but when certain other metals, particularly iron, are present there may be striking effects on the corrosion processes, which will be described later.

It should be noted here that brasses are very liable to change through 'dezincification', i.e. the dissolution or corrosive loss of zinc, which leaves a porous residue of copper.

6.4. Tin We have seen that tin was rarely used alone for the manufacture of articles in antiquity, nor, indeed, at any time in history or prehistory. This may be because of the comparative rarity of tin ores and their consequent high cost, or the relative difficulty of working pure tin. It is perhaps unfortunate as far as the archaeologist is concerned, since tin is much more resistant to corrosion than are copper, bronze, or iron, as is evidenced by the wide use of tinplate (iron coated with tin) in the twentieth century.

The corrosion products of tin are the oxide and chloride, which give a white or grey patina. Tin in pewter objects will corrode in this way.

6.5. Lead The commonest corrosion product of lead is the white carbonate, which forms a slightly porous skin, so slowing down but not entirely preventing the further corrosion of the underlying lead. It has been said that lead corrodes rapidly, but this is hardly supported by the evidence of large quantities of lead recovered from sites up to two thousand years old in temperate climates. It may be that impurities in some early products accelerated their decay, but certainly good-quality lead could survive burial for many millennia in many parts of the world.

In soils with a high chloride content a complex salt is formed on lead, intermediate between the chloride and the carbonate. This appears as a white powder, but does not adhere to the lead as well as the normal carbonate does, with the result that corrosion continues much more quickly. The chloride alone may be the fate of lead in sea-water, but in water-logged soils not containing much chloride lead is only slightly corroded.

Coatings of other colours, such as yellow, pink, and brown, have been reported on buried lead objects. The oxides of lead, of which there are several, are responsible for these rather rare effects.

6.6. Iron The all too familiar red rust of iron is a mixture of iron oxides, which are formed by a most complicated series of processes. One of the first things one learns in chemistry is that the rusting of iron needs the presence of oxygen and water, and possibly of carbon dioxide. This tends to give the false impression that rusting is a simple chemical reaction, but in fact it is mainly electrical (or electrochemical). In order to try and form a simplified picture of the process we shall now consider briefly some simple electrochemical processes, and these will also be required for explaining the corrosion effects occurring when different metals are in contact.

If a piece of metal is dipped into water a few of its atoms will be converted into positive ions, which will move away from the metal into solution. The electrons removed from the metal atoms in this process remain in the metal, giving it a negative charge. If, instead of water, we use a solution of a salt of the metal, e.g. copper sulphate solution with copper, there is the possibility of positive ions passing in either direction, out of or into the metal. If more ions enter the metal than leave it then the metal will become positively charged. Some metals behave in this way and some in the opposite way, and we measure the tendency of a metal to undergo these changes as the reduction *potential* (in volts).

When two such arrangements (of metal in its salt solution) are brought together in a particular way we can form a *cell* from which we may take an electric current. The greatest voltage we can get from our cell, under certain conditions, is easily calculated by simply taking the difference of the two reduction potentials. (It depends also on the amounts of salts in the solutions, and other factors that we need not consider here.) The values of the reduction potentials for the metals of interest to the archaeologist are listed in Table 5, which is a small part of what is called the 'Electrochemical Series'. It will be seen that for a cell made up of copper in a copper sulphate solution and zinc in zinc sulphate solution the greatest voltage available (from the appropriate arrangement) is 0·340 volts less ($-0·760$) volts; i.e. 1·100 volts.

If the two metals were joined together, i.e. the cell were short-circuited, the voltage would rapidly fall to zero and we should find that the copper sulphate solution had lost much of its blue colour because its copper ions had been deposited on the piece of copper as a loose red-brown layer. Also, a similar amount of our piece of zinc would have gone into solution. We could produce the same effects by directly adding a lump of zinc to a copper sulphate solution; the zinc becomes coated with copper as the solution loses its colour. But by this method we can get no electric current. It is only by the very special arrangement used in the electric cell that we may get something like the maximum available voltage.

How do we know (if we have not seen it done) that it is the copper that will come out of its solution and not the zinc? Quite simply by the fact that copper lies *below* zinc in the Electrochemical Series (Table 5). We say that any metal will displace from solution the ions of any metal below it in the Table (opposite).

We have listed only the metals of interest to archaeologists, but a full list would include all the metals and non-metals (and other substances besides), and in this we have the basis of an explanation of the corrosion of metals, particularly of iron.

It has been said that a perfectly pure iron would not rust, but we have no means of testing this because of the impossibility of producing a perfectly pure sample. So every piece of iron (and particularly ancient samples) will contain some impurities, and when covered with water, even as an invisibly thin film, electric

TABLE 5

The Metals of Antiquity in the Electrochemical Series

	(volts)
Zinc	−0·760
Iron	−0·441
Tin	−0·140
Lead	−0·126
(Hydrogen	0·000)
Copper	+0·340
Silver	+0·799
Gold	+1·300

cells will be set up. Since iron is near the top of our list we should find that most of the impurities in our specimen came below it, so that if a little of the impurity dissolved in the water the iron would displace it. This means that ions of iron would dissolve to take the place of the impurity ions, and this is the first stage of the rusting process.

Extensive studies of rusting that have been carried out in recent years have shown some most unexpected results. For example, rusting appears to be most rapid on iron which is *partly* immersed in water, and this is controlled by what goes on near the surface of the water, which is where the necessary oxygen supply is taken in from the atmosphere. But, strangely, it is precisely in this region that the iron rusts more slowly, and the kind of rusting above and below the water shows important differences.

We have seen that in water ions of a metal go into solution as a result of an electrical process. In doing this they must move away from the metal. After a more or less short distance these ions meet other ions (oxide or hydroxide) and form an insoluble oxide, which is then deposited above the metal surface. Thus, the rust is not formed on the surface but just above it, and the iron beneath the rust continues to be attacked, so that this kind of rust, at least, does not give protection to the metal remaining.

In the atmosphere iron rusts in a different way, because the rust is much more adherent. Also rusting is slower in the atmosphere except where there is extensive pollution or salt particles come to rest on it, which will be particularly so near the sea. In polluted

atmospheres it is the sulphur dioxide from fuels and other industrial wastes that are converted to sulphuric acid on a moist iron
surface, followed by chemical attack on the iron. There is also an
electrical process, and the results are that an adherent layer of rust
is formed with a loose layer above it. Corrosion of this kind is
greater in sheltered parts of the iron and less on surfaces that are
often washed by rain-water.

Rusting in fresh water is relatively slow and depends on the
depth of the iron below the surface, since oxygen has to diffuse
from the atmosphere down to the metal. At great depths, or in
other circumstances where the oxygen supply is limited, a black
layer of the oxide magnetite may be formed first, followed by normal red rust.

Sea-water is particularly corrosive because it contains magnesium salts. Consequently, the first corrosion products on iron in
sea-water may be green, then becoming brownish. In harbours and
estuaries there is often a large amount of decaying organic material,
which supplies sulphur compounds and increases the corrosion in
the same way as in polluted atmospheres.

It has often been suggested that ancient iron was less susceptible
to corrosion than modern iron or steel, and that this was particularly true of oriental iron. A possible reason for this was that charcoal had been used as fuel in the extraction of the iron, and this,
unlike most other fuels, is free from sulphur. The Delhi Pillar, in
India, for instance, a fourth-century iron object, is almost rust-
free above ground, but is much corroded under the soil. Recent
work suggests, however, that it is the absence of sulphur from the
atmosphere, and not in the iron, which is responsible for the remarkable state of preservation of the Delhi Pillar.

In water-logged conditions oxygen may be excluded and normal
rusting processes prevented, but there are generally alternative
mechanisms possible. There are, for example, certain bacteria
known as 'sulphur-reducing bacteria', which can get the oxygen
they need by breaking down sulphates to sulphides (SO_4^{2-} ions to
S^{2-} ions). They also require organic matter as food, and apparently a trace of iron is necessary. Sulphates and iron are very widely
available in the soil and the very small essential amounts of organic
material will usually be accessible, so that sulphate reducers can
be expected to get to work in most anaerobic environments. Their
importance lies in the fact that the sulphides they produce can

remove hydrogen from the surface of iron (an effect known as 'depolarization') and so allow rusting to occur. In fact corrosion is then much more rapid than under normal aerobic conditions. But it has been found that sulphate reducers may become dormant in the presence of certain substances, notably tannins, which on archaeological sites can be dissolved out of appropriate organic materials such as wood, and particularly bark. In such cases corrosion of iron may be negligible, and iron objects almost as good as when first deposited.

6.7. Metals in Contact   When there is a little water at any point where two metals are in contact, electrochemical cells are set up, which may profoundly change the normal corrosion processes. If the metals were pure, then we could decide with the aid of Table 5 which metal would suffer most. Even for the rather impure metals of antiquity we may still arrive at the correct answer. The rule to be applied is, as we have seen, that the metal higher in the list goes into solution, to displace from solution any ions of the other metal. Thus the metal lower down the list will be protected and the higher one will corrode more quickly than it would otherwise have done. The protective action is not likely to be complete because other substances and processes may become involved, especially with buried metals, so that the effect may be localized, or it may be found that a general but only partial protection has occurred.

Probably the most familiar combination of metals is that of iron with copper or bronze. During the Iron Ages in various parts of the world iron objects were often covered in bronze, either completely or in some kind of decorative pattern. Since both copper and tin, the constituents of bronze, lie below iron in the electrochemical series they are protected, while iron corrodes rapidly. If, of course, the iron completely rusts its protective action ceases, as it does also when the metals become separated.

Gold, at the bottom of the list, does not corrode but will tend to increase the corrosion of all other metals in contact with it.

Some metals, as a result of their corrosion, are able to preserve other materials, of organic origin, and we shall look more closely at these effects later.

THREE

ORGANIC MATERIALS

1. Introduction

Decay processes in organic materials are generally quite different from those of inorganic substances; in most cases they are much more rapid, and well-preserved material is not often found except in extreme conditions of water-logging or aridity. Very often the archaeological scientist has only a trace of material to work with, and that drastically altered chemically or badly mutilated by the action of fungi and insects, but even so it is remarkable how much information he is able to elicit from these scraps.

We have seen how inorganic substances decay by physical and chemical weathering and chemical corrosion, but we shall find that bacteria, fungi, and insects are responsible for the greater part of the decay of organic materials. Bacteria and insects need organic substances for food, and fungi, although belonging to the vegetable kingdom, also live partly on organic matter, sometimes on living plants or animals (as parasites) but particularly on dead matter (as saprophytes). The work of larger animals, from earth-worms to rabbits and badgers, must not be overlooked.

The rot sets in immediately on the death of the animal or plant, and is accelerated when left to the elements, particularly in the soil, when discarded by man. In a few cases it is possible that a state of equilibrium may be reached at which the position is stabilized and little, if any, further decay occurs until some disturbance, such as the work of an archaeologist, takes place. But for most materials the attack continues inexorably until the final disappearance of the material or object as such. Yet there may still be evidence of the previous existence of an artifact, perhaps in a dark stain in the soil, or merely the presence of an unusual amount of a particular element, which can be shown by chemical tests.

Bacteria are microscopic organisms on the border-line between the plant and animal kingdoms, but they contain no chlorophyll, and only a few types are able to synthesize their own proteins and other complex substances, others depending on plants for these, as do higher animals. British biologists classify bacteria mainly on the basis of their shapes, for example *Cocci* are single spherical cells, *Streptococci* consist of strings of individual cells, and in *Staphylococci* the cells cluster together in groups (Greek; *staphyle*, a bunch of grapes). On the other hand, American biologists have replaced this classification by a scientific division of bacteria into six orders depending on their structures and life histories.

Each bacterium consists of a protoplasmic mass surrounded by a wall, but the latter is quite different from the cellulose of plant cell-walls. Also, many bacteria have a gelatinous coating on the cell-wall, which enables them to stick together or to attach themselves to plants or animals from which they will extract their food. They are often capable of multiplying very rapidly, up to twenty million times a day, but their most powerful defensive weapon is their ability to form thick-walled and very persistent spores, which in adverse conditions may remain dormant for long periods and which are not easily destroyed. The adverse conditions may be high or low temperature or acidity of the surroundings, though some prefer acidic conditions, such as the useful Acetobacter of the human digestive tract.

Bacteria are also named from their way of life or favourite food. *Aerobic* bacteria need air (or oxygen), but *anaerobic* bacteria exist only in the absence of oxygen. *Nitrifying* bacteria can *fix* atmospheric nitrogen, i.e. use it to build up proteins; they are found in the soil and particularly in the roots of leguminous plants (peas, beans, etc.), where they form swellings.

The atmosphere always contains large numbers of bacteria and the soil many times more, so that there is never any shortage of them whenever the possibility of bacterial attack arises, but they must have water, and most of them need oxygen. This may explain the preserving effects of extremely dry and also water-logged environments as far as bacterial action is concerned, but there may still be attack by fungi, besides which there are the anaerobic bacteria to take into account.

Fungi also are very numerous and varied. They include many edible species, and many which are poisonous, and they are responsible for many plant diseases, moulds, and mildews. The life-cycles of some of these fungi are very complicated, and frequently the different stages are possible only on certain species of plant.

The familiar large 'fungi', including mushrooms and puff-balls, are merely the fruiting growths in which the spores are produced, the vegetative part being often almost invisible. It is the latter that causes damage by sending long, intertwined threads (forming the *mycelium*) into the tissues of the host plant, by which some fungi extract their food. The saprophytes attack dead vegetable matter in a similar way, and indeed, a fungus starting as a parasite may become a saprophyte when it has killed its host.

In the case of moulds and mildews the persisting evidence of their presence often consists of the spores by which the species are reproduced, but it is the mycelium that does the damage.

The methods of attack by bacteria and fungi are merely their digestive processes, but these take place *outside* the organism, whereas with the higher animals digestion is an internal process. In each case the process is a chemical attack, the organism making use particularly of acids and enzymes to break down the material being digested. Digestive juices put out by these micro-organisms can dissolve some of the simpler compounds, which can then be absorbed and used by the bacterium or fungus to build up its own tissues. Other materials, such as proteins, may require more drastic or more specific treatment to bring them into soluble form, and this usually implies attack by enzymes.

Enzymes are complex substances, often similar to proteins, which can attack specific compounds without being themselves destroyed. This means that a small amount of an enzyme can be used over and over again. One enzyme is usually designed to attack one particular substance or group of substances, and bio-chemists have shown that this is because the molecules of the two substances are so shaped that they fit together and can become joined at several important points. The mechanism has been called a 'lock-and-key' mechanism. In this way proteins, cellulose, and other complex compounds are broken down into smaller molecules, which will dissolve in water and can be absorbed through the bacterial wall or the cell-walls of the fungal mycelium. By examining the details of attack by micro-organisms we reach an explanation of the great importance of water to them. All their food must be dissolved in water before it can be absorbed, just as with all plants.

All chemical changes take place more quickly at higher tempera-tures, and this applies to the digestive processes of the micro-organisms. Although the latter are destroyed at still higher temperatures these will be well beyond any normal climatic conditions. In tropical regions, then, we shall expect decay to be much faster than in temperate zones, especially when the climate is also humid. Insects also are more numerous and more active in such climates, the termites being extremely destructive.

2. Materials of Vegetable Origin

2.1. Introduction   Vegetable *tissues*, consisting largely of cellulose and lignin after the death of the plant and rapid decay of the protoplasm, may be attacked by bacteria, fungi, and insects, besides being subjected to physical damage and attack by chemicals in the soil.

Cellulose is usually destroyed first, because it is relatively easily broken down into carbohydrates, though it may be temporarily protected by polyphenol–protein complexes. The other materials laid down after, and usually on, the cellulose, such as lignin, cutin, and suberin, are more resistant to attack. *Cutin* and *suberin* (cork) are water-proofing substances and so would be expected to be resistant. But in acid surroundings the order of attack may be changed, and lignin in particular may be destroyed before the cellulose.

Bacteria, as we have seen, cannot live in acid environments (with few exceptions), but fungi can do so, and they will attack vegetable tissues under such conditions.

2.2. Wood   It cannot be too frequently emphasized that by natural processes of decay wood can *never* be converted to charcoal. Apart from one chemical method, which could not possibly occur in nature, charcoal is formed *only* by burning wood or other organic material in an inadequate air supply (Chap. 4, p. 149).

Having disposed of a popular fallacy, let us follow the decay of wood in various circumstances. Sapwood and any other soft vegetable tissues will be rapidly attacked by bacteria and fungi in moist air or soil, but the true wood is more resistant, especially the lignified tissues.

There are many insects that attack wood, including the familiar furniture beetles and the death-watch beetle, but the wood-louse does not do so, preferring to live in the moist conditions under fallen timber. In some species of beetle it is the adult that devours the cellulose of the wood as he bores his way through it, and in other species it is the larva that is destructive. Yet other species live on fungi growing on the wood, and recent work suggests that the death-watch beetle is of this type. There are also wood-boring weevils that only attack after fungal decay has set in.

In tropical and sub-tropical regions termites (white ants) are very destructive, and may reduce most of the inside of a piece of timber to a fine dust quite quickly. The work of all these insects lays the wood open to attack by fungi and so speeds up its decay.

Many species of fungi attack wood; those which feed on the cell contents are of no importance here, but the wood-rotting fungi may be briefly mentioned. These fungi need a plentiful supply of food (cellulose), adequate moisture (usually at least 20 per cent of the weight of the wood), oxygen, and a suitable temperature. They will not grow below freezing point, which excludes them from arctic regions, but prefer temperatures around 20°C to 30°C, and so grow rapidly in humid tropical areas. They disorganize the tissues of wood by destroying the 'middle lamella', the *original* cellulose cell-walls, which in most of the cells will have been over-laid with more cellulose or lignin.

The destructive parts of a fungus are the growing tips of the *hyphae*, the thin fibres of the mycelium. These feed on the cell walls by exuding digestive juices and then absorbing the dissolved tissues as they grow in length. If the wood becomes too dry the hyphae will stop growing, but they have the ability to remain dormant for long periods, starting to grow again when sufficient moisture is available. Some species of 'dry rot' fungi can send out thick bundles of hyphae, which can pass through brick walls and concrete to reach new sources of food. In this way the rot can spread rapidly, but the normal method of propagation of fungi is by means of minute spores produced prolifically on the large fructifications and widely spread through the air.

Fungal attack on wood finally produces a fine powder, or discoloured cubes that crumble to powder when touched, but in moist soil the destruction will be continued by bacteria until no visible traces of the wood remain. But impressions of wood may be seen, or even a dark stain, in the soil. Impressions of this kind, found also in mortar, cement, and other materials, are generally of the length of a timber, showing the *grain*, and so of far less value for identification of the wood than an end-impression (cross-section) would be.

It is convenient here to say a word about wood-ash and the use of wood as fuel. The various woods have different burning characteristics, some blazing rapidly while others only smoulder, and softwoods containing resin will crackle and spit. If there is an adequate air supply and a wood fire burns quickly most of the organic materials will be completely oxidized to carbon dioxide and water (steam) and there will be very little left in the way of charcoal, but a slow-burning or air-starved fire may leave large amounts of charcoal. Wood-ash, as distinct from charcoal, consists of all the incombustible *inorganic* substances from the fuel, being largely potassium, calcium, and magnesium salts, which may often be seen as a white powder sticking to fragments of charcoal and particularly fringing the edges. They are not always seen, because many of these salts are very soluble and readily washed out by rain or soil-water. When wood ashes pass through a second, very hot, fire they may be converted into a glassy slag, and it is easy to be misled by these slags. Many non-metallic substances can form slags or glasses when strongly heated, and vitrified wheat grains look very like glass beads. It will be remembered that wood ashes were a common source of sodium and potassium salts for glass-making.

The preservation of wood in water-logged soil is a well-known phenomenon, which may be due to the exclusion of oxygen causing a suspension of the activity of bacteria and fungi. The action of anaerobic bacteria has little effect on wood. It is found that softwoods are sometimes better preserved than hardwoods in the same situation, and this is probably partly the result of the preserving action of resins in the conifers, since the resins are related to the tannins, which help to preserve leather.

Wood has also been found to be well preserved in clay, even when this is not permanently water-logged. Although clay may be almost impervious to water in bulk the individual, extremely small, clay particles each hold a thin film of water around themselves. The effect might be first the exclusion of oxygen and then possibly a very slow penetration of water from the clay into the wood, so that though the soil would not be considered water-logged the wood itself might be kept moist.

Sometimes wooden stakes were lightly charred in a fire before being set in the ground so as to preserve the buried part, but the effect is not very long-lasting. There have been instances where the whole of the uncharred wood has decayed away, leaving a cylinder of charcoal in the original post-hole.

2.3. Vegetable Fibres The resistance to decay of all kinds of vegetable fibres will depend largely on the proportions of materials other than cellulose that they contain. Flax treated by modern methods of production is almost pure cellulose, and would be attacked rather quickly by mildew, especially in warm, damp situations. Older methods would leave a certain amount of wax in the fibre, but it is doubtful whether this would have any appreciable preservative effect. Jute and some of the other bast fibres, on the other hand, contain lignin (20 per cent in jute), which protects the cellulose from attack by micro-organisms but is itself liable to break down by chemical attack, especially in sunlight. These processes cause the ends of the fibres to break off, and this was a great disadvantage in the use of jute sacks for storing flour and other foodstuffs. A further undesirable feature of jute is that it absorbs large amounts of water (up to 23 per cent), which will cause swelling of the fibres and facilitate attack by micro-organisms.

Much more might be written about the relative durabilities of vegetable fibres, but when all is said it appears that the differences between the various fibres are so slight that they are not archaeologically significant. In the soil, especially when moist and warm, decay is rapid except in very special circumstances.

As with other organic materials, extremely dry conditions may preserve fibres because there is insufficient water for the existence of most micro-organisms. Even so, chemical changes, and particularly photochemical changes (i.e. those induced by light), will take place, resulting in the weakening of the fibres, which in extreme cases may fall to dust when disturbed.

Water-logged conditions may preserve fibres by keeping oxygen from them, thus making it impossible for most bacteria to survive. But there will generally be sufficient anaerobic bacteria to cause decay. Some very special circumstances will be referred to later.

Even when fibres are completely destroyed it often happens that an impression of individual fibres or, more usually, a woven fabric remains on an adjacent object (Chap. 4, p. 152).

2.4. Pollen The common belief that pollen analysis is in widespread use for dating archaeological sites has caused the minute and beautiful pollen grains to be shrouded in mystery. It is a popular fallacy that for some obscure reason they are virtually indestructible. In fact this idea is quite mistaken. Pollen grains are formed from the same materials as other parts of plants, with double cell-walls of cellulose enclosing the living protoplasm, and these materials are subject to the same kinds of attack and decay as the rest of the plant, although the outer walls of some pollen grains are more resistant than other cellulose cell-walls.

Large differences in the durability of the various species of pollen make the interpretation of pollen analyses more difficult because, clearly, one can count only the grains that have been preserved, and nothing may be known of the many that have perished. Some pollens, in fact, last a very short time, in particular the pollen of herbaceous plants, but also that of some trees, such as the poplar. In all cases the protoplasmic contents of pollen grains disappear quite quickly, but the pollen case lasts much longer, its main attackers being the aerobic bacteria.

The essential conditions for the growth of aerobic bacteria have already been listed as air, moisture, and a temperature above freezing-point. We may add that they abhor acidic conditions. Hence we conclude that, because aerobic bacteria will not thrive there, pollen grains will be best preserved in arid or water-logged environments or in acid soils. The two latter conditions point to the importance of peat for pollen preservation, and in fact the great majority of pollen analyses have been carried out on peat deposits. But other soil types have not been entirely neglected, and pollen remains from desert sands have been studied more recently.

Other aspects of *pollen analysis* will be discussed in Part II.

Spores produced by some non-flowering plants are also very resistant to decay, even more so than pollen grains. This is especially true of the spores of ferns and club-mosses, those of bracken being of particular importance. Unfortunately, with some exceptions the identification of spores is more difficult.

2.5. Other Plant Tissues and Products The same considerations as we have discussed for wood, fibres, and pollen apply to all other plant tissues. Hard-coated seeds or fruit 'stones' are possibly the most likely of these to be found on archaeological sites, but only under the special conditions already defined. Practically any part of a plant may come to light, and it is worth noting that in acid soils preservation may occur without water-logging, especially at a considerable depth, such as under a barrow or in a deep pit or ditch.

Very interesting work has been done on the deposits of silica that some plants form in some of their cells. Grasses in particular contain quite large proportions of silica, and it is sometimes possible to destroy the organic matter and examine the remaining silica skeleton of the leaves. Some silica is also laid down in particular cells of grasses in the form of minute structures called *phytoliths* or *plant opal*, which differ in shape and size between different grasses. Except in tropical areas silica is very persistent, and there can be no doubt that phytoliths are preserved on most sites. But they are so small that the search for them under the microscope would be a laborious task, which could be justified only in very exceptional circumstances. It might then be possible to use them in a way similar to that of pollen analysis.

Gums and resins, consisting of partly broken-down cellulose molecules, would be expected to be more rapidly destroyed, and this is probably so. Ancient resin artifacts have been found in arid conditions or completely charred, in which case resins are very difficult to identify. Finally, there is evidence that some resins may be weakly antibiotic and reduce bacterial and fungal activity. They contain polyphenolic substances that resemble some of the tannins.

3. Materials of Animal Origin

3.1. Introduction   Animal tissues and products are subject to the same processes of attack and decay as are vegetable materials, but the effects may differ because of the greater diversity of substances produced by animals, in contrast to the overwhelming preponderance of cellulose and related materials in plants. We have discussed the nature of such diverse materials as skin and bone, hair and teeth, and it will be convenient for us now to consider the interaction between the environment and each of the animal substances in the same order as before.

3.2. Skins, Hides, and Leather   Untreated animal skins are subject to attack by bacteria and fungi, starting, as we have seen, in the fatty layers and rapidly spreading to the two layers of skin proper. Only under anaerobic conditions are such skins, or tanned leathers, likely to persist, and large quantities have been recovered from waterlogged situations.

Tawing with alum, or tanning with any of the various vegetable tannins, may help to prolong the life of the leather, but alum is very easily washed out of leather, as are most of the tannins. The latter are partly absorbed by the leather and the rest is chemically combined with the fibres, some tannins being more strongly bound than others. But in wet or damp surroundings all the chemically bound tannins are gradually released, and only one kind is persistent for any length of time. Breakdown of the fibre-tannin compound makes the fibres once more liable to bacterial attack and decay, which only the absence of oxygen or of moisture can prevent.

Leather recovered during excavation should be kept moist until it can be scientifically examined, as otherwise the oxygen of the atmosphere will revive dormant bacteria and initiate a rapid attack. Usually the leather will have absorbed all sorts of substances from the soil-water and will appear black or dark brown, and thorough washing is essential, followed by careful specialized treatment with neat's-foot oil. The oil is made to replace the water within the leather, and both preserves it and keeps it supple for examination and display. It may then be possible to identify the leather from the grain of the surface or from a cross-section examined under the microscope.

When leather has passed through fire and become charred it is much more difficult to identify because its structure has been distorted. It is unlikely that the origin of such charred leather can be determined, but enough of the fibre structure should remain to enable its identification *as leather* to be made.

3.3. Animal Fibres All the animal fibres consist of proteins of one kind or another, and as such they provide an ideal diet for many insects, bacteria, and fungi. They will all absorb moisture from the atmosphere, which causes the fibres to swell and makes them softer, weaker, and more susceptible to attack by all these destructive agents, and exposure to sunlight speeds up the weakening process by the slow decomposition of the keratin. Silk is also very slowly oxidized by atmospheric oxygen, and, again, more quickly in sunlight. In normal use, then, moisture, sunlight, and even oxygen are the instigators of decay, a process that starts even before the wool is shorn from the sheep's back or the silk unwound from the cocoon. When discarded, or not properly stored, articles made from animal fibres are also attacked by the all too familiar moth grubs, the larvae of various moths and beetles, and, if damp, by bacteria and mildews.

The fibres not actually devoured very soon become weakened and start to crumble, and all trace may eventually be lost. Even in arid conditions the effects of light and oxygen generally change animal fibres and fabrics made from them to an extremely fragile, brittle condition, so that they may fall to dust when disturbed.

When actually immersed in water, animal fibres will weaken more quickly. Boiling water destroys the most valuable properties of wool, making it plastic, but silk is more resistant. It is highly improbable that any finds of woollen or silk fabrics on an archaeological site will have been subjected to boiling water, but it often happens that prolonged actions at ordinary temperatures result in the same effects as much shorter treatment at higher temperatures, and this might well be so in the case of the reactions between the animal fibres and water.

In the soil all the effects already mentioned may be expected to occur more quickly, and complete destruction is likely within very few years except in arid regions. Alkaline soil-water will further accelerate the process because proteins tend to be broken down into their component amino-acids by alkalis.

All the animal fibres will burn, but when wool is removed from the flame it immediately stops burning and all the fibres are found to end in a blob of carbon. This is a test for wool; it also means that woollen material *near* a fire, but not actually in the flames, may be preserved, but silk will not. The preservation of fibres in contact with metals is referred to later (Chap. 4, p. 152).

3.4. Bones In order to study the interaction of bones with their archaeological environment one may consider the organic and the inorganic constituents separately, because the former decay mainly as a result of bacterial and fungal action whereas the inorganic part is lost by simple chemical changes. The nature of the environment will determine which of these processes is the most effective, i.e. whether the organic or inorganic parts will decay more rapidly.

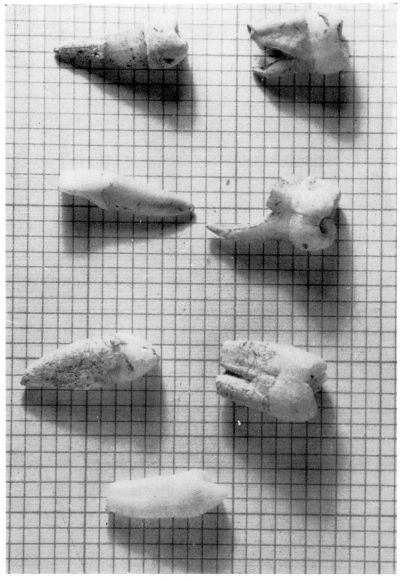

Plate VII (a) Teeth from a British Bronze Age burial mound, showing post-mortem changes, with a modern tooth for comparison.

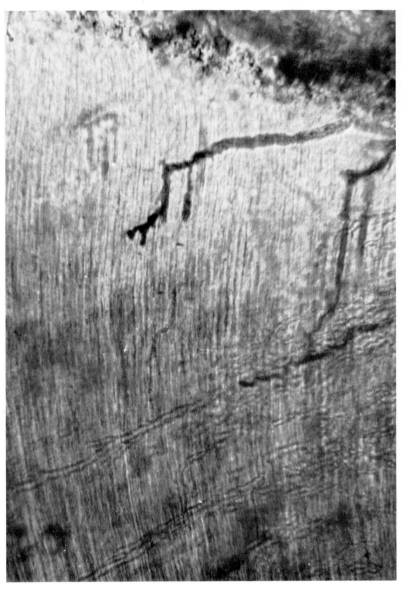

Plate VII (b) Fungus destroying the dentine of a human
(neolithic) tooth (× 50).

At first sight it would appear that the weathering and dissolution of the inorganic substances in an acid environment is the simplest decay mechanism, but in fact it is quite complicated. We can, however, express some general rules. It seems that bone will be more quickly dissolved the more acid the soil-water, i.e. the lower the pH of the soil, and this is controlled by the nature of the sub-soil and of any overlying material, the level of the water-table, and the local climate, particularly the rainfall pattern. In addition, one must not lose sight of the possibility of changes in some of these conditions over a long period of time. But if there have been no such changes then the present soil acidity will give some idea of what to expect, and this is reflected in the type of vegetation on the site. Rather sparse vegetation of a moorland type with a few birch and pine trees but mainly heather, gorse, and bracken will gener-ally be found on a sandy, well-drained soil, one which is mainly siliceous and almost without bases. This is the kind of acid soil in which bone will be rather quickly dissolved and leave no detectable trace, since there are no bases to combine with the dissolved phos-phates to form insoluble compounds, and the organic matter will also soon decay. The possibility of an increase in soil acidity since the bones were deposited must also be kept in mind.

In acid peat deposits also most of the inorganic constituents of bone will be dissolved and washed away, but if, through water-logging or other reasons, air has been excluded the organic part of bone may be preserved as a shrunken and very flexible residue.

By contrast one may find bones apparently well preserved in basic soils, where the soil-water is neutral or alkaline, such as in chalk or limestone country, provided that humic acids from upper layers do not reduce the pH below 7. Some authorities have quoted a definite pH above which bone will be preserved (or, rather, below which it will not be preserved) usually about 6·4, but there appear to be other factors involved. When we speak of preservation in this connection we mean that the inorganic con-stituents are largely unaffected. The organic part will usually have decayed by bacterial and fungal action.

There have been attempts to relate the extent of loss of organic constituents (usually measured in terms of nitrogen) from bone to the duration of burial, but environmental conditions vary so greatly that no general rules can be laid down. But bone also tends to take up certain substances from the soil, and, as might be

6

expected, similar attempts to date bones from the amounts taken up, particularly fluorides and uranium salts, have not proved entirely satisfactory. However, some sort of relative dating may be possible for bones from different levels on the same site.

Over very long periods of time bones may absorb considerable amounts of salts of calcium, iron or manganese from appropriate soils, becoming gradually and very slowly impregnated with them until they may finally have lost all their original calcium phosphate and become truly fossilized.

One other important possibility remains: the preservation of bone in very dry conditions. The absence of water makes conditions impossible for bacteria or fungi, and, of course, precludes the dissolution of the inorganic constituents. This kind of preservation, not only of bones but often of whole bodies, has most commonly been found in Egypt.

As with any organic material, burning will help to preserve bones, though only about one-third of bone is organic. The inorganic part is not greatly affected at temperatures where the organic matter is carbonized, but if more strongly heated it becomes very brittle and crumbly, and at the same time the carbon from the organic matter is oxidized to carbon dioxide and lost. These points are worth noting in connection with human cremations.

3.5. Teeth There is very little to be said about the interaction of teeth with their surroundings, because teeth are very resistant to decay in most archaeological environments. This is especially so of the enamel, since it contains practically no organic matter and will not be attacked by fungi or bacteria. The enamel will also protect the underlying dentine to a considerable extent, but the pulp will be destroyed rapidly.

In fact, dentine also is attacked by fungi, and by the saprophytic *Actinomycetes*, and although the enamel is not directly attacked it may be affected by the acid secretions of fungi (Plate VII).

The inorganic matter of teeth, the calcium phosphate and carbonate, will react in the same way as the inorganic parts of bone, though the enamel will resist longest. Hence, we might expect teeth to be well preserved in alkaline or nearly neutral soils, but poorly preserved or completely destroyed under more acid conditions.

It is interesting to note that tooth enamel, the hardest material in the body, is readily destroyed by fire, with the result that complete teeth do not usually survive a cremation. Sometimes the dentine is preserved, but the absence of complete teeth is disappointing.

3.6. Shells From the fact that shells consist entirely of calcium carbonate, with no organic substances, it will be appreciated that shells will interact with their surroundings in a very similar way to the inorganic part of bone. This means, briefly, that only acid conditions or high temperatures will appreciably affect shells chemically, though they may be very strongly abraded by the physical action of the soil, particularly of sandy soils, and also by blown sand or the rolling action on river beds or in the sea.

The *silica* skeletons of diatoms are very persistent and hardly affected by the atmosphere or the soil except in very hot, humid climates.

4. Charcoal

Charcoal is of sufficient importance on archaeological sites to warrant separate consideration. Carbon produced by the incomplete burning of *any* organic material may be called charcoal, but the term is most commonly restricted to wood-charcoal. We have seen that if wood is burnt in an ample air-supply, i.e. in a 'good draught', all its carbon will be converted to carbon dioxide or carbon monoxide, which are gases and so leave no trace. But if the air-supply is restricted some of the wood will be carbonized, i.e. reduced to elementary carbon, the same chemical element as soot or lamp-black. But where the latter are deposited in the form of fine powders either from the smoke of a fire or from the smoky flame of a lamp or candle, charcoal largely retains the original form of the wood (Plate VI), even the fine microscopic details such as cell-wall markings, multiple-perforation plates, etc.

In many parts of the world until comparatively recent times charcoal has been manufactured for use as a fuel by *charcoal-burning*. This is an unfortunate name for the process, since, in fact, it is *wood*-burning to *produce* charcoal. It was generally carried out by carefully stacking the wood to form a more or less conical pile, which was then covered with soil, turf or clay, leaving a chimney-hole at the top and holes at ground level as required to allow the appropriate amount of air to enter. It was necessary for some of the wood to burn away in order to provide the heat to convert the rest of it to charcoal, and one of the charcoal-burner's skills was in stacking and regulating his fire to produce the greatest amount of charcoal.

It might appear that to produce charcoal in this slow way merely to burn it as fuel is somewhat unnecessary, but charcoal has many advantages over raw wood as a fuel, the most important being that a much higher temperature can be attained by means of charcoal than with wood itself. The conversion to charcoal removes moisture, which tends to keep down the temperature, and many other unwanted (and unpleasant) impurities. This will be particularly important when the charcoal is to be used for metallurgical processes, as even if the process were possible with wood it would leave too many undesirable by-products, which would impair the properties of the final product.

There is very little evidence to show when charcoal-burning started in any particular country, but signs of the practice remain in many places, often as large, low, circular banks, from ten to thirty feet in diameter, showing the familiar red colour of burnt earth, and sometimes with some charcoal remaining on or near the bank.

The presence of charcoal on an archaeological site is usually taken to indicate human occupation of some kind, but there is always the possibility of a natural cause such as a forest fire, though these must have been relatively rare occurrences in most parts of the world before the arrival of cigarette-smokers and glass-bottle scatterers. Many of the extensive charcoal layers must be the result of intentional burning to remove undergrowth, or even forest trees, in opening up a settlement site, but the amount of charcoal remaining from such work can be very slight, since, with a strong wind, combustion of the vegetation could be almost complete.

Wooden huts or timber-framed buildings present a very serious fire risk, especially with open hearths in use, and we should expect to find frequent examples of the destruction of houses or entire settlements by fire, and not always attribute the loss to enemy action. Also, a little charcoal in the bottom of a post-hole does not necessarily indicate the accidental burning of a structure; the ends of wooden posts were often charred in a fire before inserting in the ground because this helped to preserve them.

Domestic hearths, metallurgical furnaces, ovens, and kilns of various kinds should all leave deposits of charcoal or ash, the quantity depending on the method of firing, air supply, type of fuel used, and other factors. So it is not possible to make any general deductions from the amount of burnt material remaining. If there is a quantity of white or pale-coloured ash then some fuel other than wood was probably used. Where charcoal fragments are fringed with white this is merely the residual salts of calcium, potassium, and sodium that have not been washed out by the percolating soil-water, for some reason which might repay investigation.

Apart from vegetation or wood charcoal other carbonized material may be important. Carbonized grain could indicate destruction of a house or granary by fire or merely the over-heating of a grain-drying oven. Such grains can often be identified and provide useful information (§2.5, p. 94).

Many dark-coloured features appear during excavation that may be mistaken for charcoal deposits. Some of these will look much paler when they dry out, but in others it is essential to confirm the presence of charcoal by examining a sample under a lens or low-powered microscope. The grain of the wood or the characteristic appearance of a cross-section must be seen if charcoal is to be confirmed, and simple tests may be carried out in order to make quite certain (Part III).

FOUR

MATERIALS IN CONTACT

In §6.7, p. 135, we discussed the mutual effects of metals in contact, noting that the result is usually the longer preservation of one of the metals and the more rapid corrosion of the other. There are many known instances of the preservation of other materials as a result of contact with substances of a quite different nature, and some of these will now be considered.

One of the most familiar effects of this kind is the preservation of organic material such as wood, leather, or fibres in the form of ropes or woven fabrics by the corrosion products of copper or bronze. This is also one of the most readily explained phenomena since copper salts are well known as fungicides; they are used, for example, for spraying potato crops, as a constituent of 'Bordeaux mixture'. When a copper or bronze object corrodes some of the copper dissolves and the solution may be absorbed by fibres or other tissues near to it, the copper salts being firmly held and inhibiting the growth of fungi and bacteria.

It is also interesting to note that in many cases of woven fabrics in contact with iron objects the pattern of the weave remains, even though the fibres themselves have disappeared, either as a mere impression in the rust or perhaps as a fossilized residue, i.e. the actual fibres have been gradually replaced by rust.

Wood is also frequently preserved by contact with iron, as with wooden handles to iron tools, but the preservative effect of the iron becomes less as the distance from the iron increases. This, in fact, is true of all such phenomena, since dissolved salts of the metal have to find their way to the organic material in order to preserve it. If the material is not close to the metal there will be a delay in the operation of the effect, during which time some decay may occur. Furthermore, at some distance from the metal the amount of metal salt deposited will be insufficient to inhibit completely the action of fungi and bacteria. Thus, the wood actually in the hole of a hammer head, for example, may be quite well preserved, but just beyond that point there might be no trace remaining.

The above examples relate to the preservation of *organic* materials by *inorganic* corrosion products, and we may also find examples of the reverse effect, that is to say, the preservation of *inorganic* materials by the action of *organic* substances. From the archaeological point of view probably the most important organic preservatives known at present are the *tannins*. These are very complex mixtures of various organic compounds, mainly of the type known as *polyphenols*. Some of these are quite simple substances, but they may be changed by oxidation or polymerization into more complex polyphenols, and it seems that their most important properties are thereby enhanced considerably. Some simple polyphenols have long been known to form coloured compounds with certain metal ions, and it may be in similar ways that the colours of the vegetable kingdom are produced. The significant fact is that polyphenols have the facility of attaching themselves chemically or physically to iron and proteins, in particular. The simpler polyphenols can in this way preserve the proteins of dead plant tissues and the similar substances in hides to form leather (tanning), but they are not very efficient in combining with iron.

On the other hand, the more complex polyphenols are more effective in all these processes and are largely responsible for the movement of iron salts down the soil profile. In addition they may strongly inhibit the activities of micro-organisms, apparently by combining with some of their vital enzymes. Thus it appears that such polyphenols may preserve organic materials both directly and indirectly by preventing attack by bacteria and fungi. But they also protect iron and copper objects by forming thin protective coatings consisting of polyphenol/metal complexes.

PART TWO

The Work of Archaeological Laboratories

ONE

INTRODUCTION

Specialization in archaeology, as in most subjects, has developed rapidly in recent years and in most western countries excavators are usually able to call on the services of those who have studied a particular archaeological period or a particular kind of artifact extensively and are able to give expert opinions on such matters as interpretation of excavation results or the origin and dating of artifacts. Occasional extensive (and expensive) reports of such studies are published, such as the large volume on the Roman *terra sigillata*, the so-called 'samian ware' of the Roman Empire, by Oswald and Pryce.

Such works are invaluable to the excavator, particularly for the dating of sites, but complementary works covering scientific investigations in similar restricted fields are not yet available, since archaeological science has developed much more recently than the archaeological arts such as typology. It may be that insufficient results are available for the production of such surveys, but it is also true to say that for many kinds of artifacts reports of scientific investigations are scattered widely among hundreds of journals of many learned societies in many countries, and the prospect of embarking on a literature survey is somewhat daunting. However, the need for this work to be done cannot be denied.

The development of new archaeological laboratories, both for basic research and for routine testing, has been a very slow process, and at present excavators in most countries have to rely very largely on the goodwill of scientists in other fields, in industrial laboratories or in educational establishments and trade research associations. Whilst such specialists are often very willing to help, and industry has sometimes benefited indirectly from the results of their investigations, one has no right to expect such co-operation and, in any case, the time and expense that can be spared from the normal work of the laboratory must of necessity be very limited.

There is certainly a need for many more archaeological laboratories, either as national institutions or in University Departments of Archaeology, but it is to be hoped that these, when they arise, will not have to be run on commercial bases so that the cost of an investigation or test may be prohibitive, as, for instance, the cost of radiocarbon dating is for most excavators at present.

In this section we shall briefly review the more important and useful investigations which might be carried out in an archaeological laboratory, but it would clearly be wasteful and futile to attempt full investigation of an artifact or series of finds unless for some exceptional and very important reason. The decision whether to ask for particular tests and on what material is a very difficult one, which can only be correctly made after considerable experience and, preferably, close contact with the specialists concerned.

Previous writers have emphasized the importance of such close contacts, of visits by specialists to sites, and, particularly for studies of soils, kilns, burnt clay, and similar materials, of sample-collecting by the expert himself. The latter procedure should ensure that in the event of unexpected results appearing from the tests there can be no doubts in the investigator's mind that correct sampling procedures have been carried out.

In all cases where the help of a scientist is required the excavator must himself be quite clear as to what information he would like to have concerning his artifacts, since only then will he be able to ask the right questions. If, for example, a piece of heavily corroded metal with traces suggesting a woven fabric upon it is submitted, the request should not be merely 'please investigate this'. The scientist would then have to decide whether the metal was to be identified or fully analysed, or its microstructure to be studied with a view to revealing the technology used in its manufacture; or does the excavator want to know why the pattern appears on the metal? It is most likely that a request for further information and a more precise enquiry would be sent to the excavator. The latter should be more specific in the first place: he might be interested in the metal alone or in the possible fabric attached, so that his request might be 'Are there any fibres preserved on this metal and if so can they be identified?' It might also help, and in any case would be courteous, to give brief details of the circumstances of the find, the nature of its environment, and details of any treatment used in cleaning or preserving the artifact. The latter is, indeed, imperative, since substances used in cleaning and preserving may interfere with proposed tests or have some effect on the object that might otherwise be assumed to be of archaeological significance.

TWO

SOILS

The practical archaeologist is interested in soils both as providing
the environment for the vast majority of his finds and as preserving
evidence of human occupation in its stratification. Earlier in this
book we looked at some common soil profiles, so as to appreciate
the continuing nature of soil-forming processes and guard against
confusing profiles and stratification. Profiles develop by natural
processes in the same material, whereas stratification arises from
the *consecutive deposition* of different materials, forming actual
superimposed layers. Stratification can be either natural or
artificial, or a mixture of each, and it is in the interpretation
of stratification that the soil scientist can give most help to the
archaeologist. But, for Palaeolithic sites in particular, a complete
physical analysis of the soil can be most informative.

Before taking samples for analysis in the laboratory the pedologist might, in certain circumstances, wish to examine the site.
There are many things he might examine, such as the shapes,
sizes, and alignments of pebbles or boulders and the general basic
and drift geology of the area, apart from a close inspection of the
features on which he has been asked to report. The pebbles, for
example, might show the direction of flow of the ice sheet that
brought them or of the ocean waves that rolled them up and down
the ancient beach.

Information about climatic changes can sometimes be deduced
from the examination of samples from each horizon in a soil profile, or, in the case of gravel beds, a physical analysis, giving the
relative proportions of the various grades, might show changes in
a river's course, besides climatic conditions at various periods.
Both physical and chemical analysis of the sand grains in a soil
sample could add considerably to the knowledge gained from the
gravel analysis, often throwing light on the history of the particles,
their place of origin, and mode of transport.

Chemically the soil scientist tends to look for particular elements or compounds as indicative of human occupation in one form or another. In a sample from an 'occupation layer', for example, he may find very small fragments of charcoal, which would be invisible to the naked eye and which would be too small for the wood to be identified, but if found over a very limited area they would clearly show that fire had been produced there by man, either intentionally or accidentally. In temperate climates he would also look for sulphates (usually as calcium sulphate), which are generally believed to show the former presence of wood-ash and might indicate the use of fire even when no charcoal is found. But the most important indicator of animal occupation is probably phosphate. In the form of calcium or magnesium phosphate this is persistent in many basic soils and acid clays but is not held in acid *sandy* soils. Where a stratum or a localized area shows a greater concentration of phosphate than its surroundings there is a strong indication of human occupation, but there may be complications, for example in the neighbourhood of farm buildings or where modern phosphatic fertilizers have been used.

The identification and characterization of *buried* soils is an important task for which the help of the soil scientist might be needed. If an old land surface has been covered by a bank or barrow-mound for a great many years it might still be possible to trace the original surface and in some cases to reveal the complete profile of a fossil soil. This would be useful if different climatic conditions were suspected, and then one might also wish to call in a biologist to examine any animal and vegetable remains within the old surface layers, especially if turf is well preserved. On the other hand, on many sites simple location of the old surface by testing for humus would be all that was required.

Finally, a word of warning. Soil science is a very wide subject of interest to workers in many different fields, such as engineering, agriculture and horticulture, geology, and biology, and to each specialist the word 'soil' has a different meaning. The engineer is concerned with the mechanical properties of soils, what weights they will bear, and so on, and the agriculturalist may concern himself only with the top-soil, to the depth of the plough or possibly to the depth to which the roots of his crops penetrate. Geologists may also restrict their interests to the topsoil, but in some branches of the science soil may be considered to extend down to the bed-rock. In view of all the different points of view and definitions of soil it is important to ensure that any specialist who is prepared to help the archaeologist with soil problems, and particularly with analyses, really understands the kind of information to be looked for. A soil specimen, for example, sent without full information to an agricultural laboratory for analysis will probably be tested only for the more important plant foods, particularly nitrogen, phosphorus, and potash, and possibly for the more important 'trace elements' which are vital for plant growth. Other substances that might be archaeologically very significant could be completely overlooked if they are of no importance as plant foods and are not actually detrimental to plant growth.

THREE

STONE

Most of the archaeological problems concerning stone will relate to stone artifacts, questions of rock type, origin, use, and technology. What information is it possible to extract from a stone tool?

In the first place the mineralogical composition of the stone could be determined by physical and chemical analysis and by special petrological techniques, of which the most important might be the examination of a thin section under the microscope. The results of such tests on large numbers of similar artifacts should enable the specialist to sort them into groups of artifacts of similar composition, and a thorough knowledge of the geology of the country might suggest possible sources of the rocks. Tests on samples from these sources could lead to positive identification of the original sites, but this last step is the most difficult of all. Success has been achieved, for example, with stone axes in Britain, and the precise location of the ancient factories that produced them can be stated for most of those available for testing.

Petrological methods rely on the identification of the constituent minerals and their arrangement and shapes as seen in the thin section. This automatically excludes flint, because this is always almost entirely composed of silica and has no observable structure that might help to determine its source. It may be that the presence of rarer elements in flint might provide the clues that would identify its source, and it would, theoretically, be possible to detect traces of such elements by means of spectrographic or X-ray methods.

Stone tools, and especially flint implements, are given names which suggest that their purposes and methods of use are clearly known, this is not so. For example, one speaks of end-scrapers, side-scrapers, burins, and points purely on the basis of the shape of the tool, without looking for signs of usage. Recent work has shown that it is often possible to see under a microscope faint scratches and other marks produced during use and from which the method of use can often be deduced. Most of the scratches at the edge of a blade will point in the direction of movement of the blade in use and so possibly reveal its purpose.

FOUR

METALS

Metallurgical and petrographic examination of good-quality metals can reveal virtually the whole history of the material since its extraction from its ore, information that may be useful to the historian of technology but will be of little interest to the general archaeologist. The latter will be more concerned to discover the source of the metal and the route by which it reached its resting place on the archaeological site, but there are many difficulties here. The main hazard is that scrap metal was often re-used by mixing in with newly extracted metal, and this might occur time after time, so that the composition of the final product would not resemble that of any 'new' metal and could not be related to any particular ore. This was especially true of bronzes, and many of the hoards of broken bronze articles that have been discovered all over Europe are believed to represent the waste-metal stocks of itinerant bronze-smiths.

Chemical analysis provides the main evidence in attempts to trace the origins of metal artifacts, and is also helpful in investigating ancient techniques of metal working. The most significant results of such analyses are the figures relating to the proportions of the minor constituents or the trace elements. For instance, a copper object may be found to contain about 95 per cent copper, with small amounts of several other metals such as iron, nickel, silver, arsenic, and antimony, with very small traces of some rarer metals. Knowing that certain copper deposits contain relatively large amounts of, say, arsenic, the expert might be able to suggest a possible source, assuming no contamination with re-used waste copper, but he will take into account the fact that a copper ore varies in composition quite considerably according to the depth from which it is mined, as a result of the weathering of the ore. Also there can be no doubt that many deposits available in antiquity were worked out long ago, so that no samples would be available for testing, even if the sites were known. These are just a few of the difficulties. With alloys the problems are multiplied because more than one source is involved.

Laboratory work on metal objects more commonly concerns their preservation, removal of corrosion products, and restoration as far as possible to their original condition. The objects of such investigations may be threefold; to assist identification, to prepare the objects for display, and to enable the surfaces to be examined for possible markings, particularly for figures and inscriptions on coins. The corrosion processes have been discussed in relation to each of the metals of antiquity, but perhaps we should emphasize the drastic effects that corrosion has on the *surface* of a metal object. This is especially important, and most readily appreciated with iron artifacts because the distortion produced by rusting is very familiar and widespread. Many quite unrecognizable iron objects are excavated and require special treatment. The quickest method of identification is by X-ray photography (Plate X), using one of the kinds of X-ray units used in industrial testing and quality control. If the first photograph does not reveal the identity of the object then another should be taken from a different angle, and it is found that the method rarely fails. The X-rays will be largely stopped by metals and other dense materials, but will pass through less dense substances. In the case of corroded iron the metal remaining, if any, will be opaque to X-rays, but the rust is fairly transparent so that the X-ray picture will show bright areas corresponding to the iron and grey regions for the rust, surrounded by blackened film where the X-rays have not been affected. The picture is, in fact, a negative.

If a metal has not become too badly corroded it may be possible to restore it almost to its original state. For iron this may be done by the use of one of the proprietary rust-removers, with scrubbing and a final thorough washing, but for other metals electrolytic reduction may be appropriate. The corrosion process is one of *oxidation* (even when the product is the chloride or carbonate of the metal rather than the oxide), and the reverse change is known as *reduction*. Electrolytic reduction is carried out by passing a current between the object and a piece of iron or a rod of carbon in a solution of caustic soda (sodium hydroxide) or washing soda (sodium carbonate). The object to be treated is suspended by means of a copper wire, which is connected to the negative pole of a battery, the iron or carbon being connected to the positive terminal. A low voltage, perhaps five or six volts, is all that is required. Bubbles of oxygen will form on the anode (positive electrode), and the reduction will be complete when bubbles of hydrogen start to form on the object itself (provided that the voltage is not too high). The whole arrangement is similar to that used in electroplating except that in the latter method a metal is deposited from a solution. Here the metal deposit comes from the breakdown of the corrosion products and so will be quite close to its original position provided that corrosion was not too far advanced. After the loose material has been brushed off and the object thoroughly washed, it should again look metallic, but may be rough or pitted.

More extensively corroded metals will not respond to electrolytic treatment, but may be reduced by the use of coal-gas. This could be a rather dangerous procedure, owing to the explosive nature of mixtures of gas and air, but under proper conditions it should be quite safe. The objects to be reduced are heated in a stream of coal-gas at a temperature of 200°C for about half an hour, and then at about 500°C for a few minutes. Reduction occurs at the lower temperature, but the further heating is required in order to sinter the fine deposit of metal, i.e. to soften the particles slightly so that they fuse together when cooled. It should be emphasized that this procedure should not be attempted by anyone except in an efficient laboratory fume-cupboard with proper safeguards against fire and explosion risks.

FIVE

POTTERY

A considerable amount of information could be deduced from a full-scale investigation of an ancient potsherd in appropriate laboratories, but how much of it would be of real value to archaeology is difficult to say. If pottery of a previously unknown type from a newly discovered culture were found then every bit of information would have its value, possibly enabling details of the methods of manufacture to be worked out: whether it was handmade or thrown on the wheel, how the glaze was applied and its composition, and the conditions of firing. Analysis of the fabric would reveal the nature of the clay used and of any modifiers, besides indicating possible sources of the material, and, finally, some idea of the date of its use might be obtained.

But few of us are ever likely to feel the need of such an extensive programme of investigation, nor to be in a position to call on the vast amount of valuable time which it would require. Except on rare occasions, when important conclusions depend on the accurate dating or the provenance of a particular find, one is happy if a firm date can be given through the older methods of typology.

Much of the information referred to above would be obtained by the examination of very thin sections of the pottery under the microscope. The technique of cutting and grinding down such thin sections takes a long time to acquire because the sections must be of uniform thickness but thin enough to be largely transparent, that is, except for grains of opaque minerals. The interpretation of the section is also a matter for a trained expert, who should be able to identify the minerals present, noting their shapes and size relationships, and to determine the nature of the surface finish. An applied slip will show as a distinct layer on the surface, distinguishing it quite clearly from, say, a burnished surface. Where a glaze has been applied its nature may be revealed together with the kind of pigment used, if the glaze is coloured.

It may also be possible to determine the area of production of the pottery by means of 'heavy mineral' analysis. In this method the sherd is crushed and the lighter mineral grains, such as silica and clay minerals, separated from the heavy minerals by flotation in a suitable liquid, i.e. the lighter minerals float and the heavier minerals sink and can be removed. All except the clay minerals would sink in water because they are denser than water, which has a density of 1, i.e. one cubic centimetre of water weighs one gramme. The liquid selected for this separation is bromoform, with a density of 2·9, which causes more of the lighter minerals to float. (Clay particles 'float' for quite a different reason—because they are extremely small.) Identification of the heavy mineral grains under the petrological microscope and counting them to find their relative proportions provides the key to the kind of geological formation from which the material came. Reference to geological survey reports should then indicate the most likely areas of production.

Analysis of pottery by other means provides alternative methods for determining its provenance. Two analytical procedures have been tested; spectrographic analysis and neutron-activation analysis. Each of these may be used to determine the proportions of several *elements* present in the pottery, regardless of how these elements are combined together to form the various minerals. They are thus complementary to the heavy-mineral analysis method.

The kind of spectrographic analysis required here is *emission* spectrography. An electric spark or arc is used to produce a spectrum of the elements in the sample. What happens is that some of the electrons in the atoms are forced into different orbits by the heat of the arc, and as they return to their normal places they emit small flashes of light, but there is such a large number of atoms involved that the total amount of light emitted may be very bright. By passing the light through a prism it is split into its separate colours or wavelengths, to give a spectrum, recorded as black lines on a photographic plate. The positions of the lines are characteristic of the particular elements and their intensities depend on the amounts of the elements present. When there are several elements present, as in pottery, there are so many lines that it may be difficult to sort them out, though this is possible by comparison with standard plates prepared from known materials. Then the composition of the sample can be worked out.

A simple demonstration of the principle can be seen when salt is thrown into a flame. An intense yellow glow is produced by the sodium ions, and if this is viewed through a prism it will be seen as two sharp yellow lines quite close together. But under the much higher temperature of the electric arc many more lines (of different colours) would be produced, giving the full sodium emission spectrum.

Neutron-activation analysis is a much more recently developed method of analysis. When a substance is bombarded by neutrons some of the atomic nuclei are transformed into nuclei of different elements, and some of these may be radioactive. That is, the neutrons have made some atoms radioactive, hence the name 'neutron activation'. The number of neutrons acting in this way will be known, and the nature and amount of radiation produced shows which atoms are involved, hence the quantity of the element concerned can be calculated. The method is not applicable to all elements, and some are difficult to estimate, requiring neutrons from a nuclear pile. But the more responsive elements can be activated by means of simple neutron generators in the form of metal foil.

Reference has been made earlier to the colour of pottery in relation to the conditions of firing such as the atmosphere in the kiln and the firing temperature. The expert may be able to answer questions on these points purely as a result of a statistical analysis of the appearance of a number of sherds, but for more precise information more accurate scientific methods are available. The firing temperature, for instance, can be determined with reasonable accuracy by following the rate of expansion of a sherd whilst it is slowly heated. As the firing temperature is reached the sherd will start to shrink very slightly because the process of sintering will be continuing from the point at which it was discontinued in the original firing.

Probably one of the most desirable developments in archaeology is the discovery of an accurate scientific method for the absolute dating of pottery sherds. Several attempts have been made to devise such methods, but at present they are of very limited usefulness. We shall briefly describe thermoluminescence dating and magnetic dating.

Clays contain minute quantities of radioactive elements, such as uranium, thorium, and potassium, and after a pot has been fired the atoms of these elements continue to decay. Radioactive decay is a natural process in which the nucleus of an atom breaks down and ejects rays which may be of three kinds, known as α-, β-, and γ-rays (alpha-, beta-, and gamma-rays). The first two are really particles, α-particles being positively charged and β-particles negatively charged. The latter are, in fact, electrons. On the other hand, γ-rays consist of radiation very similar to that of X-rays, and they may be used in similar ways. Each kind of ray leaves the nucleus with considerable energy and each can collide with and break down or displace other atoms, so that all of them, and especially α-particles, can create havoc over very small regions in a crystal. In such regions the atoms will no longer be in the normal orderly arrangement of a crystal; some will have been knocked out of place and others may have lost electrons. All the effects of radiation on crystals are known as 'crystal defects'.

When a solid, crystalline material, such as pottery, is heated to a fairly high temperature and allowed to cool slowly the atoms have time to move into their correct positions, and we may assume that there will be very few defects of the kind described above, though there will be other kinds of defect (e.g. those caused by impurities). But the radioactive substances will immediately start to create new defects. Clearly, if we knew the rate at which defects were produced and could measure the total number of defects in an ancient pot sample we should be able to calculate how long the pot has been subjected to bombardment by radioactive particles, and this period of time should give the age of the pot, or the time since it was last heated.

But one cannot determine precisely how many defects are being produced per annum. However, a reasonable estimate can be made from measurements of the present radioactivity of a sample of the pot, making certain assumptions and approximations. Then a method is required for measuring the amount of damage (or number of defects) produced since the firing of the pot, and this may be done by measuring the *thermoluminescence*.

An interesting phenomenon found in radiation-damaged materials is that when they are heated to remove the defects or 'anneal' the damage, very faint flashes of light are given out. These are generally much too faint to be seen, except in some very ancient limestones. It is sometimes possible to see the thermo-luminescence from such limestones by heating some pieces in a frying-pan in a dark room. The effect results from electrons falling back into their proper places after being displaced by radioactive particles or rays. But pottery cannot be older than about ten thousand years, compared with the millions of years since the limestone was deposited, and so the light emitted when a sherd is heated is correspondingly less. Even so, it can be detected, and measured, by very sensitive electronic devices, and the amount of light collected is taken to be proportional to the amount of radiation damage annealed during the heating process.

But scientific methods are rarely as straightforward as they seem, and many difficulties are still to be overcome. It may be that some alternative method of measuring the radiation damage might prove more convenient and accurate. At the present time it seems doubtful whether an accuracy of 10 per cent can be achieved, but even this can be useful in deciding between two quite well separated possible dates, such as in the often difficult matter of distinguishing between some types of Saxon pottery in Britain and British Iron Age pottery.

When rocks and minerals (and hence clay and pottery) which contain iron salts are heated to over 600°C and allowed to cool they become magnetized by the earth's magnetic field. This magnetization is very weak and requires very sensitive instruments for its accurate measurement, but because it has both a strength proportional to that of the earth's field at the time of cooling and the actual direction of that field, and because these remain virtually unchanged unless the material is reheated, we have the basis of methods of dating. This kind of magnetism is called *thermoremanent magnetism* (TRM), and there are two distinct dating methods making use of TRM being investigated at present.

It is known that both the strength (intensity) and the direction of the earth's field change with time, but whether these changes are cyclic, periodic, or irregular has not yet been decided, and many more measurements on firmly dated material will be needed before the methods can be put into general use.

For the magnetic-field direction method it is essential to work with baked clay or pottery that is in exactly the position in which it was fired. Then samples can be carefully marked to show the direction of the present-day magnetic field before being removed to the laboratory for measurements that will show the direction of the TRM. To define the direction fully it is necessary to measure the magnetic *declination*, i.e. the deviation of the field direction from the true geographical north–south line, and the magnetic *dip* (or inclination), the angle below the horizontal at which the compass needle will point. From the TRM measurements these two angles can be found for the samples and, if the material was baked at a time for which measurements of the earth's field are available, then dating may be possible. Unfortunately, at present relatively few accurate data are available, but the situation is improving as more accurately dated sites produce suitable baked material. Archaeologists can give considerable help by first ascertaining for what dates material is required in their own particular country or state, and arranging to inform the workers concerned should suitable material appear during excavation. In this work it is absolutely essential for the experts to select the samples themselves, measure them *in situ*, and remove them by their own special methods.

The alternative magnetic dating method involves many measurements on each sample after heating to various temperatures, and this method also requires many more well-dated reference samples before the general trend of the earth's magnetic-field intensity over archaeological time can be worked out. Early work appeared to suggest that the field intensity had decreased at the rate of about 3 per cent per annum over at least the past two thousand years, but more recent experiments in Czechoslovakia are interpreted as showing a periodical fluctuation around some figure close to the present value. The method has interesting possibilities, but no great accuracy of dating can be expected in the foreseeable future.

To return to more mundane matters: impressions made in the clay before firing often preserve important and interesting information. Impressions of grains and fabrics are not uncommon and should be examined under the microscope, as also should any unidentified marks, and impressed decoration should be inspected to determine the method of formation.

SIX

GLASS, GLAZES, AND ENAMELS

There are several mysteries surrounding the technology of ancient and medieval glass, including the apparently almost simultaneous changes in composition that occurred at various times over vast areas. This phenomenon considerably reduces the chances of tracing the source of a glass artifact from its chemical composition unless it transpires, as a result of more recent work, that there are significant differences in the nature and amounts of substances found in very minute traces (perhaps a few parts in a million million parts), or even in the isotopic composition of some constituent element. Ordinary chemical analysis, then, is rarely worth while on glass artifacts except in so far as it may reveal the nature of additives, and particularly colourants.

Modern analytical methods useful for glasses, glazes, and enamels are mainly of the non-destructive variety, including X-ray fluorescence spectroscopy and the electron micro-probe analyser. The former method is based on the fact that each element can be induced to emit its own characteristic X-rays, either by bombarding a sample with electrons, as is done in the common X-ray tubes used for X-ray photography, or by directing onto the sample a beam of X-rays of all wavelengths. In visible light we see different wavelengths as different colours; X-rays are of the same nature as light, so that a beam covering a wide range of wavelengths may be called a 'white' X-ray beam. When such a beam strikes a solid material many of the X-rays are absorbed or pass through the solid, but some are re-emitted by the atoms. These are the characteristic X-rays whose precise wavelengths are known for all the elements, and may be used as a kind of 'finger-print' to identify all the elements in any material. The method is very sensitive and non-destructive, but sometimes produces a slight discolouration of the glass in the small area used. This is readily removed by careful heating, or will slowly disappear without treatment.

Scientific methods are being described as they arise, but they will all have many other fields of application besides those for which details are given. Another such technique is that of the electron-probe micro-analyser, in which an electron beam is focused onto a very small area (about a millionth of a square metre) on the surface of the object and the X-rays produced are identified. The advantage of this technique is that small differences in composition from place to place on the surface can easily be studied, though there are circumstances where this might not be advantageous. Both these X-ray methods investigate only the surface of an object, which can differ considerably in composition from the inner parts, especially after centuries of burial in the soil.

Details of manufacturing methods can be deduced from visual examination of glass, assisted, if necessary, by the microscope. Even the bubbles that are so common in ancient glass may show, by the direction of their ellipticity, how the soft glass was worked. If the material is opaque, then similar information may be found by means of radiography with X-rays or gamma-rays, and this is particularly useful for enamels, revealing details of the mode of attachment to the underlying metal, for instance. Should an enamel prove to be almost opaque to X-rays then it must contain a fair proportion of a heavy metal, probably lead. The latter may also be detected and the amount present in a glaze or glass estimated by the beta-ray back-scatter method. Beta-rays (electrons from a radioactive substance) are absorbed by or transmitted through most substances, but heavy metals such as lead will reflect them back. The method consists of bringing a suitable screened radioactive source close to the surface and measuring the intensity of the reflected beam of beta-rays by means of a Geiger counter.

The dating of glass artifacts by typology is by no means as advanced as for some pottery types, and here again much research has been done towards providing a scientific dating method. Glass artifacts acquire a kind of patina during burial, and if it could be shown that the thickness of the patina was proportional to the duration of burial we should have the basis of a method of dating. It seems that the weathering that causes the patination is a periodic process, possibly following seasonal changes of temperature or of humidity, and that a very thin layer is produced in each season. Counting the layers under the microscope is claimed to give the approximate number of years since the glass was produced, provided that none of the flaking layers has been lost.

Natural glasses such as obsidian may be dated through the examination of a different surface effect. Fresh surfaces of obsidian take up water in a process known as *hydration*, at a steady rate, producing a very thin hydration layer visible only under the microscope. This is a continuous, homogeneous layer, not flaky as in glass, so that dating depends on measuring the precise thickness of the hydration layer. If, as is possible, the thickness increases by the same amount each year, then the age of the obsidian is readily calculated.

Obsidian and manufactured glass that contain a certain amount of uranium may be used for *fission-track dating*, but at present it seems that only very ancient natural glasses or some glasses made since about 1800 A.D. are amenable to this technique. The radioactive decay of uranium produces fast energetic particles, which damage the structure of the glass over extremely small regions around the decaying atoms. This is the same process we have already met in thermoluminescence dating of pottery, but here the effects are revealed in a different way. If a section of the glass is cut and treated with a suitable acid solution the damaged areas are attacked much more rapidly than the unaffected regions. After washing and drying the sample the damage may be seen under the microscope as small pits, which can be counted over a measured area. The amount of uranium present may be found by chemical analysis (or otherwise) and, since the rate of decay of uranium is known, the age of the glass can be calculated.

The amount of uranium in natural glasses is usually extremely small, but the effects become measurable because of the long period of time during which radiation damage has been occurring. For man-made glass fission-track dating can give accurate results only if the uranium content is much greater; more than 0·01 per cent for 2,000-year-old samples or 0·2 per cent if 100 years old. Otherwise it may only be possible to decide between two suggested dates differing by a thousand years or more. Some glass made during the past two hundred years may be dated by this method because uranium was sometimes deliberately added, either to give a yellow or green colour or, in smaller quantities, as a decolourant.

SEVEN

PLASTER, MORTAR, CEMENT, AND CONCRETE

A full-scale laboratory investigation of these building materials can add very little of archaeological significance to the information that may be obtained from visual examination and a simple grain-size analysis such as that detailed in Part III. Such analyses, together with estimations of the lime-to-sand ratios, can indicate whether materials from different parts of the same structure are likely to be contemporary, but can give no clear guidance as to dating.

Sections cut across the thickness of wall plasters will show how many applications are involved, and may disclose variations in composition, particularly where some coats contain crushed tile or pot. The thin top-coat of finer material should also be examined, as it may show the presence of pigments.

Many kinds of additives can be found in these building materials, some intentional and some accidental. Among the latter there may be small artifacts such as coins or beads, but much more common are fragments of re-used materials and of charcoal. In important cases the latter might be used for radiocarbon dating.

EIGHT

WOOD AND CHARCOAL

From what has been said concerning the structure of wood in its many varieties it will be appreciated that most of the laboratory work on wood and charcoal is related to its identification. Some species of wood, notably oak, may be readily recognized on the archaeological site by examination with a hand lens, but a higher magnification is generally required for the firm recognition of other species, and it is sometimes necessary to cut sections of one kind or another for this microscopic examination. Many archaeological specimens of wood are in a rather fragile condition and considerable skill may be necessary in order to produce satisfactory sections. Charcoal identification involves additional difficulties, not least of which are its dark colour and tendency to powder and smear. Transparent sections of such black material must obviously be very thin, but they may be produced by special cutting or grinding techniques.

As regards more fundamental work on wood and charcoal, we should refer to the three possible dating methods now available or in course of development. Of these the water-absorption method is applicable only to wood that has been permanently waterlogged. Under such conditions it appears that the micro-fibrils of the wood shrink at a steady rate, and that this affects the amount of water that the wood can absorb. Essentially the method consists of weighing the sample of wood in its water-logged state, but without any externally adhering water, then drying it and reweighing, but, as in all scientific methods, there are many important precautions which must be taken in all these procedures as well as in the selection and removal of the sample from the site. The effect varies from one kind of wood to another so that it is important to select only species for which the necessary preliminary investigations have been satisfactorily carried out and hence for which the rate of absorption of water is known.

Dendrochronology, or tree-ring dating, is a technique that has

Plate VIII   (a) The prototype Martin-Clark 'Square-array' resistivity equipment in use. (b) The Varian M-50 Proton Magnetometer in use. (c) The Varian Rubidium Magnetometer in use.

Plate IX   The 'Elsec' magnetometer at work.

aroused considerable interest during the past few years. It is well known that the age of a growing tree may often be determined by counting the growth rings seen in a cross-section of the trunk, but tree-rings contain other kinds of information also. The structure and appearance of the rings depend both on the species of tree and on various climatic factors. The simplest forms consist of annual growths, which appear quite distinct and sharply differentiated from one another, most commonly with each ring showing two less sharply distinguished regions, a broad part consisting of the spring and early summer growth and a narrower part, with smaller cells, for the late summer growth. But such seasonal effects will be seen mainly in temperate regions, although similar patterns may appear elsewhere for different reasons. It is not clear whether the formation of growth rings results from changes in humidity, temperature, daylight hours, or some other factor, and in some parts of the world the rings are not necessarily *annual* rings. Further, growth rings are sometimes quite complex, and useless for dating purposes. On the other hand, a section in which all the rings are alike in appearance and thickness is also of little dating value.

An ideal cross-section for dating purposes will show annual rings that are quite clearly distinguishable, each having a constant width all round the tree, but successive rings being of different thicknesses. Ring arrangements of this kind are called *sensitive*, because they clearly show a response to climatic variations. It is to be expected that all trees of the same species within the same geographical area or climatic region will have experienced the same climatic variations, and will have 'recorded' them as an identical succession of rings, but certain soil conditions may cause confusion. For recent historical periods it is often possible to relate the ring pattern to the recorded weather pattern, or at least to decide which particular rings correspond to seasons of exceptionally high or low rainfall, but for early historic and prehistoric times the trees themselves provide the only record. Then the method of *cross-dating* must be used.

Cross-dating means matching the tree-ring patterns in different trees (of the same species) whose lifetimes have partly overlapped. Using a whole series of such samples the pattern can be established over very long periods, providing a kind of time-scale on which the positions of the patterns of rings of undated trees may be found. This is sufficient for relative dating, but by extending the pattern from the present time right back to the archaeological period of a site it may be possible to provide an absolute date for the death of trees found there.

Whole tree sections will clearly be the most useful for dating, but some wooden artifacts may be found to be suitable, provided that the rings extending across the full radius of the tree trunk are available. Otherwise less reliable dates may be supplied if the section happens to cover a well-known period of unusual variations. Methods have also been devised for removing a small cylindrical 'core' from timbers or artifacts by means of special augers, something like the extraction of a geological core on a much smaller scale, with the object of causing the minimum of damage to the specimen. When complete sections are available it is most important to avoid losing the outer rings during excavation and transport, and it is advisable to give the expert the opportunity to supervise such work or collect his own sample.

It is convenient to describe here the method of radiocarbon dating, because wood and charcoal are the most satisfactory materials for this method, although many other organic materials may be used.

Radiocarbon, or C^{14}, is a radioactive form of carbon that is produced by the action of cosmic rays in the upper atmosphere. It then combines with oxygen to form carbon dioxide, and mixes quite quickly with the inactive carbon dioxide of the atmosphere. Chemically and biologically the forms of carbon are indistinguishable, so that the C^{14} takes part in the photosynthesis of plants and the respiration of plants and animals, and also becomes combined in various carbonates in the sea. Investigations suggest that through the operation of all these processes the percentage of radiocarbon in the atmosphere remains virtually constant, or did so before about A.D. 1890, but the Industrial Revolution vastly increased the amounts of coal and oil burnt in the western hemisphere. These fuels, sometimes called 'fossil fuels', were formed so long ago that all the C^{14} has decayed away, and the carbon dioxide and monoxide produced by burning them contains only the stable (nonradioactive) isotopes of carbon, C^{12} and a little C^{13}. The great quantities of these gases poured into the atmosphere have steadily reduced the proportion of C^{14}, and further complications have been introduced by the testing of nuclear weapons, which produces C^{14}.

During their lifetimes, then, plants and animals are continually exchanging carbon with the atmosphere, and consequently they all contain the same proportion of C^{14} as the atmosphere. This exchange ceases abruptly on the death of the plant or animal, but the radioactive decay of C^{14} continues, because it is not affected by any chemical changes and there is no known way of stopping radioactivity. In this way the proportion of C^{14} in the organic remains steadily decreases.

Now the rate of decay of a radioactive element can be measured, and is usually expressed as its '*half-life*', i.e. the time it takes to reduce the amount of the element to exactly half its original value. The half-life is characteristic of the radioactive element, and may lie anywhere between a small fraction of a second and several thousand million years; C^{14} has a half-life of about 5,568 years. This means that if there were, say, 100 grammes of C^{14}, then after 5,568 years there would be only 50 grammes left, after a further similar period a mere 25 grammes would remain, and so on. It is thus a simple matter to calculate how long the decay process has been going on if we know the amount that was originally present and can measure the amount now remaining. The initial percentage of C^{14} in the carbon of a sample is assumed to be the same as in 'modern' wood (i.e. wood of 1890); the present amount of C^{14} is measured by very sophisticated counting techniques.

Besides possible sources of error in the practical methods involved, there are some uncertainties concerning the various assumptions made. Does the proportion of C^{14} in the atmosphere remain constant, for instance (apart from recent human interference)? It may be that variations in the intensity of the bombardment of the earth by cosmic rays may have produced fluctuations in the C^{14} content of the atmosphere over several thousand years, but this is still largely a matter of conjecture. More serious doubts surround the precise value of the half-life of C^{14}, which different workers have put at from 4,700 to 7,200 years, but which has now been provisionally accepted internationally as $5,568 \pm 30$ years. It is not possible to give any one definite figure for the reliability of radiocarbon dates, but one must allow for a possible error of at least 10 per cent.

The interpretation of dates provided by either of the last two methods needs particular care. The result is the best estimate that can be made of the date at which the tree died, which could be much earlier than the date of manufacture of an artifact or the date of use of a piece of timber in a building. Radiocarbon or tree-ring dates must be considered in conjunction with other information from the archaeological context, special attention being given to the question of the possible re-use of the wood in question. In the case of beams or rafters from a house, for example, there is every chance that the wood will have been used in at least one previous construction, especially in regions where timber was in short supply. What is certain, however, is that the date of the wood will not be the date of destruction of the building; it could be the date of construction, but is not necessarily so. There is also the possibility of wood being inserted, by way of repair or re-building, at a later date than the original construction. Small wooden artifacts also could have been made from previously used timber.

NINE

FIBRES

The general procedure for the identification of textile and other fibres is first to examine the whole fibre, noting particularly the pattern of scales on the surface of the fibres, its thickness, and, if the fibre is transparent, the form of the medulla. This would be followed by the preparation and examination of cross-sections to find more information on the relative thicknesses of medulla, cortex, and cuticle, and possibly on the kind and distribution of pigments. Tests would also be made, where possible, to identify the fibres by means of dyes. There are several commercial preparations available, consisting of a mixture of several dyes, each of which will stain one of the commoner types of fibre a distinctive colour, with the exception of hair.

Unfortunately, most fibres become heavily stained during burial, and their identification by means of the staining test is therefore impossible, besides which the form of the medulla, and possibly of the scales, is not readily observable. It is also impossible in such cases to say whether the fibres had been dyed, bleached, or otherwise treated by the original users.

An interesting technique is used for examining surface scales in such circumstances. A cast is made of the surface by pressing it into a layer of softened polyvinyl acetate (PVA) and removing it when it has cooled and hardened. This reproduces the surface texture very accurately, and the cast is readily examined under the microscope. For this method to be practicable the fibres must retain some strength and not crumble during manipulation, but many archaeological samples will be too far decayed for the purpose. Often it is feasible to carry out only the microscopic examination of the whole fibre, partly because of its poor state of preservation and partly from a shortage of available material, and then identification may not be possible.

The identification of fibres from archaeological sites is important in the investigation of the historical development and uses of different types, especially of wool.

There appears to be a tendency for certain substances taken into the body to find their way into the hair. Or, it may be that, because the hair grows more quickly than other parts of the body, and also because it grows *outwards*, any substance in the blood stream at any instant may be incorporated in the growing hair, and once there it cannot be removed. Whatever may be the mechanism it is certain that human hair forms a continuous record of the diet of the individual, perhaps not a complete record, but a very interesting one.

Since the hair is often the last remaining organic material on a decaying corpse the information it contains could be extremely important, apart from its fascination. This is particularly so in cases of poisoning because it is possible to estimate, from the amount and the distribution of the poison in the hair, the dose taken by the deceased, and also the dose rate. Interpretation of the evidence is not always a simple matter and has caused controversy, as, for example, the supposed discovery of arsenic in Napoleon's hair.

Since all ancient fibres are of organic origin, theoretically it should be possible to date them by the radiocarbon method, but a rather large quantity would be required and there might be difficulties in removing absorbed materials and remains of organic dyes, so that except under very exceptional circumstances the trouble would not be worthwhile.

TEN

POLLEN AND OTHER PLANT REMAINS

Palynology is the study of pollen, more commonly called *pollen analysis* because it involves the extraction of pollen grains from a soil sample and their identification and counting. Methods are now well established and standardized, and although the microscopic work may be laborious the practical difficulties may well be negligible compared to the problems of interpretation.

Early work on pollen analysis was concentrated on peat deposits, lake sediments, and more-or-less water-logged soils, but more recently it has been recognized that much useful information can be gathered from quite different soil types, provided that they are sufficiently acid, i.e. the pH must generally be less than 5·5. But pollen grains of different plants are not all equally well preserved, and other factors also help to ensure that the *proportions* of pollen species found do not correspond to the distribution of plant types originally existing on the site. Although on many sites most of the pollen found will have come from the local vegetation cover, samples from bogs or lake deposits will have been carried there from the flora of a wider region.

Tree pollen was the first to be studied, and from large numbers of analyses it was possible to trace the changes in both kind and relative numbers of trees in forested regions since the last glaciation (in appropriate areas). By extending the analyses to include pollen of herbaceous plants the value of the results has been considerably enhanced. A typical sequence of vegetation in a postglacial period might show in the early millennia large proportions of grasses and other herbs, with a few trees such as birch and willow, followed by periods dominated by birch and pine, hazel and pine, hazel and oak, oak and elm, oak, ash, and finally beech. Since the conditions preferred by all these genera are well known it is possible to deduce the sequence of climatic changes that corresponded to the gradual changes in forest cover, and, more important to the archaeologist, the changes that resulted from the activities of man.

The removal of forest trees by man at any time, but particularly in Neolithic times, for cultivation or to provide grazing land for cattle, would permit the colonization of the cleared areas by grasses and certain herbaceous plants. A rough date for the start of such a change can be given from analysis of the pollen, but, as has already been emphasized, such a date would refer to a large geographical region and could not be specific to a particular archaeological site.

More direct evidence of cultivation is provided when cereal pollen starts to appear in the soil profile, usually associated with common weeds of cultivation such as goosefoot and plantain. When a firm date can be attached to such an occurrence, perhaps by C^{14} dating of associated artifacts, we have a date for the start of land cultivation over a large region. Arguments have recently been advanced (e.g. by Raikes) to show that there have been few, if any, major climatic changes since Palaeolithic times, and that all the ecological changes previously assumed to result from changes of climate were attributable to the activities of man.

In both dating and climatological and ecological applications of pollen analysis, stratification is important. In peat, which preserves pollen of all kinds by the exclusion of air, keeping out bacteria, there may be large quantities of pollen throughout its thickness, because the formation of the peat and the 'rain' of pollen were both continuous and contemporary. In ordinary soils the situation may be quite different. Pollen is usually associated with the mobile humus and tends to sink in the soil, though very slowly, but the presence of earth-worms causes extensive mixing, and all stratification will disappear. However, when the soil becomes acid earth-worms are discouraged and good stratification of pollen can occur, though there is usually a high concentration near the surface, decreasing gradually to zero at a depth of from eighteen to twenty-four inches. The surface concentration is a valuable guide in identifying the position of an old land surface such as those that were buried under barrows and banks.

Analysis of a series of soil samples from various depths within and below a barrow or rampart can provide valuable and sometimes surprising information. The upper layers will contain the modern pollen, but it is unlikely that any of this will have penetrated more than about two feet into the bank. Useful samples will therefore come from points below this level to well below the present ground level alongside the feature, in order to ensure that the remains of the ancient buried surface layers are fully represented. Samples from the thrown-up part of the feature should reveal details of the construction and possibly the source of the materials used. If, for instance, there is very little pollen in the soil of the structure, although conditions are favourable for its preservation, one would conclude that the feature was built up from subsoil, possibly from a ditch. On the other hand, if turf was the main constituent of a barrow, bank, or rampart this would be disclosed by the large concentrations of pollen, and, in some cases, it has been possible to see, from the changes in pollen concentration, whether the turves were laid the right way up, or inverted, or both.

On reaching a buried surface the total pollen concentration will again be high, provided that the area had not been cleared of turf or topsoil before constructing the feature, as often happened. Thus it is evident that much quite useful information might be gleaned merely from pollen *counts*, without any attempt to identify the pollen grains, but that a full pollen analysis could give, in addition, clues to the climate and vegetation cover of the region at the time of construction. In Europe and North America (but in very few other areas) where pollen sequences have been fully worked out, dating to a pollen 'zone' might be possible. *Pollen zones* are not geographical areas, as the name suggests, but periods of time, the whole post-glacial period being divided into from eight to twelve pollen zones, the number varying from one country to another according to convenience.

In particularly appropriate cases it may be possible to make rough estimates of pollen concentrations without completely separating the pollen from the soil. The layman could make use of this method himself, but he is strongly advised not to attempt the separation of pollen if this involves the destruction of inorganic matter by the use of the extremely dangerous hydrofluoric acid, which should be used only by properly trained persons under suitable laboratory conditions.

Needless to say, other plant remains offer possibilities of similar studies, but as they are generally less well preserved much less is known about them. Simple examination with a hand lens or low-powered microscope can often disclose the presence of plant remains, such as grasses and other leaves, still quite easily recognizable as the remains of turves.

ELEVEN

LEATHER

The recognition of badly decayed materials as the remains of leather, skin, or parchment is not generally difficult by means of the chemical technique of *chromatography*. There are many varieties of this method, but they may be said to involve the separation of substances in a solution or of mixed gases by passing the liquid or gas through or over a suitable solid or liquid. The different techniques depend on one or other of several physical phenomena, but all *appear* to proceed in the same way. The name was given to the method at a time when it was used only with coloured substances, although in its present-day applications it is more commonly used with colourless materials. As a simple illustration, one may use a narrow strip of absorbent paper, such as blotting paper, place a drop of a mixture of coloured liquids near one end and then immerse the same end in water. As the water soaks up the paper it carries the coloured substances with it, but to different extents, or at different speeds, thus gradually separating them. In place of paper a thin layer of a finely powdered material is now commonly used, and by careful choice of this material and of liquid solvents it is usually possible to separate very small amounts of most substances.

For the identification of decayed leather the remains are extracted with a suitable liquid, and a chromatogram is produced on which the various amino-acids (from decomposition of the proteins) are separated. The positions of these compounds on the paper or thin layer are revealed by spraying with a liquid that colours them, and, since the relative positions of numerous amino-acids are known from previous experiments, the components of the mixture can be recognized. The important indicators for leather are glycine and hydroxyproline, because the latter is rather uncommon elsewhere and large proportions of these two compounds are not known to occur together in other materials.

The identification of leather and parchment has important

applications in the history of the domestication of animals and of their breeding. It is sometimes possible to identify such materials from the grain-pattern, or the sizes, shapes, and positions of the hair follicles, but if any traces of hair remain, even the lower ends within the follicles, identification may be more satisfactory and precise. Further advantages are found in using thin horizontal sections of the skin and revealing the various features by staining. The work is clearly very specialized, and much more needs to be done on skins other than from sheep to provide more reliable results and to distinguish between species.

An interesting dating method appears to be very promising and reminiscent of the method being applied to ancient wood. For the latter the extent of shrinkage of the fibrils is measured, but for leather it is the shrinkage temperature that seems to be important. This is the temperature at which the collagen fibres of the skin start to shrink as they are carefully warmed. Modern samples show shrinkage temperatures of about 60°C, and the older the skin the lower the shrinkage temperature, in general, though no doubt the conditions of preservation, and possibly the original treatment of the skin, have some effect. The method was applied to some fragments of the (parchment) Dead Sea Scrolls and gave results agreeing with dates from other methods.

TWELVE

BONES

A complete human or animal skeleton preserves within itself all the information necessary to enable accurate estimates to be made of its age at death, its sex, and possibly its blood-group, and it may also be studied as part of a group of individuals for which measurements of stature, sizes of bones, details of pathology, and patterns of mortality are desired on which to base a picture of the mode of life of a group or race. A large number of interments excavated from a cemetery area forms an ideal human group for such investigations, but from most archaeological sites the excavator can expect to discover only the odd skeleton, and that often incomplete, though animal bones are generally more plentiful. The latter, however, rarely remain in place in a skeleton, and are more likely to be found in rubbish heaps or pits, or as a thin scatter of individual bones over the site.

It is frequently possible for the fieldworker himself to identify human and animal bones on the site or at home, provided that they are not too badly decayed or mutilated, as animal bones used as food may be. Having listed the bones and species concerned, together with other relevant information such as associated finds and possible dates, he may consider it worth passing them on to a specialist for further study on the lines suggested above.

From the examination of particular bones, especially the pelvis, the skull, and the ends of long bones, it should be possible to sex them, and, in large collections, estimate the numbers of individual males and females. This is particularly important with human remains in order to determine the sex ratio and relative mortalities of the sexes in a population.

The age at death may be estimated, if under about thirty years of age, by the state of eruption of the teeth, the joining together of certain bones, notably those of the pelvis, and the joining of the ends to the shafts of the long bones. In older people the extent of wear on the surfaces of joints and structural changes in the bones themselves may be examined. It should be noted that it may often be possible to make such estimations of sex and age at death from the fragmentary remains of bones from cremations.

A considerable amount of work has been done on the geographical distribution of the different human blood-groups at the present time, and there have been attempts to interpret these in terms of the different races of mankind and their hybridization, the evolution of blood-groups, and the effects of prehistoric migrations. The whole subject is extremely difficult, but some light may be thrown on the problems by evidence from ancient human remains. It seems that suitable material for blood-group tests may be obtained from the spongy tissue of bones, and especially ribs, of prehistoric man.

Bones should always be examined for signs of abnormality or disease, and when found should be referred to the expert for investigation; but care should be taken not to mistake chemical changes for pathological effects. The effects of acid soils, for instance, sometimes appear to be very localized, and can produce decayed areas on bones that look very much like the results of well-known diseases. Similar deception can be caused by the deposition of calcium carbonate on bones, giving the appearance of cancerous or other pathological growths.

When living roots come into contact with bones the slightly acid solution that they secrete dissolves the bony material, etching the surface. Such markings also may be deceptive, but the effects are less destructive than those of fungal mycelia, which grow right through the spongy tissue as intertwining threads, in many cases leaving very little of the centre of the bone.

Several methods have been suggested for dating bones but most of them have hitherto proved useful only for relative dating of material from the same archaeological site. Radiocarbon dating has been used, but ancient bone contains very little carbon, so that the use of large quantities is necessary in order to get acceptable results. This may not always be possible, especially with the most ancient and valuable remains. Other difficulties include the presence of modern organic material such as the roots and fungi mentioned above, and deposits of calcium carbonate from the soil.

All the other proposed dating methods for bones are analytical methods based on the estimation of the amount of some substance which is assumed to increase or decrease at a steady rate. Practically every constituent of bone has been examined for this purpose but none has been found satisfactory, all changes depending on the nature of the environment because of the interchange of inorganic materials between bones and soil-water. Reference has been made to the various analytical methods earlier (§3.4, p. 146). The fluorine and uranium atoms enter the bone by changing places with other atoms in the crystal lattice of hydroxy-apatite, the main inorganic constituent of bone. Fluorine estimation was, until very recently, a difficult technique, but because uranium is a radio-active element it may be estimated by measurement of the radio-active intensity of the sample either by counting techniques or by *autoradiography*. The particles emitted by radioactive elements affect photographic film in the same way as light or X-rays, making it possible for a bone containing uranium to photograph itself merely by remaining near a film for a convenient time. Exposure times, in fact, are quite long, especially when the uranium content is low.

Since uranium and fluorine percentages in bone increase with time of burial, and nitrogen content decreases, there seemed to be a possibility of dating by combining the results of these measurements, but this has been found to be useful only for relative dating on one site.

THIRTEEN

TEETH

In general, similar considerations apply to teeth as to bone, particularly where questions of possible dating methods are concerned, and for ageing, sexing, pathology, etc.

It is found that certain human dental characteristics vary between different races, populations, or groups, such as the number of cusps in the 'table' of a tooth, the shapes of incisors, or the congenital absence of certain teeth. The latter often results from extensive in-breeding. Investigations of large numbers of individuals can give, after statistical analysis, information on the relationships between peoples and, possibly, about large-scale migrations in the past.

The extent of attrition (wear) of teeth, both human and animal, has been used to estimate ages, which may be quite satisfactory for a small group, but in larger populations, or groups of different archaeological periods, there may be differences in attrition caused by different diets. Examples may be found in countries where, say, dwellers in highland regions have a basically different diet from their countrymen in the lowlands. Attrition is also found to be greater among peoples who consumed relatively large amounts of coarse material, including grit from the poorer-quality querns or mortars.

Dental caries appears to have been always fairly common but to have increased considerably since Neolithic times, and again the incidence of decay can be related to diet.

FOURTEEN

MOLLUSC SHELLS

The appearance in excavation reports of recent years of descriptions of mollusc (snail) shells, often without any explanation or attempted interpretation, has puzzled many archaeologists. What is the purpose of such reports? Let us first reiterate what has been said elsewhere concerning the recording of *all* information from an excavation: if it has no present value, who is to say that it will not, one day, be susceptible to new scientific methods of investigation, leading to valuable conclusions? But, this point apart, one would like to know just what might be deduced from the identification and counting of non-marine mollusc shells.

The kinds of shells we have in mind are often very small, perhaps fractions of a millimetre in diameter, and of numerous forms, including the familiar shapes of bivalves and spiral horns seen in the common larger marine forms. Much fundamental work remains to be done on these, on both modern and ancient specimens, but many of them can now be definitely identified and related to their preferred habitats or micro-climates. Hence, the most important use of mollusc shells in archaeology is as indicators of climatic conditions and the nature of the immediate environment.

Snail shells of these kinds are very abundant, and appear on most sites where the soil is not too acid, because there the shells would not persist. It appears, also, that the work of man has had comparatively little effect on the distribution of snails, so that changes in the percentages of the various classes of snails do actually reflect climatic and environmental changes.

Fresh-water and land snails are classed according to their preferred habitat types, so that any particular association of shells on a site will indicate the nature of the environment at the time the molluscs lived. The fresh-water genera or species include those that can exist almost anywhere, and are therefore of little use for our purpose, some that like slow streams or ditches with rich vegetation, those that are found in faster-moving and more wide-spread water, and a few (called 'slum species') that will stand very severe conditions. Land snails are classed as either marsh-, dry-, wood-, or open-land types. Although even one variety can give useful information it is more usual to base conclusions on statistical analyses of a reasonably large number of specimens.

As for the dating of sites from snail-shell statistics, the same remarks apply as for dating from bones and teeth; the dating can only be relative.

FIFTEEN

SAMPLING, PACKING, AND STORING

Here again we must emphasize the importance of sample-collecting by the investigator himself if at all possible. Circumstances do arise where this cannot be arranged, as, for example, where a quick emergency dig is concerned and the site cannot be kept open long enough. Then the excavator may be compelled to take his own samples or lose the opportunity of a possible laboratory investigation. In such cases the archaeologist needs to understand some of the principles of sampling.

In the present context we are considering sampling to be the collection of *representative* small quantities of large amounts of materials, and the commonest archaeological application will be to soil-sampling. Reference will be made later to other kinds of sampling.

Two aspects of sampling need to be discussed; the statistical and the practical. If a sample is to be truly representative of the whole it must include every constituent of the whole, and all the constituents must be present in the sample in the same proportions as in the whole. This, of course, is the ideal to be aimed at, but to ensure a close approach to the ideal a few general rules must be observed.

The first rule is to make sure that a sufficiently large sample is taken, but what may be large for one kind of sample may be small for another kind. One pound of a fine soil, for instance, may be too large for a sample, but one pound of a 'soil' consisting mainly of large pebbles may be much too small. In practice, therefore, one may find it convenient, for soils with both large stones and fine loam, to separate the mixture into two grades by sieving, and then to deal with the grades independently. In some cases, such as boulder clays, the large stones could be picked out by hand and discarded, since for archaeological purposes it is the finer loam that is important. On balance, it might be reasonable to estimate the size of a sample so that it will include about half a pound of the finer grades.

Further sampling will take place in the laboratory, usually by the method of *quartering*. This does not usually concern the field-worker, but he may be interested to know the procedure. Usually the soil is first dried, mixed thoroughly, and then spread over a circular area on a sheet of paper, aiming to get an even distribution of the larger particles. The soil is then divided into four equal segments, two opposite ones being selected for use and the rest stored away. The selected sample might again be quartered and the process repeated until a suitably small sample is obtained, possibly as little as one gramme.

Returning now to the practical side of sampling, the most important point to remember is that throughout the exercise there must be no possible contamination of samples, either by inadvertent mixing of samples from different strata or by subsequent changes or additions as a result of inadequate labelling, packaging, and transport.

The face of a section must first be carefully cut and cleaned. Cutting with a spade, turf-cutter, or trowel invariably transfers material up and down the section and will thus contaminate the layers. This can be avoided by lightly trowelling *horizontally*, cleaning the trowel after each stroke, or by gentle horizontal brushing to remove all loose material. Also ensure that the upper surface of the section is cleared so that there is no risk of loose debris falling into samples being collected from the face of the section. After this careful preparation an appropriate number of samples should be taken, preferably two from each layer of a stratified section, always starting with the lower levels and cleaning the trowel after each sample. Take roughly rectangular sections of soil and transfer them directly to the containers in which they are to be transported to the laboratory. Removing the lower samples first is a further precaution against contamination, and for the same reason they should never be handled. It is clearly better to collect too many samples than too few.

Since soils always contain bacteria and fungi which are liable to grow more rapidly in unsuitable storage conditions than in the ground, it is important to prevent this by drying the samples at the earliest opportunity. Air-drying is usually adequate except in very humid climates, but dust must not be allowed to settle on drying samples. When jars, boxes, or tins are used the lids may be left loosely fitted for several days, but polythene bags particularly should not be closed until the soil is quite dry. Paper bags are *not* suitable.

Unlabelled samples are quite useless, and care must be taken to see that no labels are lost or become defaced. This means that labels must be securely fixed *outside* the package.

The excavator should also seriously consider whether corresponding samples from an undisturbed section nearby might be useful to the laboratory worker for purposes of comparison. This is recommended whenever possible.

It must be very rarely indeed that sampling procedures are required for artifacts, and the methods used in taking other samples from the earth are generally quite obvious and straightforward, though there are notable exceptions. One of these is the sampling of baked clay for magnetic dating or other magnetic studies. Extreme care is necessary here, and it is doubtful whether samples would be accepted by a geomagnetic laboratory unless assurances could be given that a suitable procedure was rigorously carried out and is precisely described in the collector's report. The most important aspect of this work is that the *exact* position of each sample in the structure and, more particularly, in relation to the geographical or magnetic meridian and to the horizontal, must be indicated, usually by means of lines drawn in chalk on the sample or on a cement former in which the sample is encased.

As regards artifacts, we need to consider any special arrangements and precautions that may be necessary in packing and storing them as they await attention in the laboratory.

For perishable material, of organic origin, there are only two possibilities to be considered. Either full preserving treatment must be given immediately the object is uncovered, which is difficult to arrange on most digs, or it must be stored in such a way as to reproduce as nearly as possible the conditions under which it was found. Sometimes, where the preservation process is a very slow one, the storage arrangements may include facilities for maintaining the preservation procedure. As an example of the latter we might mention the slow removal of salt infestation from pottery by one of the methods referred to in Part III.

The reproduction of burial conditions during storage applies especially to objects found in arid or waterlogged conditions. For the former a small quantity of a drying agent, such as silica-gel, placed with the object in an airtight container should be adequate, and for artifacts from waterlogged soils some way of maintaining a damp environment is necessary. Several methods have been used, including wrapping the object in wet moss or in wet paper-pulp in an airtight container.

PART THREE

Scientific Aids for the Excavator

ONE

INTRODUCTION

So far we have attempted to give an explanation of the scientific background to the nature of archaeological sites and to the conditions in which artifacts are liable to be found. The objective now is to outline the theory and practice of some of the scientific methods that might be of value to the excavator either during the actual digging procedures or in the immediate on-site treatment of artifacts. 'On site' will include 'at home', i.e. not in the laboratory. As this book is not intended to be a treatise on practical archaeology we shall assume that the reader already has some training in or experience of the well-established excavation techniques.

TWO

EXCAVATION AIDS

The use of chemical and physical tests during excavation is a relatively recent development, which many workers seem reluctant to accept. There is a tendency to rely entirely on the old techniques, which have served so well for so long, and a feeling of irritation during the slight delays that the new methods sometimes entail. But this delay may save time in the long run and may provide answers to otherwise insoluble problems.

Many scientific aids are still in the development stage and many more, it is hoped, are still to make their début. Application of available methods is relatively rare and sporadic, and the value of a technique can be assessed only after much wider and more frequent trials. The co-operation of many non-scientists will be necessary.

Some of the physical prospecting methods described elsewhere may be modified for use during excavation. As an example of such an application let us consider the resistivity meter. This is normally used in surveying an area of ground before excavation, but by using very small probes quite closely set the method is suitable for investigating vertical faces of sections as well as for finding the limits of a feature or disturbed area encountered in digging. The Wenner configuration may be arranged by means of four three-inch or six-inch nails secured in a short length of wood, with an accurate spacing of, say, two or three inches. When working on such a small scale it is important to have exactly equal spacing of the probes and consistent depths of penetration. Instead of moving the probes one at a time the whole array is moved each time and no rotary switching is required.

Metal detectors can often be extremely useful during excavation, particularly in locating fragile metal objects just before they are reached whilst trowelling, and so preventing accidental damage. They have also been used for locating small metal objects, especially coins, and potsherds on or in old floors, and in the excavation of cemeteries for revealing the presence of grave goods. The older instruments, such as *mine detectors*, are not very sensitive, but a small area, such as a grave, can be 'swept' after removing each one-inch layer of soil: special care should be taken in excavating a spot where metal has been indicated. The new 'pulse induction' metal detectors are a big improvement on mine detectors. These are used in the same way and there is usually a choice of coil size, from about three inches to almost two feet across, to suit large area surveys down to very localized testing. Some models have a facility whereby the nature of the object detected may be deduced, although the result is by no means infallible.

The prospects for chemical testing are probably brighter. Apart from the tests for artifacts, materials, and soil types outlined in §2, p. 214, there are occasions when chemical tests can elucidate the nature and significance of textural or colour changes disclosed during excavation, or they may be used to detect features that one expects to find, or again, to delimit the area of a feature.

THREE

TESTS AND TREATMENTS

1. Soils

The examination of soils is a lengthy laboratory procedure, but simple tests on the archaeological site can be very useful, for example by indicating the nature of a stratum, or of a whole profile, distinguishing occupation levels and old surfaces. Such information may be necessary before a decision on the subsequent course of the excavation can be made, but the on-site tests will often require confirmation and extension in the laboratory, and should be regarded as only preliminary and limited in their application.

1.1. Visual Examination As with all materials for testing, inspection with a hand lens is essential, a magnification of up to ten times being suitable. Not a great deal may be learned in this way concerning the nature of the soil itself, apart from some idea of grain size and homogeneity, but many kinds of inclusions may be revealed. Foremost among these may be minute fragments of charcoal, bones or teeth of small animals, either whole or broken or burnt, shells, particularly of small molluscs, and plant remains. Suspected examples may be confirmed, or otherwise, by means of the appropriate tests below.

1.2. Carbon Place a little of the sample on the tip of a knife or on a metal can-lid and hold it in a hot flame. If the sample is wet or contains crystalline material there may be some sputtering, and it may be difficult to retain the sample on a knife tip. Any small fragments of charcoal will be oxidized, as shown by small flashes of light.

1.3. Organic Matter Uncarbonized organic matter will burn when heated, often giving off smoke with a recognizable smell. If free access of air is allowed during heating the material will be completely burnt and disappear as carbon dioxide and steam, perhaps leaving a small deposit of ash, usually grey to white. Otherwise it will first be converted to charcoal and may cause confusion.

An alternative test is to heat the sample gently in a test-tube with a little hydrogen peroxide and a drop of ammonia. This destroys most kinds of organic matter, notable exceptions being pollen grains and spores, but it has no effect on charcoal or on the soil itself.

1.4. Humus A simple test for humus is to extract a small amount of the soil by boiling it carefully with a little caustic-soda solution in a test-tube. Pour off the resulting liquid into another tube. If humus was present the solution will be stained a deep brown colour. Very dark soils are sometimes suspected of containing finely powdered charcoal. By repeating this extraction process until the solution is no longer dark-coloured it should be possible to examine the residual soil. If this is no longer dark then there is no charcoal present and the colour was entirely due to the humus.

1.5. Iron Soils containing ferric iron salts are generally brown or red, but the colour may be masked by humus or other materials. Place a little of the soil in a test-tube, cover it with dilute hydrochloric acid solution, shake it up for about half a minute, and pour off the liquid extract into another tube. Add to this a few drops of potassium ferrocyanide solution. A deep blue colour indicates the presence of iron. Alternatively, one drop of the extract may be placed on a filter-paper and a drop of the reagent solution added. The blue colour may be more obvious on the paper than in the tube when only a little iron is present.

1.6. Special Test for Iron and Organic Matter This test, reported by Biek, gives simultaneous approximate estimates of the amounts of iron and organic matter in soils or in pottery. There are, in fact, two tests involved: heating in an oxidizing atmosphere, and heating under reducing conditions.

(1) Heat a small amount of the soil (or crushed pot) in a small porcelain crucible (or on a piece of thin porcelain) above, or near the edge of, a clear flame, so that plenty of air can circulate around the sample as it is heated. A yellow or smoky flame will not be satisfactory since it will contain large amounts of carbon or un-

burnt gases. After keeping at a dull red heat for about two minutes, place carefully on one side to cool.

(2) Place a second portion of the same sample in a small hard-glass tube (a 5 cm. tube is convenient) and heat in the flame, keeping the tube at a low angle so as to help in excluding air. Note any odour given off. Some steam will condense on the cooler parts of the tube but should evaporate again as the tube warms up. Keep at dull red heat for about two minutes. Cool.

In the first heating all the iron compounds should be converted to the oxide haematite, which is red, and all the organic matter should be completely burnt. The final colour of the sample, i.e. its redness, will be a measure of the amount of iron present.

On the other hand, the second test carbonizes organic compounds but does not completely burn them, hence the colour ('blackness') indicates the proportion of organic matter in the sample. But some allowance should be made for the iron here, because it will all be reduced to the ferrous state, imparting a slight greyish tinge. The effect will be important only if the first test shows that there is a large amount of iron present.

These simple tests, which are quite quickly carried out on the site or at home, can carry a lot of information. A whole profile can be investigated in a relatively short time, and a good idea of its history, including, perhaps, the position of a buried surface, can be obtained. It is useful to draw up a Table giving, in columns, the precise depths from which the samples were taken, small samples of the soils in their original conditions, samples after oxidation and after reduction, and results of any other tests, such as pH measurements. The small amounts required for the numerous samples are easily mounted in position in the Table by pouring the soil onto a small circular area of moist, colourless glue or other adhesive. Care should be taken not to mix the samples, and this is most easily avoided by the alternative method of sticking the samples first to separate pieces of paper, shaking off the surplus when the adhesive is dry, and then cutting out a conveniently sized circle or square of the sample to stick in place in the Table. In this way a permanent record is made, which can be studied again at any later date, but it should be noted that the colours of the untreated samples will not appear to be the same as in the soil profile, mainly because they will have dried out.

1.7. Carbonates Should it be necessary to test for the presence of limestone, chalk, or calcite in a soil it is sufficient to add a few drops of dilute hydrochloric acid to a 'pinch' of the soil. If there is effervescence (fizzing) it means that carbon dioxide is being produced from a carbonate, usually as one of the above types of calcium carbonate. Since many building materials also contain calcium carbonate the possibility of the presence of building debris should be considered.

1.8. Sulphates The presence of appreciable amounts of sulphates in the soil may indicate an ancient human occupation site, though on agricultural land the source of the sulphates could well be artificial fertilizers, such as 'sulphate of ammonia'. Extract a small sample of the soil with dilute hydrochloric acid, pour off the liquid into a second test-tube and add a few drops of barium chloride solution. A white precipitate indicates the presence of sulphate.

1.9. Phosphates These may provide a more reliable indicator of occupation, by animals or humans, especially of the former presence of bones. Again extract a little of the soil by shaking in a test-tube with a good covering of hydrochloric acid. Decant the liquid into another tube, add an approximately equal amount of ammonium molybdate solution. A heavy yellow precipitate indicates the presence of phosphate. The test is very sensitive, and a slight yellow colour will mean only an extremely small amount of phosphate, probably negligible in an archaeological context. Any white precipitate should be ignored.

An alternative test recommended for chemical prospecting (q.v.) is as follows (after G. T. Schwarz, in *Archaeometry*, **10** (1967), 57–63):

A circular filter-paper is placed over a circular hole in (say) a piece of wood, so that the middle of the paper does not come into contact with anything that might contaminate it. A sample, about a quarter of an inch in diameter, is placed at the centre of the paper. Two drops of a solution 'A' are added to the sample, and then (within 30 seconds) two drops of a solution 'B'. In a few minutes a blue colour will appear if there is any phosphate in the sample. With care, and using a standardized procedure, it is possible to get a reasonable estimate of the relative proportions of phosphate in a series of samples.

The solutions used are:

Solution 'A': 5 grammes of ammonium molybdate dissolved in 100 ml. of cold water. Then add 35 ml. of nitric acid (S.G. 1.2).

Solution 'B': 0·5 per cent ascorbic acid. I have found that this is conveniently made up by dissolving a vitamin-C tablet in the appropriate amount of water, as required, because solutions do not keep well.

1.10. pH The importance of soil acidity in relation to the state of preservation of buried materials has been repeatedly stressed, and it is now convenient to explain something of the meaning of acidity and alkalinity. It is quite possible to make use of the pH scale without attempting to understand the principles behind it, and those who wish to do so may omit the rest of these first two paragraphs. For our present purposes we shall define an *acid* as a substance that produces hydrogen ions (symbol: H^+), and a *base* or *alkali* as one that combines with hydrogen ions, often because it produces *hydroxyl* ions (OH^-). The combination of these two kinds of ions forms water molecules (H_2O), as represented by the equation

$$H^+ + OH^- = H_2O,$$

and the process is that of neutralization of an acid or a base.

Water itself contains extremely small amounts of these ions, the actual concentrations being 10^{-7} gramme-ions (or one ten-millionth of a gramme-ion) of each kind in one litre of water. This is not the place to discuss the meaning of the term 'gramme-ion', so we shall merely refer to these as 'units' of concentration. If an acid is added to water it supplies more hydrogen ions, and their concentration will then be greater than 10^{-7} units, but if a base is added to water some of the hydrogen ions will be removed and their concentration will be less than 10^{-7} units. Since this method of expressing the acidity of a solution is rather cumbersome it is generally replaced by making use of an acidity scale known as the 'pH scale', which covers only a limited range but is quite adequate for many purposes, including soils. The method of expressing quantities in powers of ten (as 10^{-7} etc.) is an exponential method, and the particular 'power' or 'index' (e.g. the 7 in 10^{-7}) is called the *exponent*. The pH is correctly called the 'hydrogen-ion exponent', and is the exponent that expresses the hydrogen-ion con-

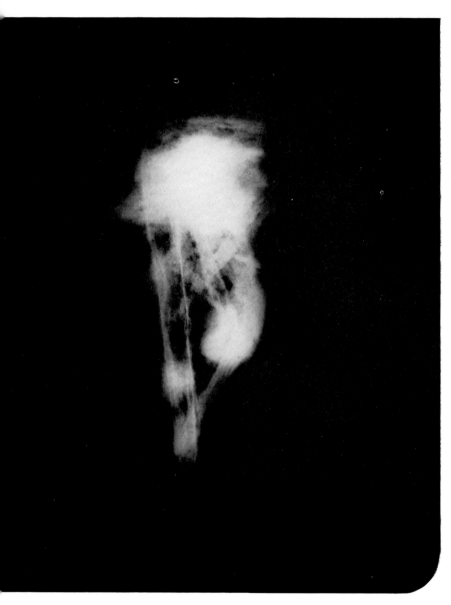

Plate X   An X-ray photograph of an 'unidentified object', which
is revealed as a cluster of rusty iron nails.

Plate XI   Aerial photograph showing crop marks in a field of
ripening barley, which revealed an unsuspected archaeological

centration, without its negative sign. Thus, pure water has a hydrogen-ion concentration of 10^{-7} units, so that its pH is 7.

The full pH scale ranges from zero to 14, values below 7 show that a solution is acid, and values above 7 refer to alkaline solutions. But solutions can be very much more acid than pH 0, or very much more alkaline than pH 14. Such solutions, however, would not be found in soils, nor, probably, in any natural circumstances.

The pH of a solution may be measured either by the use of *indicators* or by an electrical method. The latter involves the use of a *pH-meter*, which indicates the pH directly when two special electrodes are immersed in the solution being tested. Portable pH-meters are available but not really necessary on archaeological sites.

Indicator methods for finding the pH of solutions are numerous, but only the two most convenient will be described. Most people will have heard of the now obsolete *litmus*, which turns red in acids and blue in alkaline solutions. Litmus is an indicator, but not a very good one, so that it has been replaced by numerous synthetic substances. All of these change colour over a small pH range, so that we can usually say that for most practical purposes they have one colour above a certain pH and a different colour below that pH. By means of suitable mixtures of indicators so-called 'universal indicators' are produced which show a more or less gradual change of colour as the pH is increased or decreased. By adding a drop or two of such an indicator to a clear, colourless solution and comparing the colour produced with colours given by solutions of known pH, the pH of a solution may be measured. Details of the two methods follow.

Indicator papers (pH papers) provide probably the most convenient way of determining the pH of soils on the site. These are strips of paper, in booklet form, impregnated with indicators. They are made for a selection of pH ranges, but for general field use a universal indicator paper is suitable. Take a pinch of soil and moisten it with *distilled* water (which should be neutral, i.e. neither acidic nor alkaline). Tear out an indicator paper and touch one end of it on the wet sample. The solution taken up by the paper will produce a colour depending on its pH, and it is only necessary to refer to the colour chart on the cover of the book of papers to read the correct pH.

In place of papers indicator solutions may be used, and the colours produced compared with standard solutions contained in

8

sealed tubes. Because soil extracts are nearly always turbid it is necessary to use very fine tubes or the colours may be masked, i.e. the aqueous extract of the soil is taken up in a fine tube instead of on a paper. Unfortunately, the sampling tubes must be washed out each time after use, which makes the method rather slower than the test-paper method. Soil-testing outfits of this type that will fit in the pocket are commercially available.

The various methods available for pH measurement do not always give the same result when used for soils, in particular acid, peaty soils, so that when pH values are reported the precise method used should always be specified.

1.11. Spray Tests   There have been many trials in recent years of tests designed to develop silhouettes in soil plans or sections, faint traces suggesting the former presence of an artifact, human or animal remains, or other feature. The method is to spray the horizontal or vertical surface with suitable solutions that will react chemically with some residual substance in the silhouette. This kind of test is still in the experimental stage of development, but because of their great interest and promise some of the tests will be described. Since it is impossible to point out all the toxic and corrosive effects of some of the chemicals used, it is most important for the inexperienced to observe some few basic rules for safety.

Spraying should be done only in fairly still air, not in strong winds, not only in order to avoid wastage of chemicals but also to reduce the risk of damage or injury from blown solutions. It is particularly important to avoid contact of any solution with the eyes. Also, all tools, implements, and instruments should be removed to a safe distance. In fact, the substances suggested in the tests below are not particularly dangerous, but it is advisable to adopt regular safety precautions if only because other chemicals may be used later. Finally, always use the minimum practicable amounts of all chemicals.

In some of the tests it is necessary to spray more than one solution (in the order given), and separate sprays must be used. A convenient arrangement is to have several spray-containers, with an interchangeable spray, which must be washed in distilled water each time after use. Atomizer sprays are necessary (for instance the scent-spray type), with no metal parts, to give a fine mist of solution, and the jet should be held within a few inches of the surface to be covered. The soil should not be too wet, so that the solution runs down a vertical surface or spreads too much on the horizontal, nor too dry, so that the solution runs before being absorbed. Colour changes may be slight and difficult to detect in coloured soil.

Test for Iron. First decide whether a deep red or a deep blue colour will show up best against the general soil background, then use test (a) or (b) accordingly.

(a) Spray with a solution of potassium (or ammonium) thio-cyanate. A deep red colour is formed with iron salts.

(b) Spray with very little dilute hydrochloric acid, and then with a solution of potassium ferrocyanide. With iron salts this gives a deep blue colour.

Test for Phosphates. Spray, in turn, the solutions 'A' and 'B' as in §1.9, p. 210 (solution B being freshly made). Even where bones have completely decayed there may be sufficient phosphate held in the soil to give a dark stain with this test.

Test for Manganese. This is probably one of the less reliable tests, but is worth trying where it is important to decide whether there are any remaining traces of decayed organic material, particularly wood. It seems that manganese tends to accumulate in decaying organic matter. Post-hole fillings sometimes react to this test.

Spray with a little dilute caustic soda (sodium hydroxide) solution, followed by a solution of formaldoxime. Under suitable conditions a red colour should appear where manganese is present.

If the soil contains appreciable amounts of iron salts one may try a preliminary spray of Rochelle salt or of 'cream of tartar' solution to make the iron inactive before applying the test sprays. Otherwise the iron will give a similar colour.

1.12. *Particle Size Analysis* For a full soil analysis it is necessary to carry out a determination of the distribution of particle sizes, i.e. the proportions of particles of various grades, but this is a long process, and is not often essential on archaeological sites. Biek mentions a very simple test, but probably something intermediate between these two extremes will be the most generally useful.

This test is carried out in a measuring cylinder, either of 50 or 100 millilitres (ml.) capacity. Place in the cylinder a representative sample of the soil, sufficient to reach the 10 ml. mark (5 ml. for the smaller cylinder) and fill up to the top mark with distilled water. Close the top with a bung or the hand, invert, and shake vigorously until the soil is thoroughly dispersed throughout the water. Quickly set down the cylinder and start a stop-clock, or note the time. After half a minute record the depth of the soil that has settled on the bottom of the cylinder, in millilitres. Measure this depth of soil again after total times of 2, 10, and 30 minutes, and after one hour. Then leave it undisturbed until all the soil has settled and note the final depth of soil. A good light is needed to make the dividing line between the top of the sediment and the suspended soil visible, and it is a good plan to make the graduations on the cylinder clearer by rubbing a piece of chalk or other white material along the surface. The deposit of chalk in the markings makes them much clearer against a background of red or brown soil.

The six recorded depths will not correspond to any particular particle sizes, but will be acceptable for purposes of comparison of soil samples from different horizons or strata of a section, or different areas of a site. The first measurement can be taken as representing the sand grades, and it is convenient to convert each depth to a percentage of the total final depth and draw a graph of these against the time of measurement.

A steeply sloping curve shows a high proportion of particles in the size range concerned. Otherwise, the percentage of sand grades is seen in the early section and of clay grades in the last part of the curve. The method also provides a useful guide when considering whether samples of mortar or wall plaster are contemporary.

2. Metals

Occasionally it may be desirable to identify a piece of metal on the site, but the state of preservation will frequently indicate the nature of the material, and examination with a lens may be all that is required.

When chemical tests are necessary it usually means that a trace of the metal must be brought into solution, either by scraping off a very small portion and dissolving it in acid, or by the electrical method below. It is convenient to use dilute nitric acid here since all the metals of antiquity except gold will dissolve in it.

Place the minute scraping of metal in a small test-tube and add a few drops of dilute nitric acid, followed by the appropriate test solutions. If more than one metal is to be tested for, first divide the acid solution of the sample into the appropriate number of tubes, and treat each tube separately with the solutions mentioned.

Silver and Lead. Add a little sodium chloride solution. If a white precipitate forms heat the solution to see if it re-dissolves to give a clear solution. If so, and if the precipitate re-forms on cooling, then lead is present. If, on the other hand, the white precipitate persists when hot, cool the solution and then add an equal volume of ammonia solution (ammonium hydroxide solution). If now the solution becomes clear then the metal contains (or is) silver.

Copper. Whether from the pure metal or from bronze, copper may be identified by *carefully* adding ammonia solution to the acid solution of the metal in a small test-tube. (Add drop by drop, as otherwise the whole solution may shoot out of the tube.) When bubbling no longer occurs, fill up the tube with the ammonia solution. Copper will be indicated by a deep blue colour.

Iron. Use one of the tests described under §1.11, p. 213, adding about two drops of each solution to the acid solution in the test-tube. (There is no need to add hydrochloric acid in test (b).)

For metal objects which, for one reason or another, cannot be scraped to provide a sample, the electrographic method is useful. The test should be made on the least important part of the object, although, in fact, no damage should be caused if the method is carried out correctly. The process is the exact reverse of electro-plating, an extremely thin layer of metal being stripped off by electrolysis.

Clean a small area of the metal, place on it two or three thicknesses of filter-paper moistened with ammonia or sodium chloride solution, and on top of this put a small piece of clean aluminium. Make sure that the latter does not touch the metal object. Connect the aluminium to the negative pole of a six- to twelve-volt battery, and the positive pole of the battery to the metal object itself. Allow current to flow for about fifteen seconds and then disconnect the battery. The paper will now hold a very small amount of each metal in the object, and spot tests for these may be applied. Cut the paper into segments and apply one test to each segment, using one drop of each required solution, except for ammonia in the copper test, where more will be needed unless ammonia was used for moistening the paper initially.

A small electrographic tester, with enclosed battery, about the size of a small hand-torch, is manufactured, or a torch may be adapted for the purpose quite easily.

2.1. Bronze Disease Special treatment is required in order to prevent the continuation of this form of chloride corrosion after removal of an object from the ground. Small objects may be immersed in a solution of sodium sesquicarbonate, $Na_2CO_3 . NaHCO_3$, which will remove the copper chloride but not the carbonate or oxide. The latter usually give bronze objects a more or less smooth green surface, but bronze disease causes pitting and destruction of the surface. Hence, the sesquicarbonate treatment should leave the smooth surface unaffected but eradicate the copper chloride from the rough, pitted areas.

Affected areas on larger objects may be treated by applying the sodium sesquicarbonate solution with a brush, replenishing it as required, until all the copper chloride has been removed.

Protection of the remaining metal may then be provided by adding silver oxide to the cleared spots. This will react with any remaining traces of chloride to form white silver chloride, which effectively seals the surface. Small spots that are not too deeply affected may be treated directly with silver oxide without the preliminary use of sodium sesquicarbonate.

3. Pottery

Apart from washing, drying, repairing, and possibly identifying types there is very little that can be done with pottery on the site. The few tests that might occasionally be useful are also destructive and only permissible on expendable sherds. For example, perhaps two very similar sherds are found which appear to differ only in colour. It may be that they come from the same pot but have been fired under different conditions, or one or other of the fragments has been subsequently burnt, but to prove this it is necessary to carry out re-firing tests. On the other hand, similar results could probably be obtained much more quickly, and on the site, from the simple double-heating method, as described for soils. Organic matter is not to be expected in pottery as any organic additives, such as straw, will have been burnt out during the initial firing. But there could be traces of food residues or deposits of soot. Assuming these to be small in amount, comparison of the heated samples should show whether they contain the same amounts of iron and so *could* be from the same pot or batch of pots. Pieces about one-eighth of an inch square are all that is required for the tests.

Should there be any unwanted fragments of gritted ware it might be of interest to test the grit for calcite or shell by means of a drop of dilute hydrochloric acid, or for gypsum (calcium sulphate) by hydrochloric acid and barium chloride solution (§1.8, p. 209).

4. Building Materials
Visual examination followed by a few spot tests is probably all that can be done with building materials on the site. The use of a lens may help in identifying building stone, but it is not usually necessary. The lens is useful, however, for examining crushed or decayed mortar, cement, plaster, and concrete, when the nature of the material may be determinable and inclusions detected. The presence of re-used material should be noted, including crushed pot or tile, or old wall-plaster. In concretes the size and nature of the aggregate can be recorded.

Particle-size estimation may be useful in comparing samples of mortar or plaster from different walls in the same building, especially in deciding whether such mixtures are contemporary or from the same or different sources.

Again, the spot tests likely to be of use here are for carbonate and sulphate, as described under Soils (§1.7 and 1.8, p. 209). Where the walls have been completely robbed there may be sufficient mortar or plaster debris to show the outlines of buildings, or if the materials are very finely crushed they may be detectable by testing for carbonate. A series of tests might then enable the outlines of the walls to be discovered. If the carbonates have been washed out by rain-water then the residual calcium might be used in the same way, but laboratory tests would be necessary for this.

5. Materials of Vegetable Origin
There is very little the amateur can do with plant material in the field other than examination with a lens, and possibly some kind of

preservation treatment so that it may reach the laboratory without further damage or decay.

Cross-sections of wood may be examined, and any pieces of oak should be identifiable, but other kinds should be passed on to an expert for identification. It is best to avoid as far as possible impregnating any material with preservative substances, because this will almost certainly involve the laboratory in time-consuming work for its removal. Methods of storing and packing have been described above, but where wood, textiles, or other organic materials are too fragile to be moved without damaging them they should be protected with a coating of polyvinyl acetate (PVA). This is a synthetic *organic* compound and must not be used on material that might be required for radiocarbon dating as it will introduce 'modern' carbon. PVA is obtained as a solution in an organic solvent such as toluene, benzene, or acetone. All these solvents, and particularly acetone, are inflammable and may produce toxic vapours. Hence they must be used in well-ventilated conditions and well away from any naked flames. As the solvent evaporates the PVA is left as a thin, coherent film on the surface of the material, which is thus consolidated to a certain extent.

6. Materials of Animal Origin

It is not always easy to distinguish between some kinds of organic materials by examination under a lens, but there are usually simple tests that can be applied. For example, in small, discoloured fragments bone and wood look very much alike, but if small pieces are held in a flame they may be distinguished by the characteristic smell produced. If there is still doubt a test for phosphate (§1.9, p. 209) will show whether the fragments consist of bone. This test will also distinguish between bones and teeth should this be necessary.

Shells, mainly calcium carbonate, may be tested for by means of a drop of dilute hydrochloric acid.

7. Solutions Required for All the Above Tests

Concentration				
Molarity	g. per litre	Chemical name	Popular name	Formula
2	71	Hydrochloric acid	....	HCl
2	—	Nitric acid	....	HNO$_3$
2	80	Sodium hydroxide	Caustic soda	NaOH
0·25	61	Barium chloride	....	BaCl$_2$
4	—	Ammonium hydroxide	Ammonia	NH$_4$OH
2	117	Sodium chloride	Salt	NaCl
0·5	95	Sodium sesquicarbonate	—	Na$_2$CO$_3$.NaHCO$_3$
0·25	53	Potassium ferrocyanide	....	K$_4$Fe(CN)$_6$
0·5	49	Potassium thiocyanate	....	KCNS
0·1	17	Silver nitrate	....	AgNO$_3$
(§1.9, p. 209)		Ammonium molybdate	....	(complex)
—	30	Potassium sodium tartrate	Rochelle salt	KNaC$_4$H$_4$O$_6$.4H$_2$O
—	20	Potassium hydrogen tartrate	Cream of tartar	KHC$_4$H$_4$O$_6$
—	5	Ascorbic acid	Vitamin C	....
—	25	Formaldoxime	....	HCHNOH
—	—	Polyvinyl acetate (solution in toluene)	PVA	....

It is recommended that these solutions be purchased ready-made, together with 'dropping bottles' for all but the last.

8. Equipment required

It is suggested that the following list should be considered to be the minimum of equipment that should be available on any site.

Tool-box: one of the many varieties of tool-box will be found convenient for use as a container for the apparatus and all the small (about 150 ml.) dropping bottles of solutions. Wood is preferred because a metal box will be liable to corrosion from contact with some of the chemicals.

Burner: a burner of some kind is essential also. One of the smaller kinds of 'Camping Gaz' stoves has been found very convenient, with the burner itself replaced when necessary by the tube of an old Bunsen burner, although a smaller tube, with controlled air inlet, is more satisfactory. Otherwise, a small spirit lamp would be useful.

Lens: a single × 10 lens, or a three-lens pocket magnifier.

Test-tubes: a size of about 60 mm. by 8 mm. is convenient. These should be kept in a rack, which can be made by drilling a series of holes of convenient size in a $1\frac{1}{4}$-inch-thick block of wood.

Test-tube holder: a wooden one is the most convenient.

Tongs: these are necessary for holding hot objects.

Porcelain crucibles: two of these, about 3 cm. in diameter, will be suitable.

Filter-papers: two sizes will be required, although the larger ones may be cut down as required. 5 cm. and 10 cm. papers are recommended.

Sprays: these are required only if the special spraying tests are likely to be used.

pH papers: 'Universal' indicator papers will be required, with one or two other types covering the range from about pH4 to pH 8 or pH 9.

Soil-testing outfit: this is an optional extra, which may be used in place of the pH papers.

Sharp knife: this or a razor blade is essential.

Matches

Electrographic tester: optional.

Holder for filter-paper in the phosphate tests: this is simply a piece of half-inch wood with a circular hole about 4 cm. (1½ inches) in diameter, to support the paper while the test is carried out.

Distilled water container: a plastic squeeze-bottle is the most convenient for storing and using distilled water. Water from other sources must never be used for chemical testing.

Measuring cylinder: 50 ml. or 100 ml.

PART FOUR

Archaeological Prospecting

ONE

INTRODUCTION

Prospecting in archaeology may be considered as including two main objectives: the discovery of unknown sites and the precise location of features on known sites. Finding and identifying sites by ordinary fieldwork with no scientific aids is an extremely difficult process, full of traps for the unwary or untrained, and requiring, though rarely receiving, complete objectivity on the part of the investigator. Few are free from prejudices in this branch of archaeology, and it is so easy to follow red herrings. In fact this is a most fertile field for wishful thinkers. Even when not using instruments the scientific approach is necessary. This has been briefly summarized as 'experiment—theorize—test', which in field archaeology might be translated as 'observe—interpret—check'. But there are already excellent books available on field archaeology and it is not our intention to cover the same ground. We want to see what help can be expected from the use of scientific instruments.

One might suppose that any instrument that is of service in geological surveying might be useful to the archaeologist, but this is not necessarily so. The geologist is generally concerned with features on a much larger scale than archaeological sites, both in surface extent and in depth below the surface of the ground, and some of his instruments would scarcely detect many important archaeological features. Even so, it is sometimes possible, by making small adjustments in the method of application and in the form of an instrument, to adapt it to archaeological use.

Many techniques have been investigated, and most of them can give *some* useful information, but it is a question of selecting the most convenient and inexpensive instruments of widest application. Let us briefly consider some that have been used and tested on archaeological sites.

One way to locate features below ground is to send some kind of *message* through the soil and pick up and interpret the *reply*. The message may be introduced to the ground by direct contact with a small area of soil, or it may be 'broadcast' from a point above the ground.

Three interesting *contact* methods have been tried, with widely differing efficiencies. The application of *ultrasonic* methods such as are used at sea has not been successful on land. Ultrasonic waves are sound waves of very high frequency (or pitch), much too high to be detected by the human ear. In measuring the depth of the sea or detecting wrecks the ultrasonic waves are reflected from the sea-bed or wreck, i.e. an echo is produced and detected by the instrument, which thus measures the time taken by the waves to do the

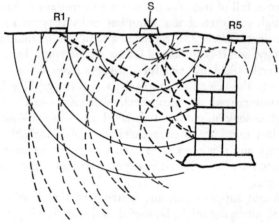

Figure 7 The passage of sound waves through the soil.

return journey. Knowing the speed at which the waves travel it is possible to calculate the depth from which the echo came.

The instrument producing and detecting the ultrasonic waves may be permanently fitted to the hull of the ship or may be lowered into the water as required. Sound waves are very easily passed through water, but unfortunately it is extremely difficult to inject ultrasonic waves into the soil. They will readily pass through the soil, but the difficulty is in getting them started. So at present the method is inpracticable on land.

The source of ultrasonic waves is a rapidly vibrating surface, but the movement of this surface is extremely small, and not powerful enough to pass on the vibrations to the soil. But it is well known that sounds of very low frequency can easily be produced, for example by striking the ground with a spade or heavy implement. It is sometimes possible to detect changes in subsoil, perhaps due to archaeological features, by this method, but a more sophisticated approach is to adapt the seismic methods used by seismologists and geologists.

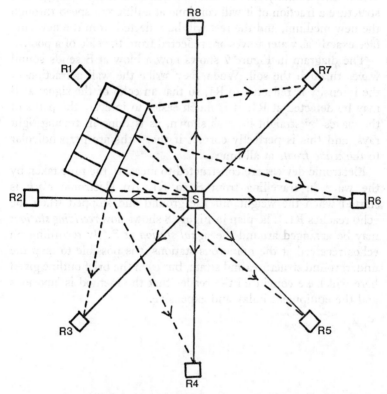

Figure 8 Plan of the arrangement of receiving stations around a seismic signal station. The effect of an underground wall is shown. Reflected waves will reach R_3 and R_7 soon after the direct signal, and *later* reflected waves will reach R_4, R_6, and R_5.

If a heavy weight is allowed to fall onto the ground it produces sound waves that travel outwards in all directions, in a similar way to the water waves produced by dropping a stone into a pool. But the sound waves are not restricted to the surface; they also travel downwards, so that, instead of picturing concentric circles as on water, we must imagine concentric hemispheres expanding, each shaped like the bottom half of a bubble as it grows. But sound waves travel at different speeds in different media. If the soil is perfectly uniform the hemispherical waves will continue in the same form, gradually becoming weaker until they fade away. When such a *wave-front* comes to another stratum or underground structure a fraction of it will continue at a different speed through the new medium, and the rest will be reflected from the new surface exactly as water waves are reflected from the side of a pool.

The diagram in Figure 7 shows how a blow at S sends sound waves through the soil. When they strike the wall a fraction of the intensity is reflected to R1, so that an echo of the signal at S may be detected at R1. It is much easier to indicate the paths of the waves by straight lines as shown, as is done in tracing light rays, and this is perfectly correct if the paths are perpendicular to the *wave-fronts* at all times.

Electronic devices are constructed to measure the time taken by the wave in travelling from S to R1. An electronic *clock* is started when the weight hits the ground and stopped when the echo reaches R1. The plan in Figure 8 shows how *receiving stations* may be arranged around the *signal station* at S. By recording all echos received at the numerous stations it is possible to map the underground structures and strata, but even the brief outline given here will have convinced the reader that the method is laborious and the equipment bulky and expensive.

TWO

RESISTIVITY SURVEYING

A much more generally useful and convenient prospecting method, for use over reasonably small areas, is the electrical resistivity method. Here the signal injected into the ground through two probes is an alternating current produced by a simple transistorized oscillator working from a small dry battery, and the *reply* is the strength of the current between two other probes. This resistivity method has superseded all other earlier types because of its speed and convenience, so that we shall not consider any other.

Again we can picture the signal entering the ground by one probe and spreading out in all directions just as the sound waves did, but there are several important differences. The electric current is much more easily injected and detected than are sound waves, and there are no reflections. Also, the current flows almost entirely through the water contained in the soil, and it is the *resistance* to this flow of current by different strata or structures that is measured.

The most popular resistivity method makes use of four steel probes, which are inserted in line in the ground to a depth of about six inches. The alternating voltage is applied between the two outer probes and the current passing between the inner probes is detected. The simple and compact transistorized electronic unit, which is easily held in one hand, effectively divides the voltage by the current to give the resistance (Ohm's Law). The instrument is, in fact, a 'bridge' device in which voltages are balanced by rotating a small knob of a potentiometer attached to a scale. The balance point is indicated either by a minimum reading on a meter or by the minimum whistle in an ear-piece. When this point is found the reading on the dial is noted and the probes may be moved to the next position.

There are several useful arrangements of probes possible, but the simplest in use, and most generally convenient, is that known as the Wenner configuration, in which the probes are equally spaced along the line of traverse. It is convenient if *five* probes are used, so that one may be moved along while a reading is being taken with the other four. The Martin-Clark Resistivity Meter is designed for use in this way and incorporates a useful rotary switch to which the five long cables from the probes are attached.

It is very important when using any measuring instrument to understand exactly what is being measured and what precautions must be taken to get the best possible results.

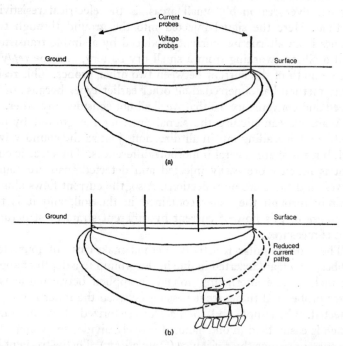

Figure 9   The passage of an electric current through the soil: (a) undisturbed soil; (b) with an underground structure.

The diagrams in Figure 9 show how the resistivity is affected by subterranean features. The full curves show some of the innumerable paths by which the electric current may pass between the probes, and how these may be cut off by features of high resistance such as masonry or hard-packed clay, as indicated by broken lines. Filled-in pits or ditches are generally more loosely packed than the surrounding soil and contain more water, so that their resistance is lower. This effect could be indicated by showing many more paths for the current in such regions.

Some features, then, by interrupting the flow of current, increase the resistance of the ground, whereas pits and ditches in particular will reduce the resistance. But rocky outcrops or intrusions will also cause increased resistance, and any damp area will reduce the resistance. For example, a traverse across a field showing cultivation ridges ('ridge and furrow') will clearly show alternating high and low resistance regions, the latter corresponding to the generally damper furrows. Factors such as these may complicate the interpretation of resistivity surveys. (Resistance and resistivity are here taken to be identical; to attempt to differentiate between them for our present purposes would amount to hair-splitting.)

The more important precautions which need to be taken in using this technique are to keep the correct spacing of probes and always insert them to the same depth. The latter is facilitated by using cranked probes, which are easily inserted by stepping on the crank until it rests on the surface of the soil. Accurate probe-spacing is more important than depth of insertion or small deviations from a straight line.

Apart from the effects already mentioned, results depend very much on the nature of the soil. Sandy soils can be almost useless for this method since they hold so little water and so have a very high resistance, which will mask any small differences arising from archaeological features. Stony soils or boulder-clay subsoils may give erratic results, complicated in the former case by difficulty in inserting the probes in their correct places and poor electrical contact with the soil. For all these reasons it is never advisable to rely on a single traverse of an area, but if this should be unavoidable then the resulting measurements should be averaged, as described later.

It is generally assumed that features at depths up to one-and-a-half times the probe-spacing will be detected under favourable conditions, and one must not overlook the fact of the sideways spread of the current. Thus, with a probe-spacing of one yard, which is convenient for general use, features up to four feet six inches down, or the same distance on either side, will affect the readings. This means, for example, that no 'run' should be nearer than five feet from any modern feature, such as a road or building, or from an excavation trench already opened.

There are many ways of recording and interpreting the results of a resistivity survey. The choice of method depends on the nature of the site, the area covered, and the personal preference of the user. For an area of moderate extent some prefer to plot lines of equal resistance in the same way as the contour lines of a map. This may reveal the positions of buried features, but it is a very laborious procedure, and, in any case, some form of 'averaging' of the observed readings is advisable. For long, narrow areas it is much more useful and convenient to draw profiles showing the variation of resistivity along definite lines across the site. This is particularly true for long, narrow features such as walls and roads, and it may be useful here to look at an actual example from such a site in order to illustrate the writer's own preferred method.

Below are given the meter readings obtained in a double 'run' across a buried Roman road, the first run being from east to west (as indicated by the arrows), the second row of figures resulting from the return run at a distance of one yard to the north of the first:

$\longrightarrow$

28 27 20 29 21 35 36 31 40 35 50 48 34 42 42 28 33 22 27 22

E   W

22 18 18 17 16 19 21 28 30 37 40 42 36 32 42 27 33 23 27 26

$\longleftarrow$

On the graph of Figure 10 line 1 was obtained by plotting the meter readings of the first run against the distance from the start of the run. The somewhat irregular form of this curve is quite a common feature of resistivity surveys, and may be caused by a more or less regular variation in ground resistance such as would result, for example, from a run across a series of cultivation ridges, or it may be partly due to instrumental errors, particularly variations in the 'contact resistance' between the probes and the ground, which would be particularly noticeable in stony ground. Although the latter effect is much less in this kind of instrument than in direct current methods (e.g. the 'Megger' tester), some small effect often remains, but this may be overcome by the 'averaging' of results.

If only a single run is possible, because of shortage of time or lack of available space, then averaging adjacent readings helps to smooth out unwanted variations. The figures following are the averages of adjacent readings and also the averages of each *three* consecutive readings, in each case for the first run only:

28 24 25 25 28 36 34 36 38 43 49 41 38 42 35 31 28 25 25

25 26 23 28 31 34 36 35 42 44 44 41 39 37 34 28 27 24

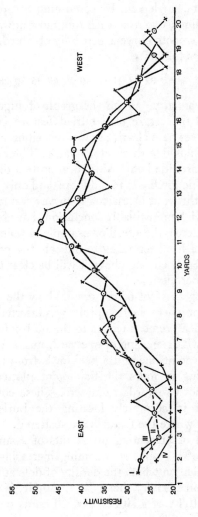

Figure 10 A simple resistivity survey: graphs showing the profile of a buried road surface. (I) The meter readings plotted as recorded. (II) The readings of the first run averaged in pairs. (III) The readings of the first run averaged in threes. (IV) Readings from two parallel runs averaged in fours.

These averages are plotted as curves II and III on the graph (Figure 10), which will be seen to be much smoother than curve I, but they have the disadvantage of making the location of features less definite, and the methods do not remove any spurious effects occurring during the single run. By combining two parallel runs, averaging *four* readings, two from each run, most unwanted effects are removed and a smooth curve is generally obtained. The calculated averages are as follows:

24 21 21 21 23 28 29 32 37 41 45 40 38 40 35 30 28 22 26

These are plotted as curve IV on the graph of Figure 10. The 'M'-shape around the centre of a buried feature is commonly found, and our curves here clearly show the position of the buried road surface and a possible ditch at 19 yards. The region of low resistivity on the east side is too wide to indicate a ditch, and, in fact, on excavation no ditch was found there, and only a very small one was found on the west. Occasionally survey results have been published from which unjustifiable conclusions have been reached from only one run across the site. For example, a point such as at $3\frac{1}{2}$ yards on curve I has been taken to indicate the presence of a ditch: from what has been said above it will be clear that such an assumption is not permissible.

The figures along the foot of the graph show the distances in yards from the point where the first probe was inserted. It is usual to assume that a measurement relates to the mid-point of the set of probes, which, with a spacing of one yard, means that the first reading refers to a point one and a half yards from zero. By the method of averaging in fours the first point plotted will then correspond to a spot two yards from zero. These considerations may be important in accurately locating the buried features, especially on a site where the features are scattered.

Another method of presenting the results of a survey, rather than in the form of a graph, is becoming increasingly popular. This is to draw a plan on which the density of dots at any point is proportional to the resistivity there. For example, if the average 'background' resistivity of a site is, say, 10 ohms on the meter, and archaeological features are giving higher readings, it may be convenient to use a dot density of one dot for every 0·1 ohm above 10 ohms. Thus a reading of 12 ohms would be shown by twenty dots, or one of 10·5 ohms by five dots, and so on. The final picture shows dark areas of high dot-density where the underground features occur. The result can be very effective, but on many sites the work of drawing the plan would be extremely laborious. No doubt this could be computerized, as has been done for some other surveying methods, but not many archaeologists have ready access to a computer.

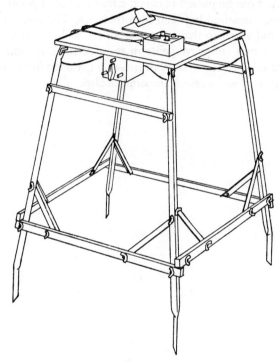

Figure 11   The Martin & Clark 'Square-array' resistivity
surveying equipment.

From what has been said concerning damp areas it will be appreciated that surveys will be affected by rainfall. Experiments have been designed in attempts to discover the best times for carrying out resistivity surveys, from which it appears that on ordinary agricultural land some time should elapse following a period of heavy rain before a survey is done. Occasional showers have only a small effect. Obviously the ground must not be water-logged, neither should it be too dry.

Martin and Clark have recently designed a 'square array' by means of which one person may rapidly survey an area. The meter and recording equipment stand on a square table the legs of which form the four probes (Figure 11; Plate VIII (a)). A probe separation of two-and-a-half feet has been selected as the most convenient, and the cables are connected to the legs through a switch so that current can be passed between either pair of opposite legs and the voltage measured between the other two. The ends of the legs are thin and sharp so that they may all be easily inserted together into the ground. Improvements in the electronic circuits are also incorporated, and the system promises a great saving of time and labour, with other possible advantages also.

THREE

GRAVITATIONAL SURVEYING

The remaining physical methods of prospecting that we shall discuss all involve a 'field of force' of some kind. The idea of a field force is not easy to picture, but everyone is familiar with the effects of two such fields, namely, gravitational and magnetic fields. We see, for example, a magnet draw a piece of iron towards itself, but we can detect no visible nor tangible connection between the two. The effect can be observed in a vacuum, i.e. where there is nothing material between magnet and iron. There is no need for us to go into any further detail here, and we shall merely conclude that there is a 'magnetic field' that draws the iron towards the magnet.

A very important thing about force fields is that they penetrate all matter within their range, whether solid, liquid, or gas, but the field may be more effective in some materials than in others. In iron, for example, a magnetic field is very effective, and hence the powerful attraction. If we made a hole inside any solid substance just large enough to hold a small magnet we should be able to see the effect on this of the field of a large magnet outside the substance. We could note just how *susceptible* is the small magnet to the effects of the magnetic field of the large magnet; or, in the language of the physicist, we could measure the *magnetic susceptibility* of the material. Thus a magnetic field will be stronger in a substance of high than in one of low magnetic susceptibility, which means that the field will be more effective in the former than in the latter. We shall return to this idea later, but first let us consider another kind of force field—gravitation.

Everything has its own gravitational field, which is simply another way of saying that everything attracts everything else, but the effect is only noticeable when extremely large bodies, such as the earth, the moon, or other planets, are involved. An artificial satellite, when it approaches the limit of the earth's gravitational field, is influenced by the gravitational fields of other planets, but itself is much too small to have any measurable effect on those planets; whereas, of course, all planets are large enough to affect each other's orbits by means of their gravitational fields.

Very sensitive instruments show that the earth's gravitational field varies from place to place. This is because gravitational effects depend directly on the mass of the body concerned. Where the rock formation consists of very dense igneous rocks the gravitational field will be higher than average, and the reverse will be true where very light or porous sedimentary rocks predominate. The effects of adjacent hills and valleys are to reduce the pull of gravity, because a high hill or mountain provides a considerable mass of rock pulling upwards, and the absence of rocks where a valley exists means the absence of attraction from that direction, which is equivalent to an attraction from above. So hills and valleys have the same effect, but variations in rock type can either increase or decrease the gravitational field.

Large archaeological features in the ground will also cause slight differences in the earth's gravitational field, and meters are available that could detect such effects, but these are so delicate and slow and difficult to use that the method is not at present suitable for archaeological prospecting.

FOUR

MAGNETIC METHODS

Magnetic prospecting depends on the effect of archaeological features on the earth's magnetic field. There are two sources of this effect: interference from materials having their own magnetic fields, and the effects of differences in *magnetic susceptibility* of materials.

The only important magnetized substance occurring naturally is *magnetite*, a widely distributed oxide of iron which, in bulk, is also known as magnetic iron ore and lodestone. The latter is not very common, most magnetite existing only as fine black grains in rocks or alluvial deposits, and hence in some soils, but it tends to be weathered to other oxides such as haematite (red) and limonite (yellow), which are not magnetic. A much more important source of magnetite is fired clay, since most clays contain some iron salts, which may be converted to magnetite during firing, either in brick- or pottery-making or when the clay is used as a hearth or kiln. As the magnetite cools it becomes magnetized by the earth's magnetic field, the direction of magnetization (i.e. the position of the 'N.' and 'S.' poles) being the direction of the earth's field at the time (see 'Magnetic Dating'). This magnetism is known as 'thermo-remanant magnetism' (TRM), and it keeps its direction no matter how the material may be broken up or moved around.

Large magnetic effects are found in the neighbourhood of burnt clay, so that kilns and hearths are very easily detected by the magnetometer, but one must take care not to be misled by the presence of modern bricks, broken, crushed or whole, which are liable to be found littering sites, particularly in urban areas.

Effects of variations in magnetic susceptibility are not so readily explained, and, indeed, not yet fully understood. We may picture certain materials, such as iron, of high magnetic susceptibility, as having the effect of concentrating the magnetic field, or of gathering the magnetism into itself. We may illustrate the effect by means of a piece of soft iron. This will not normally be magnetized and will not attract steel pins, for example, but if we touch one end of the iron with a magnet then the whole will become magnetized and the pins will be attracted to it. We may say that the iron has concentrated the magnetic field so that it is strong enough to attract other pieces of iron. But the effect will disappear when the magnet is removed. Also, a piece of aluminium, for example, will not behave in this way; it will not become magnetized because aluminium is not magnetic, or, in other words, its magnetic susceptibility is low.

In a similar way the earth's magnetic field appears to be concentrated in materials of high magnetic susceptibility and dispersed (and so weakened) in materials of low susceptibility. Iron is exceptionally effective in this way and other metals to a much smaller extent, but buried archaeological features and artifacts, and even quite small changes in the nature of the soil, will all have some effect, not necessarily easily detectable. One of the unexplained, but fortunate, effects arises from rubbish pits and filled ditches. The former differ considerably from the surrounding soil because they consist essentially of decayed organic matter, but the reasons for the effect of naturally filled ditches are far from clear.

The alteration in the earth's magnetic field by such features is known as a '*magnetic anomaly*', and may be positive or negative, i.e. it may increase or decrease the strength of the earth's field. The precise strength (and sign) of an anomaly cannot be readily calculated, and, furthermore, we cannot give a satisfactory list of features in order of their effects, because these depend on so many different factors. The anomaly caused by a filled ditch, for example, depends on the depth, width, and length of the feature, the nature of the filling and of the surrounding soil, the looseness of the filling, and possibly its water content and other matters. If one is merely locating a feature known to exist this element of doubt is no drawback, but it makes it extremely difficult to interpret the various recorded anomalies over a new site of considerable extent. This can be done with any degree of confidence only after considerable experience.

Magnetic-field strengths are measured by means of *magnetometers*, of which there are many varieties (Plates VIII, IX), but only a few kinds will have the specification needed for archaeological prospecting. The unit of magnetic-field strength is generally known as the *Gauss* (more correctly the Oersted); the average value of the earth's total field is about 0·48 G in Britain and about 0·51 G in the U.S.A. Archaeological features may change this by only a hundred-thousandth of a Gauss (10^{-5} G.), which is called 'one gamma' (1 γ), but for important features the anomaly may range from 10 γ to 1,000 γ and will vary with the distance from the feature. The magnetometer should therefore be capable of detecting changes of one or two gamma.

Because a simple magnetometer is affected by various undesirable factors such as wire fences, electricity-supply lines, electric trains, and even atmospheric changes, it is an advantage to use a magnetic *gradiometer* or a *differential* magnetometer. This is an instrument that uses two detectors and records only any difference between the magnetic fields in which the detectors lie. The detectors are usually held five or six feet apart (generally one above the other) so that the unwanted effects just mentioned will be cancelled out, and only buried or surface features will be detected, though these may include undesirables of perhaps geological origin.

The first magnetometer used in archaeology, and still the only one in common use, was the *proton magnetometer* (or proton gradiometer), but it has certain disadvantages, notably the need to make measurements while the instrument is stationary. Other instruments, which give continuous readings while the detector is steadily carried along, will probably supersede the proton magnetometer shortly, but these are not yet widely available. We shall therefore describe the proton gradiometer.

A *proton* is the nucleus of a hydrogen atom, which behaves in some ways as though it were spinning like a top, and also *precessing*. The latter is the circular movement of the axis that is noticed when the speed of a top begins to fall; we see the top still spinning around its axis, but the axis itself is now slowly moving around, the top being no longer upright. The proton precession depends on the strength of the magnetic field in which it finds itself, and in the earth's field it precesses at about 2,000 revolutions per second. But it will do this only if it is 'flipped over' from its normal position, which is done by means of an alternating current of the same frequency (i.e. 2,000 cycles per second). When this alternating current is cut off the protons flip back to their original positions, and in so doing they send out a faint signal, which can be picked up by a suitable coil of wire and detected by electronic circuits in a similar way to radio signals. The signal received is of the same frequency as the precession frequency, and so depends on the magnetic-field strength.

The gradiometer has two such detectors, and records the difference between the two signals. If the detectors (called 'bottles') are in identical surroundings the two signals will be identical and will be heard in the loud-speaker as a high steady note. The instrument is made to actuate the 'bottles' (a process called 'polarization') for $2\frac{1}{2}$ seconds and then automatically switch over to detecting the response, also for $2\frac{1}{2}$ seconds. For no anomaly (equal signals) the high-pitched note lasts for the whole of the $2\frac{1}{2}$ seconds' listening period, but when the bottles are in different magnetic fields a 'beat' is heard, which fades away before the end of the listening period. The frequency of the beat, i.e. the number of beats per second, is used to measure the anomaly. The beat frequency is equal to the difference between the two individual frequencies.

A very large number of protons must react in the detectors in order to give an appreciable signal, and it is found that the best substance for general use is methyl alcohol, with water almost as good. These liquids both contain a large proportion of protons, but they must be very pure when used for this purpose. The liquid is contained in a plastic bottle around which is wound a very long coil of copper wire, the whole being finally encased in a plastic material for protection. The result is a heavy 'bottle', two of which are attached to a stout pole about seven feet long, one bottle being about a foot from the ground and the other five or six feet higher. An assistant is required to move this cumbersome structure from point to point across a grid of strings, holding it steady at each intersection for at least $2\frac{1}{2}$ seconds while the reading is taken, and it is desirable to have another assistant to note the results. There must be no magnetic material, such as iron or steel, near the bottles, which means that the assistant concerned must carefully survey his clothing and remove any offending articles (including tags on shoe laces) before starting the archaeological survey.

Results of the magnetometer survey may be recorded in many ways. Some workers plot the anomalies on a plan, using symbols to indicate the size of the anomalies, but these plans would seem to be rather confusing and difficult for another worker to follow. Some prefer to join together by a line points of similar anomaly-values, making a plan resembling a contour map. This is a laborious process but does give an instantaneous impression of regions of high or low anomaly, and often indicates the approximate shapes and positions of underground features. Another alternative is to plot graphs of anomaly-strength against distance from the starting point, giving curves with peaks showing the regions of high anomaly and depressions showing regions of low anomaly. One advantage of this method is that one can compare the shapes of the curves with those of predicted curves for various kinds of simple buried structures, but there are many difficulties to overcome, and anyone intending to make frequent use of a magnetometer should first consult the literature, including the manufacturer's instruction book and, in particular, articles such as those appearing in *Archaeometry* (for example in 1964 and 1966) and in *Prospezioni Archeologiche*. Recent studies have made use of computers to produce magnetic survey plans.

Two of the other magnetometers referred to above that have been tested on archaeological sites are the 'fluxgate gradiometer' and the 'rubidium magnetometer'. The former works on principles that can be explained in terms of the classical ideas of magnetism and electricity, and can be said to be based on the effect of a magnetic field on an arrangement very like a transformer, with a core of specially designed magnetic alloy. The rubidium magnetometer makes use of the magnetic effect on the optical spectrum of the metal rubidium, but the theory of each kind is too complex to be detailed here. Each of these may attain a sensitivity of one gamma. It should also be possible to design suitable magnetometers making use of the Hall effect, which could be electronically much simpler than the other types mentioned.

The fascinating story has recently been published of the use of a caesium magnetometer in the successful search for the ancient Greek city of Sybaris in Italy.

FIVE

OTHER ELECTRICAL METHODS

A device originally designed for the detection of metal objects in the ground but found to respond also to changes in the soil itself, as in pits and ditches, uses the 'pulsed induction' technique. This does not involve the earth's magnetic field, but the instrument transmits a magnetic field, from a large coil in short pulses into the ground, where it interacts with metals and the soil. The rising and falling magnetic field produces currents in a metal, which then send out their own magnetic fields. These are detected by a receiving coil, and the strength of this signal can be made to indicate not only the presence of a metal object but also its depth below ground level. Development of the method is proceeding, but even with the increased sensitivity that is expected it will still suffer from the fact that each reading takes at least ten seconds, as the coils must be stationary when a measurement is made.

The Soil Conductivity Meter promises to be a very useful instrument of moderate cost, easy to operate, and giving continuous readings. Conductivity is the reciprocal of resistivity, and so one would expect results similar to those of the familiar resistivity meter. The difference is that the conductivity method does not require the insertion of probes into the ground, but instead transmits a signal similar to a radio signal, which is re-radiated by metal objects in the same way as with the induction method. Again the unexpected soil effects have been found, and, in fact, excellent response to small post-holes has occurred with a prototype instrument. Reports on trials of such instruments will be found in the periodicals listed in the bibliography.

SIX

AERIAL PHOTOGRAPHY

No review of surveying or prospecting methods in archaeology would be complete without some reference to the use of aerial photography. This is now a well-established and familiar method, but the reasons for the revelation of archaeological features and the limitations of the method are not always understood.

Vertical photographs are the most generally useful, but success depends so much on the climate, weather conditions, type of soil and crop (if any), time of year, and time of day that many failures may occur before a positive result is achieved.

There are two kinds of marks that may reveal archaeological features on aerial photographs: shadow marks and crop marks. Shadow marks may appear when the sun is low in the sky, so that the ground is illuminated by almost horizontal rays and even slight irregularities will throw appreciable shadows and be high-lighted on the sunny side. In this way the remains of ploughed-out banks and filled ditches that are not noticeable at ground level may be revealed on the aerial photographs. Similar effects arise under a light covering of snow, especially when wind-blown, as the snow tends to accumulate in slight hollows or against the windward side of very low banks, so 'developing' a pattern not normally visible.

Crop marks (Plate XI) arise because of some difference in crop growth above buried features as compared to adjacent areas. There may be several causes. Differences in moisture content of the soil will occur; for example, a filled-in ditch is generally more loosely packed than the undisturbed soil and so will hold more water, causing better crop growth in rather dry areas or seasons, in terms of either height or colour. On the other hand, masonry not too far below the surface will tend to produce a drier environment, either by draining away the soil water or by making the roots search further afield for their water, producing short-stemmed and paler corn crops, or pale, weak, and sparse root-crops. The effects are more pronounced at the end of a dry period, although under wet conditions, and with some kinds of underground structures, water may be retained so that the outline of a structure shows up on the aerial photograph as darker lines or areas. All these effects may show also in the early spring growth, though they are generally not so pronounced as towards the end of the growing season.

In extreme cases a combination of shadow mark with crop mark might give results when each alone has failed. It should also be noted that the effects change as the crop grows, and there are certain periods at which the best photographs can be obtained, such as the onset of ripening of corn, or when the ears of barley start to turn downwards. Anyone wishing to engage in large-scale aerial surveying for archaeology must learn quite a lot about farm crops and grassland, local climate and short-term weather conditions. But many of us must rely on photographs taken for other purposes, perhaps by local or central government departments, and we must not expect much help from these. In particular we must not be dismayed if no signs of any kind of archaeological feature appear, as the chances of hitting on suitable conditions on a single flight are remote. Also, such photographs are frequently taken at an angle rather than vertically; it is then much more difficult to fix the precise position of any feature in relation to useful landmarks, and the shapes of such marks may be considerably distorted.

When studying aerial photographs it is important to be able to distinguish between archaeological features and marks produced by normal farming methods or other modern activities. Cornfields or hayfields often show, during and after harvesting, a very regular pattern, often with a small rectangle in the centre with diagnosis to the corners of the field. Other farming operations may produce patterns also, and there are often very misleading marks left by tractors, because only a portion of the tracks may be visible. Other pitfalls to watch for include sports fields, sewers, gas and oil pipe-lines, and the filled-in pits left by uprooted trees. Several of the latter have been reported as 'pit rows', sometimes even confirmed by excavation. Grubbed-up hedgerows usually leave a slight bank, which may show up as either a shadow or a crop mark, and the positions of manure heaps are shown by the small areas of better-grown crops. The best advice to follow when looking for archaeological features on aerial photographs is to be always suspicious, especially of an extremely clear and obvious mark.

Experiments with colour photographs and with infra-red

cameras have been carried out more recently, with interesting results and showing great promise. The spectrum produced when white light is split into its component colours is seen in the rainbow, the colours passing from red on one side to violet on the other. *Infra-red (below red)* light is beyond the red and is invisible to human beings. It consists of radiation of longer wavelength than visible light and is, in fact, the form in which *heat* is radiated. It may be detected by means of instruments which measure very small heat changes, but because it is of the same *nature* as visible light it is also detected by specially made photographic films. The difference is that an infra-red photograph does not pick up shadows or crop marks, but minute amounts of radiant heat, and it appears that crops growing at different rates or under slightly different conditions give off different amounts of heat. Several quite unsuspected sites have recently been discovered by this method. A further refinement is to take several (usually nine) photographs of the same site with a series of infra-red films sensitive to different wavelengths of radiation. Archaeological features may show up on one or more of the films, but possibly not on all.

SEVEN

CHEMICAL METHODS

Finally, brief mention should be made of chemical methods of prospecting. For the discovery or delineation of archaeological sites chemical tests for phosphates have been used, but such methods must of necessity be slower than the instrumental methods or aerial photography. In fact it is recommended that chemical testing of this kind should be used only in conjunction with one or more of the other methods. The chemical element *phosphorus* is a constituent of many animal products in addition to being the main component of bone. On the decay of such substances most of the phosphorus remains in the form of *phosphates*, which are not easily washed out of the soil and are quite persistent. The main difficulty of this surveying method is that it does not distinguish human occupation from animal occupation. Hence, considerable care is necessary to avoid areas where domestic animals congregate or where victims of cattle disease have been buried. Results may also be vitiated in fields where modern phosphatic fertilizers have been applied.

The method consists of collecting small samples (about 50 g., or 2 oz.) at regular intervals across the area to be surveyed. For large areas the intervals may be from 25 to 50 yards, but when locating a site whose position is approximately known, or finding the limits of a known site, much closer spacing of samples may be used. The samples may be placed in plastic bags and the tests carried out in a laboratory, at home, or even on the site, as the equipment required is quite simple and cheap. Stratification of a section can also be tested in this way to reveal occupation levels, identify burial sites, and for many other purposes. Details will be found in Part III.

APPENDIX

The Glossary is intended for use as a quick, independent reference source where the busy practical archaeologist may look for a brief description of the nature of any material or for the definition of a scientific term, but a definition has been followed by a more detailed explanation where this has appeared to be necessary.

Substances and materials that can be represented by a chemical formula are listed in Table 6. To a chemist a formula is a kind of shorthand, which conveys quite a lot of information, especially when combined with others in a chemical equation, but for our present purposes it is merely intended to indicate the elements a compound contains, and their relative proportions. A list of symbols for the chemical elements is provided as Table 7.

Chemical nomenclature is something of a mystery to non-scientists, and an attempt has been made in Table 8 to give a brief explanation of some of the common forms used in naming compounds. It will be noted that there are several frequently occurring groupings of elements which are called *radicals*, and that these also, besides single atoms, may gain or lose electrons to form ions; some of these are tabulated.

TABLE 6

Inorganic Compounds, Alloys, and Minerals

Name	Chemical formula	Description
Agate	$SiO_2 . xH_2O$	A chalcedonic silica
Alabaster	$CaSO_4 . 2H_2O$	A fine-grained gypsum
Albite	$NaAlSi_3O_8$	Sodium felspar: a silicate mineral
Anhydrite	$CaSO_4$	Anhydrous calcium sulphate
Anorthite	$CaAl_2Si_2O_8$	Calcium felspar
Apatite	$Ca_5F(PO_4)_3$	A fluorinated calcium phosphate, widely distributed in rocks and in bone and teeth
Aurichalcum	Cu/Zn alloy	About 22 per cent zinc, with lead, tin, and iron
Azurite	$2CuCO_3 . Cu(OH)_2$	Blue copper ore: a basic copper carbonate
Brass	Cu/Zn alloy	
Bronze	Cu/Sn alloy	

TABLE 6 (*continued*)

Inorganic Compounds, Alloys, and Minerals

Name	Chemical formula	Description
Calamine	$ZnCO_3$	A zinc ore with hexagonal crystals: zinc carbonate
Calcite	$CaCO_3$	Calcium carbonate hexagonal crystals
Carnelian	$SiO_2.xH_2O$	Red or brown varieties of chalcedony
Cassiterite	SnO_2	Stannic oxide: yellow, brown, or black tin ore
Chalcedony	$SiO_2.xH_2O$	Partly colloidal, partly crystalline silica
Chert	$SiO_2.xH_2O$	A coarse flint: a form of chalcedony
Copaline	Approx. $C_{10}H_{16}O$	A dark yellow amber found in London Clay
Corundum	Al_2O_3	Aluminium oxide: alumina—white hexagonal crystals
Electrum	Au/Ag alloy	Gold with about 25 per cent silver: a white alloy
Felspars	—	Alumino-silicates of sodium, potassium, and/or calcium
Galena	PbS	Lead sulphide ore, with a little silver: grey, cubic crystals
Gypsum	$CaSO_4.2H_2O$	Hydrated calcium sulphate: flat, usually white, crystals
Haematite	Fe_2O_3	Ferric oxide: hexagonal, often flat, crystals, but often in round, lustrous lumps; red, black, or grey
Halite	NaCl	Rock salt, or common salt: white cubic crystals
Hornblende	—	Complex silicates of iron, magnesium, aluminium, calcium, and sodium, always containing hydroxyl ions
Hydroxyapatite	$Ca_5(OH)(PO_4)_3$	Apatite in which fluorine has been replaced by hydroxyl (perhaps partly)
Illite	—	A clay mineral
Jasper	$SiO_2.xH_2O$	Opaque, deeply coloured varieties of chalcedony mainly crystalline

Table 6 (*continued*)

Inorganic Compounds, Alloys, and Minerals

Name	Chemical formula	Description
Jeweller's Rouge	Fe_2O_3	A form of ferric oxide used as a polishing powder and red pigment
Kaolin(ite)	$Al_2SiO_5(OH)_4$	China clay
Limonite	$2Fe_2O_3 . 3H_2O$	Hydrated ferric oxide: yellow to brown
Magnetite	Fe_3O_4	Ferroso-ferric oxide: black or dark grey cubic crystals
Malachite	$CuCO_3 . Cu(OH)_2$	A basic copper carbonate ore: green
Marble	$CaCO_3$	Metamorphosed limestone
Mica	—	Complex alumino-silicates of potassium, magnesium, and iron, with hydroxyl and fluoride ions; flaky
Natron	$Na_2CO_3 . 10H_2O$	'Washing soda': white crystals
Obsidian	—	A volcanic glass
Ochres	$Fe_2O_3 . xH_2O$	Colour depends on the extent of hydration: yellow to red or brown pigments
Olivine	Mg_2SiO_4 to Fe_2SiO_4	Green minerals with various proportions of magnesium and iron
Opal	$SiO_2 . xH_2O$	Colloidal silica: opaque white or coloured by impurities
Orichalcum		See *Aurichalcum*
Orthoclase	$KAlSi_3O_8$	Potassium felspar
Pewter	Pb/Sn	Alloy of lead and tin or antimony and tin
Plaster of Paris	$CaSO_4 . H_2O$	Partly dehydrated gypsum
Potash alum	$K_2SO_4 . Al_2(SO_4)_3 . 24H_2O$	See *Alums* in Glossary
Pyroxenes		Complex silicates of iron and magnesium, with calcium, sodium, and aluminium
Quartz	SiO_2	Hexagonal crystals: white, but often coloured by impurities
Quartzite	SiO_2	Quartz crystals cemented together with silica
Quicklime	CaO	Calcium oxide; with water it becomes very hot and forms *slaked* lime

10

TABLE 6 (*continued*)

Inorganic Compounds, Alloys, and Minerals

Name	Chemical formula	Description
Serpentine	$Mg_3Si_2O_5(OH)_4$	A rather soft green mineral: may contain some iron
Silica	SiO_2	Silicon dioxide: the commonest of all minerals
Slaked lime	$Ca(OH)_2$	Calcium hydroxide, made by adding water to (i.e. slaking) quicklime
Soapstone	$Mg_3Si_4O_{10}(OH)_2$	A form of talc: amorphous white, grey, green, red, or black
Steatite		See *Soapstone*
Talc	$Mg_3Si_4O_{10}(OH)_2$	A very soft mineral: white or greenish, with a soapy feel ('French chalk')
Tinstone	SnO_2	The mineral *cassiterite*
Tufa	$CaCO_3$	Calcium carbonate deposited around springs in limestone areas
Tuff		A fine-grained volcanic ash

Organic Compounds

Amino-acids	—	More or less complex compounds containing one or more of each of the groups $-COOH$ and $-NH_2$: constituents of proteins
Cellulose	$(C_6H_{10}O_5)_n$	The main constituent of plant cell-walls, consisting of very long chains of links with the formula shown (glucose units). The number 'n' may be very large, but is variable, giving molecules weighing from 40,000 to 120,000 times the weight of a hydrogen atom
Glycine	NH_2CH_2COOH	The simplest amino-acid
Hydroxyproline	$C_5H_9O_3N$	An amino-acid found in breakdown products of the protein collagen

TABLE 6 (*continued*)

Organic Compounds

Name	Chemical formula	Description
Methane	CH_4	'Marsh gas', formed by the decay of organic material; a constituent of natural gas
Monosaccharides	$C_6H_{12}O_6$	Simple sugars, of which there are several with this general formula, e.g. glucose, fructose
Polysaccharides	—	More complex sugars formed by the combination of two or more monosaccharides, with the exclusion of water
Proteins: Collagen Cutin Fibroin Keratin Ossein Sericin Suberin		Complex organic compounds containing C, H, O, N, S, and sometimes P. They are built up from many amino-acids arranged in a very definite order for each kind of protein, and each has a different selection of amino-acids, by which it may be identified
Starch	$(C_6H_{10}O_5)_n$	Starch differs from cellulose in having branched and cross-linked chains of glucose units; a means of food storage in plants
Succinic acid	$C_4H_6O_{10}$	A constituent of amber
Sucrose	$C_{12}H_{22}O_{11}$	Cane sugar, a disaccharide

TABLE 7

The Chemical Elements

The symbols for all elements mentioned.

Element	Symbol	Element	Symbol
Aluminium	Al	Calcium	Ca
Antimony	Sb	Carbon	C
Argon	A	Chlorine	Cl
Arsenic	As	Cobalt	Co
Bromine	Br	Copper	Cu

TABLE 7 (*continued*)

The Chemical Elements

Element	Symbol	Element	Symbol
Fluorine	F	Nitrogen	N
Gold	Au	Oxygen	O
Helium	He	Phosphorus	P
Hydrogen	H	Potassium	K
Iodine	I	Rubidium	Rb
Iron	Fe	Silicon	Si
Lead	Pb	Silver	Ag
Magnesium	Mg	Sodium	Na
Manganese	Mn	Sulphur	S
Molybdenum	Mo	Thorium	Th
Neon	Ne	Tin	Sn
Nickel	Ni	Uranium	U
Radon	Rn	Zinc	Zn

1. Chemical Nomenclature

Most *inorganic* compounds have names consisting of two parts, (a) a basic part, or positive ion, usually a metal (which includes sodium, potassium, calcium, etc.) and (b) an acidic part, or negative ion, which may be a non-metallic element (such as chlorine, oxygen, etc.) or a group of elements, called an *acid radical*. Some of the latter are listed in Table 8.

Part (a) of the name is never changed (e.g. sodium is always sodium), but part (b) may carry a prefix or a suffix (or both), which is intended to indicate its nature and to distinguish it from other related compounds. Table 8 also includes some of the commoner prefixes and suffixes, with their meanings.

There are also *systematic* names for all *organic* compounds, but these become unmanageable for the complex organic materials with which we have been mainly concerned, so that it is much easier to use the specific or common names for these.

TABLE 8

The Nomenclature of Inorganic Compounds

ACIDIC (NEGATIVE) IONS

Symbol or formula	Name	Example
Cl^-	Chloride	NaCl, sodium chloride (common salt)
Br^-	Bromide	KBr, potassium bromide (formerly used as a sedative)

TABLE 8 (*continued*)

The Nomenclature of Inorganic Compounds

ACIDIC (NEGATIVE) IONS

Symbol or formula	*Name*	*Example*
I^-	Iodide	—
NO_3^-	Nitrate	KNO_3, potassium nitrate, (Chile saltpetre)
SO_4^{2-}	Sulphate	$(NH_4)_2SO_4$, ammonium sulphate (sulphate of ammonia fertiliser)
PO_4^{3-}	Phosphate	$Ca_3(PO_4)_2$, calcium phosphate
MnO_4^-	Permanganate	$KMnO_4$, potassium permanganate (used as a wood stain, etc.)

PREFIXES

per-	means that the substance contains more than usual of some element (especially oxygen) or radical	Potassium permanganate, $KMnO_4$ (potassium manganate is K_2MnO_4)
hypo-	means that the substance contains less than usual of some element or radical	Sodium hypochlorite, $NaClO$ (a common disinfectant) (sodium chlorite is $NaClO_2$, sodium chlorate is $NaClO_3$, and sodium perchlorate is $NaClO_4$)

SUFFIXES

-ide	means that the acidic part consists of *one* element	Chloride ion, Cl^- (exception; CN^-, the cyanide ion)
-ate	means that the acidic part contains oxygen	Sulphate ion, SO_4^{2-}
-ite	means that the acidic part contains less oxygen than the last	Sulphite ion, SO_3^{2-}
-ous ⎫ -ic ⎬	means that the metal concerned can combine with either less or more of an acid radical	Ferrous oxide, FeO Ferric oxide, Fe_2O_3

GLOSSARY

Acid   A substance that provides hydrogen ions when dissolved in water. This is a simplified definition, but quite adequate for general purposes. The modern view is that the hydrogen ions themselves constitute the acid, and that there are many other species that may behave as acids.

Acidity   A measure of the amount of acid in a solution. From the definition of acid above it is clear that the acidity of a solution may be measured in terms of the concentration of hydrogen ions (i.e. the number or the weight of hydrogen ions in one litre of solution). The symbol for 'hydrogen ion concentration' is $[H^+]$. (*See* pH.)

Agglomerate   A deposit of volcanic debris with particles larger than about 2 mm. diameter, in a matrix of volcanic ash.

Aggregate   The material of gravel grade or larger in a concrete; the hard-core.

Alkali   An alkali is strictly a *strong* base, and a base is a substance that will neutralize an acid, or reverse the effects of an acid. Metal hydroxides are bases, and the hydroxides of the 'alkali' metals (e.g. sodium and potassium) are alkalis.

Algae   Simple plants of the Thallophyta group, including many green and red species responsible for the colour of stagnant water, and some of the seaweeds.

Alpha-particles   Positively charged particles thrown out from the nucleus of some radioactive atoms. An α-particle is actually identical with the nucleus of an atom of helium, and it can readily take up two electrons to form such an atom of helium. It therefore has a charge equal and opposite to that of two electrons, i.e. two positive charges. Its weight is four times the weight of a hydrogen atom, i.e. its *atomic mass* is 4.

Alums   Double sulphates of general formula X_2SO_4. $Y_2(SO_4)_3.24H_2O$, which all crystallize in the same form. 'X' can be sodium, potassium, ammonium, etc., and 'Y' can be aluminium, chromium, iron, etc. Potash alum (X = potassium, Y = aluminium) is colourless, but many alums are deeply coloured.

Anhydride   The anhydride of a substance may be converted into that substance by the addition of water. For example, sulphur trioxide (SO_3) is the anhydride of sulphuric acid because it forms this acid when it combines with water, thus: $SO_3 + H_2O = H_2SO_4$.

Anther The male organ of a flowering plant, which produces and contains the pollen grains.

Arthropoda Animals with jointed appendages (Greek *arthron*, a joint).

Ashlar Square-dressed stone used in building. All faces are finely dressed and all corners and edges are square. If all the stones in a row of a wall are of the same thickness, then the wall is of coursed ashlar, but if they are of various thicknesses and shapes the wall is of uncoursed ashlar.

Atom The smallest particle of an element. The simple picture of an atom as consisting of a positive nucleus, accounting for all the weight, and electrons orbiting around the nucleus, may be used to explain many phenomena, but by no means all.

Bacteria Microscopic organisms belonging to the plant kingdom. They lie on the border-line between plants and animals, and most contain no chlorophyll.

Basalt A fine-grained igneous rock consisting mainly of the ferro-magnesian minerals. Usually dull black, grey, or green.

Base A substance that will neutralize an acid or reverse the effects of an acid.

Basic Rocks Rocks that contain relatively high proportions of the metals and smaller proportions of silica. They often contain the *mafic* minerals, i.e. those containing silicates of magnesium and iron.

Bast The phloem of the vascular tissue in woody plants, consisting of fibres and sieve-tubes.

Bedding Stratification of sedimentary rocks. The bedding plane is the plane in which the material was originally deposited. When stone is laid in the same way in building it is said to be base-bedded, but when the bedding planes are vertical and parallel to the face of the wall it is face-bedded.

Beta-particles Electrons emitted by some radioactive atoms.

Bilateral Symmetry An object is said to have (or show) bilateral symmetry when each half is the mirror-image of the other.

Bivalves Molluscs with two shells hinged together, as in the mussel or oyster.

Bloom   The form of iron extracted by early methods, consisting of small grains of the metal mixed in a spongy mass of slag. The iron was separated by hammering, or forging.

Boll   The fruit of the cotton plant, containing the seeds with their long cotton fibres.

Boulder-clay   Clay mixed with boulders of various sizes transported and deposited by glacial action.

Brackish Water Water with a slight salty taste.

Braunerde   A nearly neutral soil type with an A(B)C profile. The name is German for 'brown earth', but not all braunerdes are brown.

Bronze Disease The corrosion of bronze by the formation of copper chloride, a process that continues after removal of the bronze from the soil and can be arrested by the application of silver nitrate.

Bulb of Percussion A bulbous protrusion, which is left on a flint core after removal of a flake by percussion. It forms immediately below the striking-platform. A corresponding depression may be formed on the flake.

Burnishing   Producing a fine, smooth surface by rubbing with the hand or some smooth material. Pottery and wall-plaster were often burnished by means of flattish, smooth pebbles.

Canaliculi   Minute 'canals' that connect together the lacuni (cavities) and canals in bony tissue. In living bone the lacuni contain cells whose 'limbs' extend into the canaliculi. They distribute material from the blood throughout the bone.

Cancellous Tissue The spongy tissue of bones.

Canine Teeth   Teeth corresponding to the long, conical teeth of a dog (Latin *canis*, a dog).

Cannon-bone   A bone of the lower leg of some animals, formed by the fusion of the tibia and fibula.

Carbohydrates Organic compounds in which the ratio of hydrogen to oxygen atoms is the same as in water, i.e. two to one. For example, glucose is $C_6H_{12}O_6$.

Cartilage   A tough but flexible substance, which may take the place of bone, cover articulating surfaces of bones, form the flexible part of the nose, etc. Temporary cartilage is the forerunner of bone in the infant animal.

Cells   The fundamental structural units of all plant and animal tissues, generally too small to be seen with the unaided eye. Plant cells are distinguished by their cellulose cell-walls.

Charcoal   Carbon produced by the incomplete combustion of organic compounds. Complete combustion, i.e. in a plentiful supply of air, would convert all organic compounds into carbon dioxide and water (and the oxides of any other elements present), leaving virtually no solid residue. With insufficient air some carbon is oxidized only as far as carbon monoxide and some remains in the solid elemental form. The oxidation may be completed by burning in air—a useful test for charcoal.

Chlorophyll   The green colouring-matter of plants, which plays a vital part in photosynthesis. It contains magnesium (Greek *khloros*, green; *phullon*, leaf).

Chromatography   A method of separating mixtures of various substances. Solutions may be taken up by absorbent paper or a thin layer of powder supported on a glass plate. Mixtures of gases are passed through a column packed with a suitable powder. (Greek *khroma*, colour; *grapho*, write.)

Cleavage   The way in which a mineral tends to split. Cleavage planes, along which the crystal is most easily split, are planes *across* which the chemical bonds are relatively weak.

Climax Soils   A soil in which the full profile has been formed but which has not yet been fully developed. As long as existing climatic conditions persist the soil will not produce any new horizons but will merely show changes in the relative thicknesses of the existing horizons.

Cocci   Spherical bacteria (Greek *kokhos*, a grain).

Colloidal   A state of matter in which very small particles of one substance are distributed throughout another substance. Each substance may be either solid, liquid, or gaseous. A mist is a colloidal dispersion of very small water droplets in air; pumice is colloidal gas bubbles in solidified lava; emulsions are colloidal dispersions of an oil in water or of water in an oil.

Compound   A substance containing two or more different elements chemically bound together. Chemical bonding involves the rearrangement of the electrons of the atoms.

Conchoidal Fracture   Fractures of rocks or minerals are said to be conchoidal when the surfaces formed are curved and possibly show a series of minute curved cracks, with some radial marks also, resembling the markings on conch shells.

Conglomerate Gravel cemented together to form solid rock. The gravel may be of any size or shape, but with more-or-less rounded corners, and may be mainly of one or two sizes or a completely unsorted mass. When the gravel is from a scree, with sharp-edged fragments, the rock is called breccia.

Coprolites Fossilized animal excrement.

Corium The inner, and most important, layer of the skin of an animal.

Cortex The walls of the central cells of an animal fibre.

Crustacea Hard-shelled animals, such as crabs, shrimps, etc.

Cryptocrystalline Consisting of very small, sub-microscopic, crystals (Greek *krupto*, hide).

Cullet Scrap glass re-used in glass-making.

Cupellation Separation of metals by heating on a *cupel*, an absorbent stone. One of the constituents, usually as oxide, sinks into the cupel, leaving the other more or less pure metal.

Cusps The surfaces of teeth that meet when the mouth is closed.

Cuticle The outer skin, or epidermis.

Dead-burnt When gypsum is heated so that all the water of crystallization is driven off, the product (anhydrite) will not set when water is added, as the hemi-hydrate (plaster of Paris) will. It is therefore said to be 'dead-burnt'.

Declination The magnetic declination at a point on the earth's surface is the angle between the position of a compass needle and the true north.

Dendrochronology Tree-ring dating.

Denticles The bony growths in fish that correspond to teeth in mammals.

Dentine The hard bone-like material that forms the greater part of a tooth. It contains much less organic matter than bone.

Dentition The characteristic arrangement of the teeth in a species of animal, or the arrangement in a particular specimen.

Desert Gloss In deserts flint artifacts may appear highly polished, either from the polishing action of the sand or the re-deposition of colloidal silica on the surfaces. This is known as desert gloss.

Devitrification The slow change from the vitreous (glassy) state to the crystalline state. In old glass the process may start with the formation of very small crystals here and there, the glass becoming cloudy as the extent of crystallization increases.

Dezincification The preferential corrosion of zinc in some brasses, which leaves the surface rough and pitted.

Diatoms Microscopic marine and fresh-water organisms con-sisting of single cells, often sticking together in groups. They contain silica, which sinks to the ocean or lake floor when the diatoms die, forming deposits known as 'diatomaceous earths', e.g. kieselguhr.

Dicotyledons Flowering plants that produce two seed-leaves. The latter are present in the seed and may have quite a different appearance from the later leaves.

Digitigrade Walking on the toes only.

Distal The part of a long-bone that is further from the trunk. The nearer end is the proximal end.

Dip At any point on the earth's surface the magnetic dip is the vertical angle at which a compass needle will set if suspended in a vertical plane.

Dolomite A double carbonate of calcium and magnesium: white unless stained by impurities.

Drumlin An oval mound of boulder-clay pointing in the direc-tion of the ice-flow that shaped it. This may or may not be the same ice-flow as that from which the clay was deposited.

Electron The unit of negative charge. A sub-atomic particle that weighs only about 1/1,850 part of the weight of an hydrogen atom, and has a negative charge. Elec-trons in atoms move in definite orbits around the nucleus, and they are responsible for all the chemical properties of atoms and molecules, and the formation of chemical bonds. Although electrons *as such* do not appear to exist within the nucleus of an atom they are often ejected from the nucleus during the changes which result in radioactive decay.

Element A substance that cannot be broken down into simpler substances. In terms of modern physics one might define an element as a substance in which all the atoms have the same electronic structure, i.e. the same number and arrangement of orbital electrons.

Eluvial   Washing out, or washed out.

End-moraine   A bank or ridge formed of material deposited by the retreating front of a glacier.

Enzyme   A biological catalyst, i.e. an organic compound which enables a biochemical change to take place without itself being consumed in the process.

Epidermis   The outer skin (Greek *epi*, upon; *derma*, the skin).

Epiphyses   The ends of long-bones.

Erratics   Rocks carried by glaciers and deposited far from their original sites.

Esker   A ridge of sand or gravel lying at right-angles to a former ice-front. Eskers are the remains of beds of streams that ran on or under the ice near the melting front. The streams were running between walls of ice, which prevented the spread of the deposits laterally.

Face-bedding   When building stone is laid with the bedding planes parallel to the face of the wall it is said to be face-bedded.

Faience   A paste of powdered quartz and alkali with a little water. When baked it forms a semi-vitreous mass intermediate in nature between baked clay and glass.

Fibrils   Sub-microscopic fibre-like structures formed by the adhesion of large numbers of more or less spherical protein molecules. They form the cell-wall material of some vegetable fibres.

Flocculation   The formation of large particles by condensing together large numbers of colloidal particles. This can often be done simply by adding a salt.

Flotation   A process for separating the light and heavy particles in a soil, etc. Particles denser than the liquid used will settle, but less dense material will float on the surface. It is particularly useful for separating the 'heavy' minerals from a sand, using bromoform, which has a density of 2·9 grammes per cubic centimetre.

Froth-flotation is a newer method for separating a metal ore from the gangue (waste material). A froth is formed by blowing air through a suspension of the mixture in water containing a frothing agent (similar to a detergent). Only the lighter material is carried away by the froth.

Follicles   The roots of hairs, just below the surface of the skin.

Foraminifera   Very small sea creatures with hard shells often
                    perforated with many minute holes (Latin *forare*,
                    pierce).

Forging   The process of alternately hammering and heating in
                    order to remove slag from impure iron, or simply to
                    shape a piece of iron.

Fossil Fuels   Coal, petroleum, and natural gases, so called because
                    they are produced by the decay and alteration of
                    plant or animal matter.

Fossil Soil   A soil profile that has been preserved by having been
                    covered and protected by a structure such as an
                    earthen bank, barrow, or rampart.

Freestone   A fine, homogeneous sedimentary rock without any
                    preferred splitting planes, which may therefore be
                    cut and laid in any direction.

Fresco   Decoration of walls by applying pigments directly to
                    wet, freshly applied plaster.

Gamma   One gamma ($1\,\gamma$) is one hundred-thousandth part
                    (10^{-5}) of a Gauss (see below).

Gamma-rays   Electro-magnetic radiation (i.e. of the same kind as
                    light) emitted by some radioactive elements. They
                    are similar to X-rays in penetrating power and may be
                    used in similar ways.

Gauss   The unit of magnetic field strength. Physicists no
                    longer use the term in this way, but it is convenient to
                    retain it when using magnetometers.

Gel   A kind of colloidal solution consisting of small par-
                    ticles of a solid dispersed in a liquid, the solid
                    particles forming a sort of skeleton, which gives the
                    gel a certain rigidity. Gels contain more of the solid
                    material than do *sols*, and with increasing concentra-
                    tion one may often pass from sol to gel and then to
                    paste. The name is derived from gelatine, which in
                    turn is from the Latin for jelly.

Glycine   The simplest amino-acid, formula: $C_2H_5O_2N$.

Gneiss   Coarse-grained metamorphic crystalline rocks show-
                    ing a banded structure.

Greenstones   Kinds of green, basic rocks.

Half-life   The time taken for a given amount of a radioactive
                    element to be reduced to just half its weight.

Hard-core   See *aggregate*.

Hardness (of water)   A hard water is one that contains the carbonates and/or sulphates of calcium and/or magnesium. These salts form a scum with soap. The hardness used to be measured by finding the quantity of a standard soap solution required to produce a permanent lather, but more precise methods are now used.

Hardwoods   Deciduous trees, in contrast to the conifers, which are called softwoods. This does not mean that the wood of conifers is in fact always softer than other woods.

Hipparion   An extinct member of the Horse family, which walked on three toes.

Horizon (soil)   A distinct layer in a soil profile.

Hydration   The chemical incorporation of water by any substance or material. Hydrated solids contain water molecules that occupy definite places in the crystal lattice; without the water quite a different crystal form would be produced. For example, anhydrite is $CaSO_4$ and forms prismatic or tabular crystals, whereas gypsum, $CaSO_4.2H_2O$, a hydrated salt, crystallizes as flat lozenge-shaped crystals. This water is 'water of crystallization'.

Hydraulic Lime   A lime containing clay that will set hard under water or in the absence of air.

Hydroxyl Ion   The ion OH^-, which is a base because it neutralizes a hydrogen ion, forming a water molecule.

Hyphae   The long, fine vegetative growths of a fungus, which penetrate the organic matter on which it feeds. The whole mass of hyphae form the mycelium.

Hypodermis   The fatty tissue beneath the skin of an animal (Greek *hypo*, below; *derma*, the skin).

Illite   A clay mineral consisting of particularly thin, flat particles, used as a slip on pottery to produce a high gloss on firing.

Incisors   The front, cutting teeth of mammals.

Inert Gases   The gases helium, neon, argon, krypton, xenon, and radon, which do not combine with other elements to form compounds of the normal kind. In fact, until quite recently they were thought to form no compounds whatever: hence the name. They all occur in the atmosphere in small amounts, and radon is produced in the radioactive decay of radium.

Infra-red Light Light of wavelengths greater than that of red light, i.e. beyond the red of the spectrum, and therefore invisible. By the use of sensitive dyes photographic films can be made to respond to infra-red light.

Inner Bark The phloem of the stem of a flowering plant, containing vessels, sieve tubes, and bast fibres. It plays an important part in the transport of the sap and forms a useful source of food, just below the bark, for 'food-gathering' peoples.

Ion An ion is formed when an atom, a group of atoms, or a molecule loses or gains one or more electrons.

Ion-exchange Some large molecules have loosely-held ions, which are readily exchanged for other ions in a solution in contact with the ion-exchanger. Clay behaves in this way in the soil, and the zeolite minerals, which were the first water-softeners used before synthetic ion-exchange resins were produced.

Ionic Crystal A crystal consisting of positive and negative ions arranged in a regular three-dimensional pattern.

Iron pan A more or less hard deposit of iron oxide or of iron salts, formed by the re-deposition of iron carried down the soil profile by the soil-water, perhaps in combination with the humus.

Isotopes Atoms of the same element, which differ only in the number of neutrons in the nucleus, and hence differ in weight. 'Radiocarbon', for example, is the isotope of carbon known as C^{14}. The main isotope of carbon is C^{12}, and there is always a very small proportion of C^{13} in carbon. The superscripts are the *isotopic masses*, i.e. the weights relative to the hydrogen atom.

Jet A black mineral, which can be considered as an early stage in the formation of coal from wood.

Lake A coloured complex formed when a dye is adsorbed by (i.e. held on the surface of) solid particles. Aluminium hydroxide is particularly efficient in forming lakes, especially when it is produced in its gelatinous form suspended in water. Lakes may be formed in the mordanting process.

Lateral Moraine Rock fragments from the sides of a valley, which fell onto the edge of a glacier and were deposited when the latter retreated.

Latex   A milky sap containing fine particles of rubber, starch, or protein suspended in water.

Lattice   A crystal lattice is a regular arrangement of points in a crystal, each point being occupied by one of the atoms, ions, or molecules forming the crystal.

Linters   Short fragments of fibres. These must be removed from the long fibres before spinning.

Loam   Any soil containing particles of sand, silt, and clay grades.

Loess   Deposits of wind-borne soil, predominantly of silt grades, which were derived from glacial deposits during very cold, dry periods closely following the retreat of glaciers.

Lumen   The central open part of a fibre, which was originally occupied by the living cell contents.

Magma   Molten rock material within the earth's crust or poured out on the earth's surface.

Medium   An adhesive substance mixed with a pigment to form a paint.

Medulla   The central pith in the stem of a flowering plant (Latin marrow).

Medullary Rays   Radial series of conducting cells in plant stems, which transport food materials between the medulla and outer parts of the stem.

Metamorphic Rocks   Rocks that have been fundamentally changed since their original formation, usually as a result of high temperatures or pressures.

Middle Lamella   The thin layer of cellulose, often embedded in lignin or other material, between adjacent plant cells. It was, in fact, the original cell-wall.

Mildews   Varieties of parasitic fungi.

Moder Humus   A loose, crumbly form of humus in which the plant remains are only partly decayed, largely as a result of the activities of worms. Found on acid soils under deciduous forests. Leaf-mould.

Modifier   Glass modifiers are fluxes added during the manufacture of glass or glazes to reduce the melting point.

Molars   The teeth used for grinding the food (Latin *mola*, a grindstone).

Molecule   The smallest particle of an element or compound that can exist separately. In some *elements* (e.g. helium) the molecule is one atom, but in many elements (e.g. oxygen) there are two atoms in a molecule.

	Compounds must have at least two atoms in a molecule, because they contain at least two kinds of atom, but there may be many more. Cellulose, for example, contains many thousands of atoms in a molecule.
Mollusca	A sub-kingdom, or *phylum*, of animals with soft bodies and often with hard shells, e.g. oysters, snails, and slugs.
Monocotyledons	Flowering plants that produce only a single seed-leaf.
Monomer	The unit from which a polymer is built up.
Mor Humus	Raw humus, consisting of plant remains decomposing very slowly and not mixed with the soil. Found on acid sandy soils, especially under pine woods and on heath-land.
Moraines	Rock fragments of any size or shape deposited from ice.
Mordant	A substance applied to textile material before dyeing, for the purpose of binding the dye to the fibres.
Mortar	Material used for binding together bricks or stones in building. It is usually made by mixing lime, sand, and water.
Moulds	Fungi that produce woolly mycelia on damp surfaces.
Mucilage	A dilute solution of a gum, formed from the breakdown of cellulose in some plants, such as seaweeds and lichens.
Mudstone	A fine-grained sedimentary rock in which the flat grains have a random orientation. They will break easily in any direction, with curved fracture planes.
Mull Humus	The most completely decayed form of humus, in which the plant remains are no longer recognizable as such and the humic materials are evenly distributed throughout the 'humus layer' of the soil, being held on the surfaces of the soil particles.
Multi-seriate	Medullary rays formed of several thicknesses of tissue cells, as seen in cross-section, compared to uniseriate rays, which consist of a single series of cells.
Mycelium	The mass of intertwining hyphae formed by many fungi.
Nekton	Microscopic free-swimming organisms (cf. plankton).
Neutron	A sub-atomic particle of the same weight as the proton but uncharged. Neutrons and protons together

make up the atomic nucleus, and either may be ejected from a nucleus by bombarding with appropriate high-energy particles.

Noble Gases See *Inert Gases*.

Nodes This word is derived from the Latin for 'knot' and is used in many ways; for example, the swollen joints in a stem or fibre, the 'fixed', or unmoving, points on a vibrating string, and a hard tumour.

Nucleus The central part of an atom in which all the weight of the atom is concentrated. It is extremely small even in comparison with the diameter of the atom itself, so that the chances of other particles striking an atomic nucleus are very small. Hence, when atoms are bombarded with high-energy particles only a small fraction of the particles will produce changes in the atomic nuclei.

Oolitic Limestone Deposits of calcium carbonate consisting of spherical particles cemented together. The limestone is usually deposited around minute sand grains, and the particles may be of any size up to about a quarter of an inch in diameter. Oolites are generally more porous and hence more easily weathered than other limestones, but this may depend on the cementing medium.

Opal (plant) Plant opal, or *phytoliths* (= plant stones), are deposits of silica found in certain cells of grasses.

Opus Signinum A water-resisting plaster or cement containing crushed or powdered pottery or tiles, or tufa. A kind of pozzolanic mortar.

Oxidation Originally the addition of oxygen to or the removal of hydrogen from a substance, but now defined as an increase in the proportion of electro-negative (i.e. acidic) components in a compound, or the removal of electrons from any species (atom, ion, or molecule).

Palynology The study of pollen.

Panning The method of extracting gold from sediments by washing away the lighter material in a shallow pan, leaving the heavier gold granules in the pan.

Papyrus An early writing material made from the pith of the plant *Cyperus papyrus*. Strips of the pith, laid crosswise in layers, were beaten with sticks until they became firmly stuck together by the natural gums.

Parchment	A writing material consisting of thin layers split from calf-skin and suitably dressed.
Patina	A more-or-less thin surface layer developed on stone or metal by chemical or physical alteration of the material, e.g. the green carbonate patina on a bronze coin, or the white patina on flint.
Pedicle	A small stalk-like structure, as the bony protrusion of the skull left by a discarded antler.
Periosteum	The thin membrane closely enclosing a bone.
pH	A scale of acidity ranging from 0 to 14. A neutral solution has a pH of 7, acid solutions have pH less than 7, and alkaline solutions greater than 7.
Phloem	The inner bark of a tree (Greek *phloios*).
Phytoliths	See *Opal (plant)*.
Plankton	The microscopic floating organisms of sea or fresh water.
Plantigrade	Walking on the soles of the feet (Latin *planta*, sole).
Plumping	The swelling and partial putrefaction of hides by soaking in water.
Podsol	An acid soil found in cool temperate regions, showing a clearly defined bleached horizon (A_2) and iron- and humus-enrichment of the B-horizon (Russian: ash-grey soil).
Pollen Zones	Time-zones, or periods, during which a particular type of vegetation cover existed in an area from which pollen has been analysed.
Polymers	Large molecules formed, either naturally or artificially, by condensing together a number of monomer units, usually of one or two kinds. Rubber, for example, is a polymer built up of many isoprene units, cellulose consists of glucose units strung together, and the molecule of the synthetic polymer 'bakelite' contains phenol and formaldehyde units.
Pozzolanic Mortar	See *Opus Signinum*.
Premolars	The teeth before the molars, i.e. in front of them in the jaw.
Primary Clays	Clays remaining on the site of the rock from which they were formed by weathering. Also called residual clays. On the other hand, clays that have been transported by water or ice and deposited far from their origins are called *secondary* clays.
Profile (soil)	A vertical section of the soil, from surface to bedrock.
Proton	An atomic particle carrying one unit of positive charge and of unit mass relative to hydrogen, because

it is identical with the nucleus of a hydrogen atom. All atomic nuclei contain protons, and all but hydrogen also contain neutrons.

Protoplasm The living contents of a plant or animal cell (Greek *protos*, first; *plasma*, moulded).

Protozoa Single-cell animals.

Proximal Describes the part of a bone (etc.) nearer to the centre of an animal (cf. distal).

Puering Partially putrefying a skin before tanning.

Pulp The filling of the pulp-cavity of a tooth, containing blood vessels and nerve fibres.

Pyroclastic Rocks Rocks formed from material thrown out of a volcano with the escaping gases, e.g. agglomerate and tuff.

Quicklime Calcium oxide (CaO). It reacts vigorously with water, giving off much heat and converting some of the water into steam. The product is *slaked lime*, calcium hydroxide, $Ca(OH)_2$.

Radioactivity Changes occurring in the nucleus of an atom, by which radiation is produced, and resulting in the transformation of the atom into a different element. It may be natural or artificially induced, but in either case it cannot be controlled or stopped, and is not affected by temperature changes nor the way in which the atoms are chemically combined.

Raw Humus See *Mor Humus*.

Raw Soil A soil with an incompletely developed profile.

Reduction The opposite of *oxidation* (q.v.).

Relaxation Shrinkage Shrinkage caused by the return of wool fibres, when wet, to their original lengths, having been stretched during spinning and weaving.

Relict Soil Re-deposited material from an older soil profile. May cause confusion when a new soil profile is formed in such a relict soil.

Retting Soaking bast fibres in water until they are partially *rotted*.

Rhizome A swollen creeping underground stem.

Ring-porous Wood Wood in which the large vessels are formed only in the spring, so that they appear, in cross-section, as rings of large cells separated by rings of small xylem cells.

Ripple Marks   The concentric marks on the surface of a conchoidal fracture.

Ruminants   Animals that chew cud (Latin *rumen*, throat).

Salt Infestation When a porous material, such as pottery, remains for a long time in sea-water or very wet soil it accumulates large quantities of salts. This is salt-infestation. On drying, the salts crystallize within the pores and may cause serious damage.

Saltings   Shallow depressions near the sea in which salt was produced by evaporating sea-water. Salt-pans.

Scale-cell   The thin, hard scales covering the surface of animal fibres.

Schist   A metamorphic rock showing a finely banded structure in which the mineral grains are clearly visible and may appear to be elongated, as though crushed.

Scudding   Scraping the fatty layers from the inside of a skin.

Sedimentary Rocks Rocks formed by sediments deposited from water or as wind-blown silt (loess). The individual particles may be visible, and the stratification, or bedding, is usually clear. Clay, sandstone, and lime-stone are common varieties.

Shale   A fine-grained sediment consisting of small flat particles, usually of clay or mica. They split readily along bedding planes because the flat grains tend to be aligned parallel to these planes.

Shrinkage Temperature The temperature at which fibres start to shrink when warmed. The basis of a method of dating leather collagen fibres.

Sieve-tubes   Structures in the phloem of stems with the end walls between cells perforated like a sieve.

Sickle-gloss A high polish found on flint after prolonged use in cutting corn or wood. Also called corn-gloss.

Silica-gel   A gel consisting of a skeleton of small silica particles in water. When some of the water is driven off by heating the gel becomes solid and may then be used as a desiccator since it readily takes up water, either from the liquid or the vapour.

Sintering   When a compressed powder is heated the separate particles may start to soften at a temperature well below their normal melting point, and will then stick together on cooling. This phenomenon of sintering occurs during the firing of pottery, and is now used in the manufacture of porous materials, e.g. sintered glass for filters.

Slaked Lime   See *Quicklime*.

Slate   A fine-grained sedimentary rock, formed of clays, which has been changed by pressure into a thin-layered structure having good cleavage planes. The latter do not usually coincide with the original bedding planes because the pressure will not have been applied directly across the bedding planes.

Slum Species   Types of fresh-water snails that can exist under very extreme or adverse conditions.

Softwoods   Coniferous timbers.

Sol   A colloidal suspension of small solid particles in a liquid.

Stigma   The part of the female organs of a plant which receives the pollen.

Streak Test   An important test used in the identification of minerals. The sample is rubbed along a piece of unglazed porcelain and the colour of the streak is noted. This may be quite different from the apparent colour of the bulk sample, and many coloured minerals are too pale to produce a coloured streak.

Streptococci   Bacteria that consist of strings of single-celled individuals (Greek *streptos*, a torc; *coccos*, a grain).

Susceptibility   Magnetic susceptibility is a measure of the effect of a magnetic field on a material, i.e. the relative strength of the magnetic field *within* the material.

Tanning   The preservation of hides by impregnating them with aqueous extracts of tannins, such as oak bark. The tannin combines chemically with the fibres of the skin and leather is formed.

Tawing   The preservation of hides by dressing them with salt or alum. The effect is short-lived because the salts are easily washed out.

Tempera   Painting with pigments mixed with a medium other than an oil, such as a gum, size, or egg-white.

Terracotta   Pottery fired below about 900°C.

Thermoluminescence   The production of light by heating. As applied to dating pottery it means light produced when radiation-damage is annealed from pottery by heating. Electrons returning to their proper places in crystals give off their surplus energy as flashes of light.

Thermo-remanent Magnestism   The magnetism remaining in baked clay when it cools down after being heated in a magnetic field. In pottery and archaeological features of burnt clay it is assumed that the field was the earth's magnetic field, and estimates of the direction and intensity of the latter may be made from measurements of the thermo-remanent magnetism (TRM).

Ungulates   Hoofed animals.
Uniseriate Wood in which the medullary rays seen in transverse section consist of only one row of cells. In the vertical plane they will, of course, be many cells in height.
Vascular   Having vessels, as in wood (Latin *vas*, a vessel).
Vellum   Fine parchment made from calf skin.
Velvet   The covering of soft skin on immature antlers.
Vessels   Long tubes in woody tissues formed by the fusion of many cells. Along these are transported the food and waste products of the plant.

Wolf-teeth The fourth premolars of a horse, which are only occasionally present.

Xylem   The wood of stem or root (Greek *xulon*, wood).
X-rays   X-rays, or Röntgen rays, are very short-wave electromagnetic waves, i.e. of the same form as light but of much shorter wavelengths than visible light. They are produced when a beam of electrons, from a hot wire filament, impinges on any material. The wavelengths of the most intense lines in the X-ray spectrum are characteristic of the elements concerned.

SELECT BIBLIOGRAPHY

BIEK, L. *Archaeology and the Microscope* (Butterworth, London 1964).

BROTHWELL, D. and HIGGS, E. (Eds.). *Science in Archaeology* (Thames and Hudson, London 1963).

BUNTING, B. T. *The Geography of Soil* (Hutchinson, London 1965).

COOK, J. G. *Handbook of Textile Fibres: Vol. 1. Natural Fibres* (Merrow, Watford, England 1968).

CORNWALL, I. W. *Bones for the Archaeologist* (Phoenix House, London, 1956).

—— *Soils for the Archaeologist* (Phoenix House, London 1966).

DESCH, H. E. *Timber: its Structure and Properties* (Macmillan, London 1962).

DIMBLEBY, G. *Plants in Archaeology* (John Baker, London 1967).

HODGES, H. *Artifacts* (John Baker, London 1964).

KUBIENA, W. L. *The Soils of Europe* (Allen & Unwin, London 1953).

LEVEY, M. (Ed.) *Archaeological Chemistry: a symposium* (University of Pennsylvania Press, Philadelphia 1968).

OSWALD, F., and PRYCE, T. D. *Introduction to the Study of Terra Sigillata* (Gregg Press Ltd., London 1966).

RAIKES, R. *Water, Weather and Prehistory* (John Baker, London 1967).

ROSENFELD, A. *The Inorganic Raw Materials of Antiquity* (Weidenfeld & Nicholson, London 1965).

SNEYERS, R. *Stones Also Die*, in UNESCO *Courier* (UNESCO, Paris 1965).

WELCH, P. S. *Limnology* (McGraw Hill, New York 1952).

WOODROFFE, D. (Ed.). *Standard Handbook of Industrial Leathers* (The National Trades Press Ltd., London 1949).

LABORATORY FOR ARCHAEOLOGY AND THE HISTORY OF ART, OXFORD. *Archaeometry* (Published twice annually) (Cambridge University Press, Cambridge).

INDEX